EVERETT M. ROGERS

Diffusion of Innovations.

THE FREE PRESS, *New York*

COLLIER-MACMILLAN LIMITED, *London*

TO MY WIFE

PREFACE

                            This book is
directed both to advanced college students enrolled in sociology courses and to students of the other social sciences (such as anthropology, economics, history, and psychology) who are concerned with diffusion. (For this reason, sociological concepts are defined when they are introduced.)

More than five hundred publications on the diffusion of innovations are reviewed here. The innovations studied range from new drugs among physicians to hand tools among primitive tribes, and from driver training among public high schools to hybrid corn among farmers. Although a generally consistent set of findings has emerged from these studies, a search of the literature shows little attempt to summarize and evaluate available results and theories on the spread of ideas. This volume synthesizes these findings and theories.

One evidence of the need for this synthesis is the lack of diffusion among the various traditions of diffusion research itself. For example, educators have largely ignored the diffusion findings of rural sociologists, and anthropologists have paid no attention to either one. Nearly all the understandings about the diffusion of ideas are monopolized by several small cliques of research workers.

This book is based not only on the five hundred available diffusion research studies but also upon unpublished research and personal discussions with American and European diffusion researchers. My tour of European research centers in 1961 uncovered many diffusion studies not available in the United States.

Additional diffusion studies are continually appearing. Several yet unpublished works have been inspected through the generosity of their authors, and are cited here as "in press." It is perhaps significant that few of the studies encountered after the first draft of this manuscript was prepared entailed major revisions of the present book. Most of the recent findings simply added additional confirmation to generalizations already apparent.

Because of the great number of diffusion publications, some observers fear that this area is becoming barren ground and that the choice research topics have already been harvested. Perhaps this volume can aid in suggesting fruitful locations for "digging" by pointing out leads for needed research. This book suggests that students of diffusion have been working where the ground was soft; that is, where they could secure research resources. The challenge for future research is to expand the area of digging and to search for different objectives from those of the past. Perhaps there is a need to dig deeper, in directions that theory suggests. Although the main emphasis is upon research findings, a theoretical framework is presented mainly to complement and order these findings. In this manner, the empirical findings are placed in a more logical context.

This book must of necessity be somewhat multidisciplinary, as is the research on which it is based. However, these data are analyzed in a framework that is chiefly sociological and social-psychological.

The audience anticipated is not only college students but also change agents, whose purpose is to diffuse innovations. Emphasis, therefore, is placed upon what is known about diffusion as well as on what needs to be discovered.

I wish to acknowledge the Iowa and Ohio Agricultural Experiment Stations for sponsoring my research on the diffusion of innovations, some of which is reported here for the first time. The Foundation for Research on Human Behavior also provided research resources. Special thanks for help go to Gene Havens and Joe Crymes at The Ohio State University, Rabel Burdge at Pennsylvania State University,

Al Bird at Michigan State University, Larry Campbell at Monsanto Chemical Company, Gary Eichholz at the University of South Florida, and to Anne van den Ban at the University of Wageningen, Netherlands. Students in my courses and graduate seminars are to be commended for their patience with earlier drafts of the manuscript.

My interest in the diffusion of innovations began when I was an Iowa farm boy. After high school and college training in modern agriculture, I found my home community somewhat less than impressed with my stock of innovations. The resulting frustration was later guided into a lasting research interest by Dr. George M. Beal in graduate seminars at Iowa State University. My investigation of the diffusion of innovations has continued through eleven major research projects to the present volume.

E. M. R.

CONTENTS

Preface   vii

CHAPTER I Introduction   1
    Interest in Diffusion Research   3
    Research on the Diffusion of Innovations   4
    Purpose   6
    Innovation That Failed: Water Boiling in a
        Peruvian Town   7
    Elements of Diffusion   12
    Summary   19

CHAPTER II Traditions of Research on Diffusion   21
    The Lack of Diffusion of Diffusion Research   21
    Research Traditions   22
    Anthropology   24
    Early Sociology   28
    Rural Sociology   31
    Education   39
    Industrial   43
    Medical Sociology   45
    Relationships Among the Traditions   52
    Summary   55

CHAPTER III Culture, Norms, and Diffusion   57
    Importance of Culture in Diffusion   57
    Traditional and Modern Norms   59
    Measuring the Traditional-Modern Dimension   62
    Social System Norms and Individual Innovativeness   70
    Needed Research   72
    Summary   75

CHAPTER IV The Adoption Process   76
    Learning Theory   76
    Decision-Making   77
    Adoption as a Process   79

Stages in the Adoption Process   81
Adoption of Home Canning in a Georgia County:
A Case Illustration   86
Discontinuances   88
Are There Adoption Stages?   95
Sources of Information by Stages   98
The Adoption Period   105
Summary   119

CHAPTER V Characteristics of the Innovation   121
The Pill That Failed   122
Characteristics of Innovations   124
Characteristics and Rate of Adoption   134
Overadoption   142
Summary   146

CHAPTER VI Adopter Categories   148
Normal Adopter Distributions   152
A Method of Adopter Categorization   159
Adopter Categories as Ideal Types: Salient Values   168
Characteristics of Adopter Categories   171
Self-Images of Adopter Categories   188
Changes in Adopter Categories over Time   189
Summary   191

CHAPTER VII Innovators as Deviants: In Step with a
                         Different Drummer   193
Past Views of Innovators   194
Innovators and Inventors   195
Deviation   196
Are Innovators Deviants? A Research Study   198
Discussion   205
Summary   206

CHAPTER VIII Opinion Leaders and the Flow of Ideas   208
Opinion Leaders   208
The Two-Step Flow of Communication   211
The Interaction Effect   215
Importance of Personal Influence   217
Functions of Personal Influence   223

Distribution of Influence 226
Measuring Opinion Leadership 228
What Is Known About Opinion Leaders 232
Barriers to the Flow of Ideas in a Social System 247
Needed Research 250
Summary 251

CHAPTER IX The Role of the Change Agent and the
                  Consequences of Innovation 254
Role of the Change Agent 255
Commercial Change Agents 261
Cross-Cultural Diffusion of Innovations 267
Social Consequences 271
Windfall Profits 276
A Strategy of Change 278
Summary 283

CHAPTER X Predicting Innovativeness 285
Past Prediction Studies 286
Prediction with Multiple Correlation 287
A Configurational Approach to Prediction 292
Future Approaches to Prediction 295

CHAPTER XI Toward a Theory of the Diffusion and
                  Adoption of Innovations 300
Theoretical Approach 301
Diffusion of an Innovation 303
Adoption of an Innovation 305
Generalizations and Hypotheses 308

Bibliography 317
Diffusion Research Cited 317
General References Cited 353

Index 359

Diffusion of Innovations

CHAPTER I

Introduction

> Our problem is to learn why, given one hundred different innovations conceived of at the same time—innovations in the form of words, in mythological ideas, in industrial processes, etc.—ten will spread abroad while ninety will be forgotten.
>
> GABRIEL TARDE,* 1903, p. 140

The annals of world history are charged with dynamic accounts of armed warfare, depicting in graphic detail how the culture of nations and men has been altered. Yet some of the greatest struggles encountered by mankind have been not with the sword but with ideas that diffused into their daily lives and emerged as cultural changes. The explosion and shock of innovations on the minds of people are just as real and devastating as the nuclear missiles of modern military machines (Reed, 1961).

The results of technological change are apparent everywhere. One example is found in American agriculture. The average farmer supported four others plus himself in 1820. By 1940 this figure was 12, by 1961 it was 27! Other indications of technological change are the number of new medical drugs released per year, increases in United States man-hour productivity (3 per cent per year), the widespread adoption of industrial automation, and the thousands of new household products available each year. And, Americans are not satisfied to change just their own culture. United States

---

* All references cited are listed in a bibliography at the end of the book.

technical assistance workers are seeking the adoption of innovations throughout the less developed areas of the world.

Americans spent $10 billion on research and development
in 1960, and this will increase to about $21 billion in ten
years. Yet this tremendous research cost is an unrealized
public investment until the resulting innovations are diffused
to and adopted by the intended audience. As this fact has become apparent in recent years, attempts have been made to
speed the diffusion of research findings.

In spite of Americans' generally favorable attitude toward
science and technology, a considerable *time lag* is required
before an innovation reaches wide acceptance. This is true
despite the economic benefits of the innovations studied. For
instance: A 40-year time lag was found between the first
success of the tunnel oven in the pottery industry and its
general use (Carter and Williams, 1957). Over 14 years were
required for hybrid seed corn to reach complete adoption in
Iowa (Ryan and Gross, 1943). About 50 years elapsed after
development of a new educational practice before its adoption by all public schools (Ross, 1958). Put in another way,
the average American school lags 25 years behind the best
practice.

Similar time gaps have been found in other studies of innovations. For example, the average U.S. farmer could support 50 other persons (rather than 27) if he adopted already
developed innovations. In fact, two U.S. Department of Agriculture experts stated, "People develop and apply technology in agriculture in a way that reminds us of a slow-
motion game of leapfrog, in which the time between advancing leaps is months or years or decades" (Green and LeRay,
1960, p. 31). So while large sums are invested in developing
innovations and communicating them to intended audiences,
there are important time lags before these innovations reach
widespread adoption.

One implicit or explicit purpose of many diffusion studies
has been to determine methods by which diffusion can be

hastened. The accomplishment of this goal is obviously important to modern America and particularly to its foreign defense position. It is clear that research alone is not enough to solve most problems; the research results must be diffused and adopted before their advantage can be realized. In fact, the benefits of diffusion research itself cannot be secured until the findings are diffused. One reason for the present volume is to encourage the widespread understanding of diffusion research.

However, it should not be assumed that the diffusion and adoption of *all* innovations (for instance, a new narcotic among drug addicts) is necessarily desirable. In fact, this book will review studies of nonrecommended and uneconomical innovations that are generally undesirable for both the individual adopter and for society.

Also, although the diffusion of most desirable innovations requires a considerable time lag, there is a certain inevitability in their diffusion. Most attempts to prevent diffusion from occurring have been unsuccessful over a long time period. Examples are the ancient Chinese attempt to maintain sole knowledge of gunpowder, and United States efforts to prevent diffusion of the secret of the atomic bomb. In fact, it is probably inevitable that most of the smaller countries of the world today will eventually gain knowledge of nuclear weapons.

INTEREST IN DIFFUSION RESEARCH

Dr. Joe Ackerman, Director of the Farm Foundation, Chicago, tells of an experience that illustrates the developing interest in the diffusion of innovations. The Farm Foundation invited a committee of Midwestern rural sociologists studying diffusion to confer in 1955. The committee, after carefully reviewing the literature, made a report succinctly stating general conclusions from diffusion studies. The sociologists, sure no one else would be interested in the document, felt that only 25 copies should be mimeographed. The Foundation Director, however, convinced them to have 5,000 copies printed. By 1962, 80,000 additional copies had been distributed throughout the world, with translations available in Dutch, Spanish, and other languages.

In 1955, two Iowa State University sociologists developed a visual presentation illustrating the diffusion of farm innovations. Six years later they had given this presentation over 160 times to all types of professional change agents such as salesmen and dealers, advertising agency personnel, extension workers, and industrial managers. Their presentation has done much to popularize both the theory and the research findings on the diffusion of innovations.

RESEARCH ON THE DIFFUSION OF INNOVATIONS

The number of research studies on diffusion, as well as the attention paid to these investigations, has increased in recent years. For example, over 172 different research studies dealing with educational innovations have been completed since 1938. Agricultural innovations have also received wide research attention. Rural sociologists have completed over 286 diffusion studies since the classic investigation of hybrid seed corn adoption by Ryan and Gross (1943).[1] In many respects, hybrid corn is symbolic of the farm innovations that have

1. A recent review of literature by Rogers (1960) indicated diffusion to be the second most popular research topic among contemporary rural sociologists.

been studied. The Ryan and Gross analysis probed into a remarkable number of areas currently being investigated by students of diffusion.

The 506 diffusion studies reviewed in this book have some remarkably similar findings, but little attempt at comparison of the results has previously been made. It should also be pointed out that, although many studies have been completed, much of the research in this field has yet to be done. Areas of needed research will be mentioned at several points in this book.

The variety of innovations that have been investigated is illustrated by these examples:

1. Smallpox inoculation among medical doctors in England and France in the eighteenth century (Miller, 1957), and an antibiotic drug among Illinois physicians (Coleman and others, 1957).

2. Fertilizers, 2,4-D weed spray, bulk milk tanks, and other new agricultural ideas among farmers (Lionberger, 1960).

3. Driver training, remedial reading programs, and other educational innovations among schools (Ross, 1958).

4. Birth-control methods among Puerto Ricans (Hill and others, 1959).

5. New fabrics, wild rice, electric blankets, and other homemaking ideas among housewives (Beal and Rogers, 1957; Opinion Research Corporation, 1959).

6. Child-rearing practices among U.S. mothers (Brim, 1954; Maccoby and others, 1959).

7. Radio sets among ham operators (Bowers, 1938).

8. High-draft spinning among firms in the cotton processing industry (Sutherland, 1959).

9. Gasoline motors and fish-raising among Thailand peasants (Goldsen and Ralis, 1957).

In spite of the diverse characteristics of these innovations, there are many basic similarities running through the findings from these research studies. These basic similarities form the backbone of this book.

PURPOSE

Although scholars in several traditions of research have studied diffusion, there has been little "diffusion" among these traditions. For instance, medical sociologists, educators, anthropologists, and rural sociologists are mostly unaware of each others' findings. Every research area reaches the point where greater returns are available from a synthesis of the findings already available than from investing resources and efforts in additional research. Summaries of diffusion research findings have been made in agriculture by Lionberger (1960) and in education by Ross (1958). However, no author has yet attempted to point out the *common threads* running through *all* the research traditions on the diffusion of innovations. Such is our task.

The main purpose of this volume is to synthesize and evaluate available research findings and theories on the diffusion of innovations. If the reader has time to read and digest 506 research reports, he does not need this book. However, many research publications on diffusion are difficult to secure; some are theses in university libraries, others are out-of-print bulletins or research reports. A function of the present volume is to make this fugitive literature more widely available. One hoped-for result of this book is to prevent unnecessary duplication of research efforts in the future. Areas of needed research will be suggested by an approach to a theory of the diffusion and adoption of innovations.

Most diffusion research has been accomplished by means of the sociologist's favorite digging tool, the personal interview. Despite certain methodological shortcomings, the general body of research on the diffusion of innovations is extensive and impressive. The author will attempt to not only set forth major conclusions from the studies cited but also tell briefly *how* these findings were obtained. Then the reader can judge the authenticity of the findings for himself.

Many of the findings are organized around a series of generalizations which summarize the evidence available about the relationships between two or more concepts. Truth claims have been established for these generalizations, yet they seldom can be considered to be principles until much more research is completed. As such, the generalizations range somewhere between hypotheses and principles. Additional generalizations need to be added to the present list as further research findings become available.

Case examples and illustrations punctuate the present volume. The following case illustration suggests the complex factors involved in the spread of new ideas. The case describes the failure of a health campaign to secure the boiling of drinking water in a Peruvian town. Perhaps as much can be learned from analyses of diffusion failures as from successes, although relatively few such studies have been completed.

INNOVATION THAT FAILED: WATER BOILING IN A PERUVIAN TOWN[2]

A major concern of a public health service in Peru is to introduce such hygienic measures as boiling contaminated water. After two years' effort in Los Molinos, a rural town of 200 families, a local hygiene worker visiting individual homes persuaded only 11 housewives to boil water. The

2. This case illustration is adapted from Wellin (1955, pp. 71–103). Used by permission.

change agent, Nelida, was aided by a physician who gave occasional public talks on water boiling, and by 15 housewives who were already boiling water before Nelida arrived.

In spite of the considerable efforts to secure adoption of water boiling, one wonders why diffusion of the innovation failed. In order to answer this question, one must understand the people of Los Molinos and their culture.

Los Molinos

Most people in Los Molinos are peasants who work for local plantations as field hands. Water rusts no pipes in Los Molinos. It is borne directly from stream and well by cans, pails, gourds, and casks. Children are the most frequent water carriers; it is considered inappropriate for those of courtship age or for married men to carry water. There are three sources of water: a seasonal irrigation ditch, a spring, and a public well. All are subject to pollution at all times and show contamination whenever tested. Of the three, the irrigation ditch is most commonly used. It is close to most homes and children can be sent to fetch the water; it has the advantage of running rather than being stagnant. People like its taste.

It is not feasible to install a sanitary water system, but the incidence of typhoid and other water-borne diseases could be lowered by boiling water before consumption. Nelida, during her two-year period in Los Molinos, paid several visits to every home but devoted especially intensive efforts to 21 families. She visited every one of these selected families between 15 and 25 times; 11 of the families now boil their water regularly.

Let us look at the people behind these figures by describing three housewives, one who boils water to obey custom, one who was persuaded by the health worker, and one who rejected the innovation.

Mrs. A: Custom

Mrs. *A* is about forty and suffers from sinus; she is labeled by the town as a "sickly one." Every morning, Mrs. *A* boils a potful of water and uses it throughout the day. She has no understanding of germ theory; her motivation for water boiling is supplied by a complex local custom of "hot" and "cold" foods. The basic principle of this belief system is that all foods, liquids, medicines, and other materials are inherently hot or cold, quite apart from actual temperature. In essence, hot-cold distinctions serve as a series of avoidances and prescriptions, especially in health and illness behavior.

Cooked water and illness are closely linked in Los Molinos. According to custom, only ill people use boiled or "hot" water. Once an individual is considered sick, it would be unthinkable for him to eat pork ("very cold") or to drink brandy which is "very hot." Raw water is also "very cold." Extremes of hot and cold must be avoided.

Local people learn from earliest childhood to dislike boiled water. Most residents can tolerate boiled water only if flavoring is added such as sugar, cinnamon, lemon, or herbs. Mrs. *A* prefers a dash of cinnamon. At no point does the notion of bacteriological contamination of water enter the cultural beliefs. By tradition, boiling is aimed at eliminating the innate "cold" quality of unboiled water, not the bacteria. Mrs. *A* drinks boiled water in obedience to custom; she is ill.

Mrs. B: Persuaded

The *B* family came to Los Molinos a generation ago but is still strongly oriented to their original home in the mountain highlands. Mrs. *B* worries about the lowland diseases that she feels infest the Los Molinos community. It is partly because of this anxiety that the change agent, Nelida, was able to persuade Mrs. *B* to boil water.

Nelida is a friendly authority to Mrs. *B* (rather than a "dirt inspector," as some other housewives perceive her) who imparts lowland knowledge and brings protection against dangerous lowland diseases. Mrs. *B* not only boils her water, but has also installed a privy and sent her youngest child to the health center for an inspection.

Mrs. *B* is still marked as an outsider to the Los Molinos community by her stumbling Spanish and highland hairdo. She can never achieve more than marginal social acceptance in Los Molinos. Because the community is not an important reference group to her, Mrs. *B* deviates from the group norms on innovation. Having nothing to lose socially, Mrs. *B* gains in personal security by heeding Nelida's friendly counsel. Mrs. *B*'s practice of boiling water neither improves nor worsens her marginal position. She is grateful to Nelida for teaching her how to neutralize the danger of contaminated water.

Mrs. C: Rejector

This housewife stands for the majority of Los Molinos families who were not convinced to boil their drinking water by the health campaign. Mrs. *C* does not understand germ theory in spite of Nelida's explanations. How, she argues, can microbes fail to drown in water? Are they fish? If germs are so small that they cannot be seen or felt, how can such delicate things survive in water? There are enough *real* threats in the world to worry about—poverty and hunger—without bothering oneself about animals one cannot see, hear, touch, or smell. Mrs. *C*'s allegiances to traditional standards are at odds with the notion of boiling water. An avid subscriber to the hot-cold complex, she feels that only the sickly need to drink boiled water.

Several housewives, particularly those of lower social

status, are rejectors because they cannot boil water even if they were convinced of the idea's value. These women plead a lack of time to gather firewood and to boil water. The poor can less afford the cost of fuel than can middle-status housewives. The poor often work as field laborers along with their husbands, leaving them less time to boil water for their families.

There is also a difference in how middle- and low-status housewives perceive Nelida. Most poor families see the health worker as a "dirt inspector" or a "snooper," sent to Los Molinos to pry for dirt and to press already harassed housewives to keep cleaner houses. Because these lower-status housewives have less free time, they are not so likely to visit with Nelida about water boiling.

The poor are also less likely to have contacts outside of the community; they are largely bound to the horizons and cultural values of Los Molinos. Holding more firmly to local tradition, the lower-status persons tend to show greater resistance to new ways and to regard innovations as threats to established custom.

Conclusions

An intensive campaign by a public health worker in a Peruvian town of 200 families to secure the boiling of drinking water was largely unsuccessful. The reasons for the failure of the water-boiling campaign can be traced largely to the cultural beliefs of the Los Molinos people, particularly their customs dealing with hot and cold foods and illness. Boiling water makes it less "cold" and, hence, appropriate only for ill persons. But if one is not ill, he is prohibited by the cultural norms from drinking boiled water. Only the least integrated individuals could afford to defy the community norm on water-boiling. An important factor affecting the adoption rate of an innovation is the cultural values of the potential adopters.

The present case illustration also demonstrates the importance of group relationships in the adoption or rejection of an innovation. Mrs. *B* was socially an outsider to the community although she had lived there many years. The health worker was a more important reference group to Mrs. *B* than was the Los Molinos community. The result was Mrs. *B*'s conversion to boiling water. Among lower-status housewives like Mrs. *C*, greater distrust for the change agent was evident, less time and resources were available for water boiling, and understanding of germ theory was less complete. Mrs. *C*, like the majority of housewives in Los Molinos, rejected the idea of boiling water.

ELEMENTS OF DIFFUSION

The definitions of terms presented in this section will be utilized in the remainder of this book. Some concepts have already been intuitively defined through their usage, but there is need to specify more exact meanings for terms. They are given to help dispel some of the "fertile disorder of ideas" that has occurred about certain key concepts.

There are four crucial elements in the analysis of the diffusion of innovations: (1) the *innovation*, (2) its *communication* from one individual to another (3) in a *social system* (4) over *time*.

These four elements are generally similar to those listed by Katz (1961) as essential in any diffusion study: (1) the tracing of an innovation, (2) over time, (3) through specific channels of communication, and (4) within a social structure. In fact, Laswell[3] once described all communications research

3. Found in Smith and others (1946, p. 121).

as inquiry into *"who* says what, through *what channels* (media) of communication, to whom [with] what . . . results."

1. The Innovation

An *innovation* is an idea perceived as new by the individual. It really matters little, as far as human behavior is concerned, whether or not an idea is "objectively" new as measured by the amount of time elapsed since its first use or discovery. It is the newness of the idea to the individual that determines his reaction to it.

Viewing an innovation as any new idea gives wide scope to this definition. Innovations might include, for example, social movements, clothing fads, the twist, compact cars, and the steel ax. When a more restrictive definition is required, innovation can be preceded by an appropriate adjective such as "technical," "organizational," or some more specific term (Ruttan, 1959). Most, but not all, innovations discussed here are technological innovations.[4]

2. Communication

Diffusion is the process by which an innovation spreads. The *diffusion process* is the spread of a new idea from its source of invention or creation to its ultimate users or adopters.

The essence of the diffusion process is the human interaction in which one person communicates a new idea to another person. Thus, at its most elemental level of conceptu-

4. Technological innovations are new developments or combinations of the material, as distinguished from the nonmaterial, culture. It should be pointed out that even in the case of technological innovations, it is the *idea* about the new material product that is diffused as well as the object itself.

alization, the diffusion process consists of (1) a new idea, (2) individual A who knows about the innovation, and (3) individual B who does not yet know about the innovation. The social relationships of A and B have a great deal to say about the conditions under which A will tell B about the innovation, and the results of this telling.

3. In a Social System

A *social system* is defined as a population of individuals who are functionally differentiated and engaged in collective problem-solving behavior. The members of a social system are individuals, although these individuals may represent informal groups, industrial firms, or schools. The social system under analysis in a diffusion study may consist of all the farmers in one county, the physicians in a community, or the members of an aborigine tribe.[5] Each of the members in a social system can be differentiated from the others. All of the members cooperate at least to the extent of having some common problem which they are seeking to solve.

There is a continuum of types of adoption decisions ranging from individual choice to group decision.[6]

1. Many innovations are adopted by an individual regardless of the decisions of other individuals in a social system. Of course, the decision-maker may be influenced by others in his system, but the adoption decision is largely an individual one.

2. One intermediate point on the continuum from individual choice to group decision is the type of innovation requiring prior acceptance by the majority of the social system's members before individual adoption decisions can be made.

5. By implication, the innovation under analysis is relevant to all members of the social system.
6. As suggested by Katz and Levin (1959) and Katz (1962).

An individual may wish to adopt, but he cannot do so until others join him. One example is adoption of a group activity, the sun dance, by Indian tribes (Voget, 1948). Another example is central-station electricity for farmers; other community members must accept the idea before an individual can adopt. There is little utility in construction of a family fallout shelter unless most of one's neighbor also adopt the idea.

3. Some ideas are adopted by a group decision that forces acceptance even upon those who are unwilling. An example is fluoridation of city drinking water.[7] Once the community decision is made, the individual has little choice. Fluoridation was recommended by dental health experts about 1950 as a means of preventing tooth decay, and there was a rapid adoption in the early years of diffusion. By the end of 1952, opposition to fluoridation became organized and the rate of adoption slowed down. By 1961, only about one-third of persons served by waterworks were drinking fluoridated water, and fluoridation was rejected by communities in about 80 per cent of the local referenda. This example suggests that the diffusion of ideas requiring group decision may be a more complex process, especially where opposition to the idea is organized, than in the case of innovations requiring individual choice. The adoption of fluoridation by communities would undoubtedly be aided if an "antifluoridation pill" were available which the opponents of fluoridation could put in their own water to neutralize the fluoride added to city water supplies. Such a hypothetical antifluoridation pill, in effect, changes the idea from one requiring group decision to one requiring only individual decision.

The norms of the social system and the status of individ-

7. There has been a proliferation of research studies in recent years on how communities adopt or reject fluoridation. For example, see Davis (1959), McNeil (1957), Plaut (1959), Gamson (1961 and in press), National Analysts (1961), Simulmatics Corporation (1961a), and a special issue of the *Journal of Social Issues* (in press).

uals *A* and *B* in the social structure of the system affect the diffusion of ideas. The importance of this social structure in the analysis of diffusion was emphasized by Katz (1961) ". . . It is about as unthinkable to study diffusion without some knowledge of the social structures in which potential adopters are located as it is to study blood circulation without adequate knowledge of the structure of veins and arteries." A new idea can be traced as it spreads through a social system just as a radioactive tracer is followed by scientists as it courses through the bloodstream.

A *norm* is defined as the most frequently occurring pattern of overt behavior for the members of a particular social system. The norms in a social system may be *traditional* and discourage the adoption of new ideas, or they may be *modern* and encourage the use of innovations. Of course, an individual may be a member of more than one social system, and the norms of each of these social systems may vary on the traditional-modern continuum.

As one illustration of the importance of social system norms, the author once visited two Netherlands agricultural communities located about five miles apart. The norms of the two communities were a sharp contrast between traditional and modern. Farmers in the traditional community had not yet adopted farm ideas that had been successfully utilized for twenty years in the modern community.

Not all individuals in a social system play equivalent roles in diffusing ideas. One individual may tell only one other person about an innovation while another person will diffuse the new idea to many others. For example, individual *A* may tell not only individual *B*, but also *C, D, E,* and *F* about the innovation.

The individuals like *A* in a social system, who often tell many others about new ideas, are called opinion leaders. *Opinion leaders* are defined as those individuals from whom others seek information and advice. Sociometry is one

method for mapping the lines of opinion leadership among the individuals in a social system.

So far, only diffusion within a social system has been considered, but it is obvious that the new idea must enter the social system from some source. The idea may be invented or created within the system or it may enter from an external source. One individual is more cosmopolite than another because he received the new idea from a source outside of the social system. *Cosmopoliteness* is the degree to which an individual's orientation is external to a particular social system.

Opinion leaders are most often members of the social system in which they exert their influence. In some cases individuals with influence in the social system are professional persons representing organizations external to the system. A *change agent* is a professional person who attempts to influence adoption decisions in a direction that he feels is desirable. A change agent usually seeks to secure the adoption of new ideas, but he may also attempt to slow the diffusion and prevent the adoption of certain innovations.

4. Over Time

What happens after individual *B* learns about a new idea from individual *A?* Under certain conditions *B* may decide to adopt the new idea. *Adoption* is a decision to continue full use of an innovation. This definition implies that the adopter is satisfied with the innovation.

The *adoption process* is the mental process through which an individual passes from first hearing about an innovation to final adoption. Five stages in the adoption process are: awareness, interest, evaluation, trial, and adoption. The adoption process differs from the diffusion process in that the adoption process deals with adoption of a new idea by one

individual while the diffusion process deals with the spread of new ideas in a social system, or with the spread of innovations between social systems or societies.[8]

An example is presented in order to clarify the meaning of adoption. Farmer *A* first learned of hybrid seed corn by reading a farm magazine in 1933. He was not convinced of the worth of hybrid seed until 1936, when he discussed the idea with his neighbor. Farmer *A* purchased one bushel of seed in 1936, and by 1938, planted 100 per cent of his corn acreage in hybrid varieties. When did Farmer *A* adopt hybrid seed?

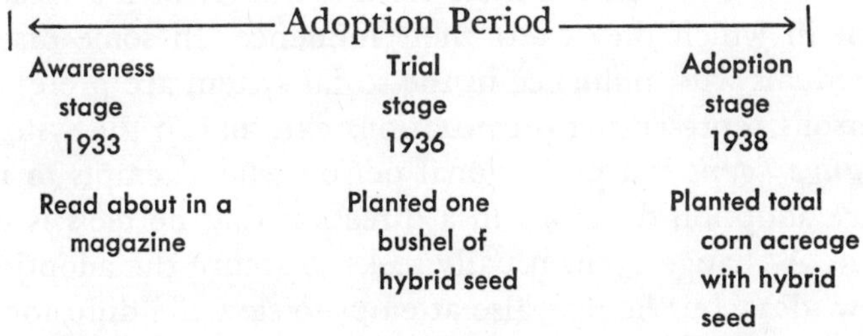

← ———————— Adoption Period ———————— →		
Awareness stage 1933	Trial stage 1936	Adoption stage 1938
Read about in a magazine	Planted one bushel of hybrid seed	Planted total corn acreage with hybrid seed

FIGURE 1-1. THE ADOPTION PERIOD FROM AWARENESS TO ADOPTION

According to the definition used in this book, Farmer *A* (Figure 1–1) adopted in 1938, when he decided to continue full use of the idea. The *adoption period,* from 1933 to 1938, is the length of time required for an individual to pass through the adoption process from awareness to adoption.

Farmer *A* later became dissatisfied with hybrid seed and discontinued adoption in 1941 when he planted all of his corn acreage in open-pollinated seed. A *discontinuance* is a

8. There is some disagreement among diffusion researchers as to whether the diffusion process ends when the individuals in a social system (1) are aware of, or (2) have adopted the new idea. The author prefers the latter viewpoint, and it is most prevalent among diffusion writers. This view of the diffusion process implies that it includes the adoption processes for the individuals in the social system.

decision to cease use of an innovation after previously adopting. Discontinuances are thus one type of rejection. *Rejection* is a decision not to adopt an innovation. In the present example, if Farmer *A* had decided in 1938 never to plant his total acreage in hybrid seed, he would be a rejector.

If Farmer *A* adopted hybrid seed in 1938, and the average farmer in his community adopted in 1935, he is less innovative than the average member of his social system. *Innovativeness* is defined as the degree to which an individual is relatively earlier in adopting new ideas than the other members of his social system.[9] Rather than speak of Farmer *A* as "less innovative than the average member of his social system," it is handier to refer to him as in the "late majority" adopter category. This "shorthand" notation saves words and aids clearer understanding. *Adopter categories* are the classifications of individuals within a social system on the basis of innovativeness. The five categories utilized here are innovators, early adopters, early majority, late majority, and laggards.

Both the measure of innovativeness and the classification of individuals into adopter categories are based upon the *time* at which an innovation is adopted.

SUMMARY

There are four essential elements in any analysis of the diffusion of an idea: (1) the innovation, and (2) its communication from one individual to another, (3) in a social system, (4) over time. An *innovation* is an idea perceived as new by the individual. *Diffusion* is the process by which an innova-

9. By "relatively earlier," the author means earlier in terms of *actual* time of adoption rather than whether the individual perceives he adopted the idea relatively earlier than others in a social system.

tion spreads. The *diffusion process* is the spread of a new idea from its source of invention or creation to its ultimate users or adopters. A *social system* is a population of individuals who are functionally differentiated and engaged in collective problem-solving behavior. *Adoption* is a decision to continue full use of an innovation. The *adoption process* is the mental process through which an individual passes from first hearing about an innovation to final adoption. *Innovativeness* is the degree to which an individual is relatively earlier in adopting new ideas than the other members of his social system. *Adopter categories* are the classifications of individuals within a social system on the basis of innovativeness.

CHAPTER II

Traditions of Research on Diffusion

Research on mass communications and on the acceptance of new farm practices may be characterized as an interest in campaigns to gain acceptance of change. Despite their shared problems, these two fields have shown no interest in each other.

ELIHU KATZ, 1960

In 1955, the author chanced upon an education journal devoted to reviewing research studies on the diffusion of new educational ideas. This was the first convergence between two research traditions, education and rural sociology, that had both been investigating the spread of new ideas for over 17 years!

The development and convergences of the six major traditions of research on the diffusion of innovations are described in this chapter.

THE LACK OF DIFFUSION
OF DIFFUSION RESEARCH

Scientists, whatever their particular specialty, are likely to bemoan the lack of adequate communication about research methods and results in their field. One would hope that this would not be characteristic of the diffusion field, however, where researchers are studying how ideas spread.

Nevertheless, any review of available literature on the diffusion of innovations must arrive at one conclusion: There has been very inadequate diffusion of diffusion research findings among diffusion researchers. For example, two of the intellectual traditions on diffusion were ably represented on the same campus of one large university and within five blocks of each other. After several years of widely acknowledged research, these two sets of scholars had little under· standing or appreciation of each others' findings.

Other evidences of inadequate communication among the traditions of research on diffusion are plentiful. A study of the adoption of farm innovations in Australia did not cite one of the 120 available publications on this topic. One of the Australian authors indicated in a private communication to the present author that they were aware of some of this similar research, but there is no evidence in their book that this knowledge affected their analysis in any way (Katz, 1959). Students of the diffusion of educational ideas have only a minimal understanding of sociological or anthropological studies on the diffusion of new ideas (Mort and Cornell, 1938, p. 42), and have never become aware of how new drugs spread to doctors or how farm innovations are adopted. Also, the anthropology field is completely unaware that any other tradition on the diffusion of innovations exists.[1]

The reasons for these communication barriers between those researching the diffusion of ideas will be presented later, as well as some of the implications of this partitioning. Let us see how each of these research traditions developed.

RESEARCH TRADITIONS

A *research tradition* is a series of research studies on a similar topic in which successive studies are influenced by

1. One exception is Hochstrasser (1955) who reviewed several rural sociology studies.

preceding investigations.[2] Thus, inspection of a research tradition allows us to trace the academic ancestry of a particular study.

Katz (1961) and Katz and Levin (1959) consider *diffusion* studies as those tracing the movement of (1) a given new idea, (2) over time, (3) through specific channels of communication, and (4) within a social structure. In order to qualify as a research tradition on diffusion, researchers in a field must have studied each, or at least most of these four elements. Katz and Levin (1959) imply there are seven major research traditions: (1) sociology, (2) early sociology, (3) anthropology, (4) market research, (5) mass communication (including mainly studies of how new drugs diffuse to medical doctors), (6) rural sociology, and (7) technical assistance.

In the present chapter, six major diffusion traditions are examined: (1) anthropology, (2) early sociology, (3) rural sociology, (4) education, (5) industrial, and (6) medical sociology. Six major diffusion traditions are easily delineated, yet almost every behavioral science has some interest in the diffusion of new ideas. Anthropology deals with the effect of culture on the spread of innovations, particularly in less developed societies. Public health deals with the diffusion of health information and practices. One specialty in speech is concerned with the spread of new speech forms. Marketing has to do with the purchase of new products. Collective behavior is concerned with fads, fashions, and social movements.

The Katz and Levin (1959) list of traditions includes market research while the present listing does not. There are relatively few research studies available in this field. It is probably true, however, that much ". . . of interest in the field of Marketing may be in the files of private agencies . . ." (Katz and Levin, 1959).

2. The term "research tradition" was first utilized by Katz (1956 and 1961) in his writing on the convergence of two of the traditions described in the present chapter, the rural sociology and the medical sociology traditions. Ross (1958) analyzed the influences of one study upon another *within* the education research tradition, but he did not use the term "traditions."

The present list of traditions includes education (172 studies) and industrial (12 publications), which were omitted from the Katz and Levin list. The medical sociology tradition includes the 21 drug studies, plus 16 additional analyses of medical innovations, such as polio vaccine. "Medical sociology" seems a better label for this expanded field than "mass communication," a term preferred by Katz and Levin (1959). These authors also include "technical assistance" as one tradition; I categorized these studies under the relevant discipline (such as anthropology) in which they were done.

It is possible, of course, to classify the research traditions on any topic by a number of different criteria. For example, the present traditions are categorized along the lines of (1) the *type* of innovations studied (such as drugs, farm ideas, and educational methods), and (2) the *discipline* to which the researchers belonged (such as anthropology, sociology, and education).

In the ensuing sections, the six major traditions will each be described in detail.

ANTHROPOLOGY

The anthropology diffusion tradition is certainly the oldest of the six to be discussed here. It has had considerable influence on the early sociology, rural sociology, and medical sociology traditions, but less on the education or industrial traditions. The other five traditions, in turn, have had no recognizable effect on later diffusion studies in the anthropological tradition.

In the early days of anthropology, a major argument raged as to whether diffusion or parallel invention was more important. That is, the question was whether ideas were independently invented in two different cultures, or whether an idea was invented in one culture and diffused to the other.

Certain groups of scholars in the early days of anthropology were labeled by such terms as "British diffusionists" and "German diffusionists." This suggests the crucial importance of the diffusion concept throughout the history of anthropology. However, the early diffusionists were actually little concerned with the *process* of diffusion.

As the field of anthropology developed, a great number of anthropological studies were concerned with investigating the acceptance of Western modern ideas by primitive societies. In spite of the proliferation of these "acculturation" studies, they contribute relatively little to the main themes of this book. Anthropologists have generally been more concerned with the exchange of ideas between societies than with the spread of an idea within a society.

However, Kroeber (1923) and Wissler (1923) published anthropological works that directly influenced many later diffusion studies, both in the anthropology and in other traditions. For example, Wissler (1923, pp. 111–121) traced the diffusion of horses from the Spanish explorers to American Indian tribes. Linton (1936, pp. 324–336) set forth a concise summary of current anthropological knowledge of diffusion for his time. He was probably one of the first academics to recognize that the characteristics of an innovation affect its rate of adoption.

Anthropologists have tended to emphasize the social consequences of innovation more than any other diffusion tradition. An example is Sharp's (1952) analysis of the effects of the adoption of the steel ax by an Australian native tribe.

Steel Axes for Stone-Age Australians[3]

The consequences of the acceptance of steel axes by a tribe of Australian aborigines offers an illustration of research in

3. Adapted from Sharp, "Steel Axes for Stone-Age Australians," in Edward H. Spicer (editor), *Human Problems in Technological Change.* New York: Russell Sage Foundation, 1952, pp. 69–92, by permission of the publisher.

the anthropology tradition on diffusion. The tribe is the Yir Yoront, who travel in small nomadic groups over a vast territory in search of game and other food. The central item in their culture was the stone ax, which the Yir Yoront found indispensable in producing food, constructing shelters, and obtaining warmth. It is difficult to imagine a more complete revolution than that precipitated by the adoption of the steel ax as a replacement for the stone ax.

The method of study used by Sharp (1952)—and by most of his colleagues in the anthropology tradition—to investigate the Yir Yoront is that of participant observation. A participant observer studies a culture by taking part in its everyday activities. In the 1930's an American anthropologist was able to live with the Yir Yoront for 13 months without seeing another white man. Because of their isolation, the natives were relatively unaffected by modern civilization until the establishment of a nearby missionary station in recent years. The missionaries distributed a great many steel axes among the Yir Yoront as gifts and as pay for work performed.

Before the days of the steel ax, the stone ax was a symbol of masculinity and of respect for elders. The men owned the stone axes, but the women and children were the principal users of these tools. The axes were thus borrowed from fathers, husbands, or uncles according to a system of social relationship prescribed by custom. The Yir Yoront obtained their stone ax heads in exchange for spears through barter with other tribes. The bartering took place as part of elaborate rituals at seasonal fiestas.

When the missionaries distributed the steel axes to the Yir Yoront, they hoped that a rapid improvement in living conditions would result. There was no important resistance to the shift from stone to steel axes, as the aborigines were accustomed to securing their tools via trade with others. The steel axes were more efficient for most tasks, and the stone axes rapidly disappeared among the Yir Yoront. However, the steel ax contributed little to progress; the Yir Yoront used their new-found leisure time for sleep, "an act they had thoroughly mastered."

The missionaries had distributed the steel axes to men, women, and children alike. In fact, the young men were more likely to adopt the new tools than were the elders, who maintained a greater distrust for the missionaries. The result was a disruption of status relations among the Yir Yoront, and a revolutionary confusion of age and sex roles. Elders, once highly respected, now became dependent upon women and younger men and were often forced to borrow their steel axes.

The trading rituals of the tribe were also disorganized. Ties of friendship among traders broke down, and interest in the fiestas, where the barter of stone axes for spears had formerly taken place, declined. The religious system and social structure of the Yir Yoront became disorganized as a result of inability to adjust to the innovation. It is important to note that the steel ax alone did not cause all the social changes among the Yir Yoront, but it was central to most of these cultural disorders.

Later Developments in Anthropology

Sharp's analysis of the adoption of the steel ax by the Yir Yoront illustrates the relative importance placed by the anthropology tradition upon determining the social consequences of innovation. The case of the steel ax should be contrasted with some other anthropological analyses where the innovation studied caused few serious consequences for the adopters' society. An example is Suttles' (1951) investigation of the adoption of potato-growing among a Pacific Northwest Indian tribe.

Probably one of the best-known writings in the anthropology tradition on diffusion is the book by Barnett (1953) entitled *Innovation*. The author is mainly concerned with describing the adoption of innovations at the psychological level, although the concept of the adoption process is not specifically utilized. The data used by Barnett came from six cultures ranging from modern American society to Pacific Northwest Indian tribes. Barnett's discussion of why individuals adopt new ideas is more theoretical than empirical.

In most recent years the anthropology tradition has altered its attention somewhat to emphasize analyses of cross-cultural programs of technical assistance. In many of these research reports, the anthropologists show that the technical assistance planners failed to take fully into account the cultural values of the target audience. The number of change programs analyzed by anthropologists that failed probably outnumbers those that succeeded.[4]

EARLY SOCIOLOGY

The intellectual tradition known in the present book as early sociology can trace its beginning to Tarde. At least 15 different research publications appeared in this tradition during the period from the late 1920's to the early 1940's. The real significance of the early sociology tradition lies neither in the volume of investigations nor in the sophistication of their research methods (as judged by today's standards), but in the influence of the early sociologists' writings on later students of diffusion.

Tarde (1903) proposed several pioneering ideas that have been developed and tested by later diffusion researchers. For instance, Tarde suggested that the adoption of new ideas followed a normal, S-shaped distribution over time. At first,

4. Examples of this type of anthropological report are Dobyns (1951), Bliss (1952), Mead (1955), and Erasmus (1961).

only a few individuals adopt the new idea, then great numbers of individuals accept the innovation, and finally the rate of adoption slackens. Tarde (1903, pp. 87–88) also suggested that the greater cosmopoliteness of innovators (than of later adopters) was one reason for their early acceptance of new ideas. Probably Tarde's greatest contribution was his insights into the process by which the behavior of opinion leaders is imitated by other individuals.

One of the first empirical investigations by an early sociologist was Chapin's (1928) analysis of the diffusion of the city manager plan of government. Chapin utilized secondary sources of data, as did most other early sociologists. He followed Tarde's lead in showing that the adopter distribution for the city manager idea in the United States followed an S-shaped "growth curve." Many other early sociologists[5] were concerned with determining the S-shape and normality of adopter distributions.

Another common theme in several of the researches in this tradition was the concern with determining the ecology of diffusion. For example, both Pemberton (1936b) and Bowers (1938) investigated rural-urban differences in the rate of adoption of radios. The type of innovations studied by early sociologists was limited by their availability from records or other secondary sources, as is shown by the following list: (1) political attitudes (Rice, 1928), (2) postage stamps (Pemberton, 1936b and 1938), (3) compulsory school laws (Pemberton, 1936b), (4) city manager government (Chapin, 1928, and McVoy, 1940), (5) patents for cotton machinery (Davis, 1941), and (6) PTA organizations (Pemberton, 1937).

Most early sociologists traced the diffusion of a single innovation over a geographical area. One exception was McVoy (1940), who constructed an "index of progressiveness" composed of 12 new ideas in state government. This index was an

5. Examples are Pemberton (1936b and 1937), Davis (1941), and Bowers (1938).

early attempt to measure a more general innovativeness dimension. It set a precedent that later researchers, particularly in the rural sociology tradition, were to follow in great numbers.

Bowers' (1937 and 1938) investigation was probably the first study in the early sociology tradition to utilize other sources of data in addition to those from available government records. He contacted a sample of 312 ham radio operators in the United States by mailed questionnaire in order to determine the influences that led to their adoption of radios. Bowers (1938) was the first researcher to find that personal influences were more important (than impersonal influences) for earlier adopters than for later adopters. He concluded, "The diffusion . . . becomes more organized and proselyting as it becomes entrenched."

The number of amateur radio operators in the United States had increased sharply from about 3,000 in 1914, to 46,000 in 1935. Bowers attempted to determine whether this adopter distribution followed a normal shape, and concluded that it was generally an S-shaped normal curve except for a plateau near the middle of the distribution. In a fashion similar to others in the early sociology tradition, Bowers (1938) traced the relationship of such ecological factors as city size, region, and urbanness to the rate of adoption of ham radios.

The motivating interest for the early sociologists was mainly in the diffusion of innovations which promised to contribute to major social changes (Katz and Levin, 1959). The early sociologists, with the exception of Bowers, did not emphasize the adoption process by which an individual decides to adopt, nor did they concentrate upon the processes by which individuals influence others to adopt or reject ideas. These limitations derived in part from the dependence of early sociologists upon secondary sources of data, and the fact that the unit of adoption was most often a state, city, or organization, rather than a single individual.

The early sociologists were aware of the anthropologists Lowie, Wissler, and Kroeber, but seemed to make relatively little use of the anthropologists' ideas. The early sociologists' studies, in turn, contributed indirectly to findings reported in later chapters, but the early sociologists' findings are only rarely cited.

RURAL SOCIOLOGY[6]

The research tradition that has produced the greatest number of publications and studies on the diffusion of new ideas is rural sociology. Most of these studies deal with the transmission of farm innovations from agricultural scientists to farmers. Rural sociology is probably ". . . the only research tradition within the social sciences that can boast so long and so continuing a concern with the social aspects of diffusion" (Katz, 1961).

The background of the tradition dates back to the 1920's when administrators in the USDA Federal Extension Service instigated evaluations of their program's effectiveness. One handy evaluation measure for this adult education agency was the adoption of innovations recommended and promoted by the Extension Service. Typical of these studies are those by M. C. Wilson.[7] One of his earliest studies included data from

6. Because the author is himself involved as a participant in the tradition described in this section, it may be somewhat inevitable that the viewpoint of the rural sociology tradition is thus affected. Katz (1960) analyzed the convergence of two traditions, rural sociology and mass communications, from the latter discipline's viewpoint. He stated, "It would be interesting if a rural sociologist would tell it from his point of view." This section is thus an acceptance of the invitation.

7. Wilson's studies of the 1920's certainly influenced later studies in the rural sociology tradition, but actually he was neither trained in rural sociology nor associated with a department of rural sociology at the time of his diffusion studies.

7,802 families in ten states (Wilson, 1927). It was mainly concerned with the effectiveness of different Extension methods in securing adoption of recommended innovations. As early as 1925, Wilson and his associates were studying the ratio of adopted innovations to the relative costs of their diffusion (Wilson and Gallup, 1955).

Little further research was completed in the rural sociology tradition until 1940 when Kollmorgen (1941) investigated the adoption of farm ideas by German-Swiss farmers and non-German-Swiss farmers. Diffusion became part of the mainstream of rural sociology in the early 1940's. Hoffer (1942) studied the adoption of farm practices by Michigan celery growers of Dutch descent, and Ryan and Gross (1943) investigated the diffusion of hybrid seed corn in Iowa. The latter is the classic study in the rural sociology tradition. In fact, the hybrid seed corn study is undoubtedly the most widely known rural sociological study of all time.[8]

Hoffer's (1942) study was initiated at the insistence of the director of the Michigan Agricultural Experiment Station. He was puzzled as to why the Dutch celergy growers in Michigan refused to adopt disease-control sprays developed by agricultural scientists. Hoffer found his respondents' values on frugality were a major barrier to the adoption of new celery-growing ideas. Even if a farmer could purchase a new spray for fifty dollars in order to save his celery crop worth thousands, he would reject the idea because of his attitude that the way to save money was not to spend it. Hoffer's study is perhaps most noteworthy for its experimental design which included a "control" sample and a "treatment" sample, who received mailings of the bulletin in Dutch and in English. To this extent, the Hoffer study is a marked departure from the *ex post facto* type of research design predominant in all the traditions on diffusion.

8. A study that has perhaps received wider attention outside of rural sociology is Kollmorgen's (1947) analysis of the Old Order Amish.

The Hybrid Seed Corn Study

The Ryan and Gross (1943) investigation of the diffusion of hybrid seed corn, more than any other study, influenced the methods, findings, and interpretations of later students in the rural sociology tradition. The Iowa Agricultural Experiment Station study was initiated because of (1) the significance of hybrid seed corn as an element of agricultural technology in the 1930's, (2) its characteristics, which made it ideal for sociological study,[9] and (3) the personal interest of Bryce Ryan in cultural change.

Neal Gross was a young graduate student in rural sociology at Iowa State College. He actually knew little about rural people and nothing about securing information from them in research interviews. His first research task, Professor Ryan told him upon his arrival in Ames, would be to interview farmers concerning their adoption of hybrid seed. Someone told Gross that Iowa farmers arose at six A.M., and so the next morning he was waiting at daybreak in the barnyard of his first respondent. The story goes that by that evening he had completed 21 research interviews. In fact, Gross averaged about 14 interviews per day during the data-gathering period in 1941! This is particularly amazing when one considers that a rate of four interviews per day is considered average by modern rural sociologists.

A total of 345 farmers were interviewed in two small Iowa communities, Grand Junction and Scranton (Gross, 1942). Twelve farmers with less than 20 acres were discarded as well as 74 respondents who entered farming after hybrid corn began to diffuse.[10] Thus, the final number of respondents was

9. These characteristics included the fact that hybrid seed diffused over a little more than a decade in Iowa, so the researchers felt farmers would be able to recall information about their adoption decision.

10. Ryan and Gross (1943) recognized that some of their respondents were not living in the two communities at the time they adopted hybrid seed. The researchers did not explicitly recognize that some of the adopters had left farming by the time of data-gathering in 1941.

259. All but two of these farmers had adopted hybrid seed when the data were gathered in 1941.

The innovation was the result of years of intensive research by agricultural scientists. The hybrid vigor of the seed did not continue in the second generation, so farmers had to purchase hybrid seed each year, while previously they had selected their own open-pollinated seed. The major advantage of the innovation was a 20 per cent increase in yield. Hybrid seed was not available until 1928 or 1929, but it was almost completely adopted by 1941. Lively commercial interests and the Iowa Extension Service aided the diffusion of the new idea.

The major findings[11] from the hybrid study are:

1. The first use of hybrid seed followed a bell-shaped (but not exactly normal) distribution when plotted over time (Ryan and Gross, 1943). Gross (1942) classified four adopter categories[12] on the basis of their first use of hybrid seed. The social characteristics, such as age, social status, and cosmopoliteness,[13] of both the earliest and the latest adopters were then determined.

2. Three stages in the adoption process were recognized by the researchers: (1) awareness, or first hearing about the new idea, (2) trial, or first use, and (3) adoption, or 100 per cent use.

3. The adoption period from awareness to complete adoption averaged about nine years for all respondents. About 5.5 years were required for the period from awareness to trial, and 3.5 years for the span from trial to 100 per cent use.

11. Publications from the study are Gross (1942 and 1949), Ryan and Gross (1943 and 1950), Gross and Taves (1952), and Rohwer (1949). These reports are supplemented through private communication with both Dr. Ryan and Dr. Gross by the author.

12. An innovativeness scale was constructed of eight new farm ideas other than hybrid corn, but it was not utilized to classify the respondents into adopter categories.

13. In fact, the hybrid study was one of the first to establish the relationship between cosmopoliteness and innovativeness.

4. The typical farmer first heard of hybrid seed from a salesman, but neighbors were the most influential source in leading to adoption. Salesmen were more important information sources for earlier adopters, and neighbors were more important for later adopters.

Several criticisms of the hybrid seed corn investigation may be pointed out.

1. The study was based upon both the existing anthropological and early sociological writings and research on the diffusion of innovations. Nevertheless, the Hoffer (1942) study of Michigan celery growers[14] and the educational diffusion research of Mort and Cornell (1938 and 1941) at Columbia University were ignored.

2. No analysis of opinion leadership in the diffusion of hybrid seed was attempted, although the sample design, which consisted of a complete enumeration of two communities, would have made the use of sociometric questions easily possible. ". . . Information was simply collected from all community members as if they were unrelated respondents in a random sample" (Katz and Levin, 1959).

3. Ryan and Gross defined "aceptance" as first use of hybrid seed (the trial stage), and largely ignored the adoption (100 per cent use) dimension in the data they had gathered. Thus, Gross's (1942) four adopter categories are actually classified on the basis of the time they *tried,* rather than *adopted* hybrid seed.

In spite of these possible shortcomings, however, the scope and depth of the hybrid corn analyis is impressive for its time. A number of subsequent studies have made important advances on the basis of leads set forth by Ryan and Gross (Katz, 1961). However, a great number of later rural sociological studies have followed an unimaginative "factors-related-to-innovativeness" approach. The results add very

14. Professor Ryan, in a recent private correspondence, indicated to the present author that his attention had been called to the Hoffer (1942) study, but by then the hybrid corn analysis was largely completed.

little, in many cases, to present knowledge of how new ideas diffuse except further verification of previous findings.

Later Developments in the Rural Sociology Tradition

The first study in the rural sociology tradition to utilize a sociometric analysis was that of Coleman (1946) in his analysis of the adoption of soil conservation practices by Illinois farmers. The importance of peer influences upon farmers' adoption decisions, which had been suggested in previous studies, was emphasized by Coleman's research. Nevertheless, rural sociologists ". . . have never mapped the spread of a particular innovation against the sociometric structure of an entire community" (Katz, 1960).

Two of the important scholars in this tradition entered the field in the late 1940's. Herbert F. Lionberger (1949 and 1951) in Missouri originally directed his research toward the investigation of the sources of farm information used by low-income farmers. Lionberger (1953, 1955, and 1959) later became more interested in tracing the importance of community norms, traditionalism-modernism, social status, and opinion leadership in the informal transmission of new farm ideas via word of mouth.

Eugene A. Wilkening, a contemporary of Lionberger in this tradition, first studied adoption by North Carolina farmers (1949, 1950a, 1950b, 1951, 1952a, and 1952b), and then by Wisconsin farmers after 1951. Wilkening's North Carolina studies were the first to utilize a social-psychological approach to determine relationships among attitudes, values, and group attachments, and innovativeness. Wilkening's efforts in Wisconsin have particularly centered around the influence of the farm family on adoption decisions (1953, 1954a, 1954b, and 1956).

Since the mid-1950's, there has been a great proliferation

of research studies by rural sociologists.[15] Most of these studies have been financed by state agricultural experiment stations or the USDA (but also in very recent years by agricultural companies). Federal and state agencies spend sizable sums for research on agricultural technology. Their administrators have been convinced of the value of sociological inquiry to trace the diffusion of these research results to farm people. Most rural sociologists are employed by state agricultural universities, and the proximity of these sociologists to state Agricultural Extension Services has affected the tradition.

In recent years, several U.S. rural sociologists have completed research studies in foreign countries using essentially similar methods to those found in the U.S. Examples are Polson and Pal (1955) in the Philippines, Wilkening (1962) and Wilkening and others (1960) in Australia, and Lindstrom (1958) in Japan. A number of foreign nationals, often trained in the U.S. in rural sociology, are now engaged in diffusion research in their home countries. Among these are van den Ban (1953, 1957a, 1957b, 1958, 1960a, 1961a, and in press), Rahudkar (1958, 1959, and 1961), Bose (1961), and Barnabas (1958 and 1960). The contemporary international outlook in the rural sociological tradition provides a cross-cultural test of the propositions generated by research in the U.S. and abroad.[16]

After a relatively slow development in the 1930's and 1940's, the number of studies in the rural sociology tradition increased rapidly in the 1950's and early 1960's. Ryan and

15. When the number of diffusion research studies in rural sociology is plotted by year, the distribution appears to approach a familiar S-shape that has not yet reached the second point of inflection.

16. Another trend in the rural sociology tradition is to analyze not only farm innovations, but also new homemaking ideas (Abell, 1952; Wilkening, 1952a; Bonser, 1958b; Harris, 1956a; and Rogers and Havens, 1961c), new educational ideas (Keitlow and Duncan, 1956), and public health ideas (Belcher, 1958; Lowry and Hay, 1957 and 1958; Hay and Lowry, 1957 and 1958; Belcher and Hay, 1959 and 1960; and Lowry and others, 1958).

Gross's analysis of the diffusion of hybrid corn led directly to investigations of correlates of innovativeness (which are reviewed in Chapters VI, VIII, and X of this book), and information sources at stages in the adoption process (Chapter IV). Four other general types of research in this tradition are (1) social system norms on innovativeness (Chapter III), (2) characteristics of innovations (Chapter V), (3) opinion leadership (Chapter VIII), and (4) the role of change agents (Chapter IX).

Compared to most other traditions, rural sociologists studying diffusion have probably been in closer contact *within* their tradition. The Rural Sociological Society annually devotes several sessions of papers to diffusion, and many studies are published in the Society's journal, *Rural Sociology.* Semiannual meetings of Midwestern rural sociologists studying diffusion are sponsored by the Farm Foundation, and out of these conferences have grown several summary publications and bibliographies (NCRS Subcommittee, 1955, 1956, 1959, and 1961). A recent summary of rural sociological research has appeared in book form by Lionberger (1960).

One general criticism of the rural sociology tradition, which has been voiced by rural sociologists themselves,[17] is the lack of attention to sociological theory. There is a noticeable tendency for many rural sociology diffusion studies to approach raw empiricism, with little emphasis upon the sociological significance of the findings.

The rural sociology tradition probably has received more favorable evaluation from outsiders than from its own members. For instance, Katz (1956) stated that rural sociology ". . . is an island of communications research deriving from a sociological tradition which has taken account of the fact that 'farmers talk to other farmers' and that such interaction has consequences for the response of individuals and groups. . . ."

17. Examples are Lionberger (1952 and 1960).

EDUCATION

The education diffusion tradition is one of the largest in number of studies (150 are listed in a recent bibliography by Ross, 1958), but this tradition is probably one of lesser significance in terms of its contributions to understandings of the diffusion of ideas. The education diffusion studies illustrate strong intercommunication within the tradition, but no close attention to any other diffusion tradition.[18] Ross (1958, p. 553), after his review of education diffusion studies, concluded, "Seldom has dispersed research in some phase of education been so well articulated and formed such an integrated pattern as a whole." It is interesting to note that neither the field of education nor educational sociology has paid much attention to the educational diffusion studies. There is no reference to any of these diffusion reports in the major educational sociology books.

The majority of education diffusion studies have been done at one institution, Columbia University's Teachers College, under the sponsorship of one researcher, Paul Mort. He was described as the "guiding force" in all the education studies (Ross, 1958, p. xi). The ancestry of the education tradition traces to the early research by Mort and others on school finance in the 1920's. They were trying to show the value of local control over school financial decisions. One advantage, Mort felt, was that local control lead to greater "adaptability," the key concept in almost all of the Columbia University diffusion researches that were to follow (Mort, 1960). Adaptability, essentially a synonym for innovativeness, was defined as "the capacity of a school to take on new

18. A rare exception to this statement is the first publication in this tradition (Mort and Cornell, 1938), where several sociologists and anthropologists, such as Ogburn (1922) and Wissler (1923), were cited. Cocking (1951) cited Ogburn (1922) and Linton (1936).

practices and discard outmoded ones" (Ross, 1955, pp. 173–174). Mort and Cornell (1938) stated:

To operate schools today in terms of the understandings of a half century ago is to waste school funds and school time. Adaptability, or the capacity to meet new needs by taking on new purposes and new practices, is indispensable to the effective functioning of any school system.

There is little doubt in this statement, or in any of the Columbia University education diffusion publications, that innovativeness of schools is perceived as desirable.

There is probably little need to review the 150 education studies at Columbia University in detail because this task has already been fulfilled by Ross (1958), even to the extent of showing the influence of one study in this tradition upon another. Most of the Columbia University research studies were published as D.Ed. theses or as Teachers College reports. It is interesting to note that the financial support for these studies came largely from the public schools being studied! The total research budget for Columbia University education diffusion investigations was over one-quarter million dollars in 1959 (Mort, 1960). Most of this financial support was donated by an annual fee from (1) each member of the Metropolitan School Study Council, mostly public schools in the New York City area, and (2) member schools in the Associated Public School Systems, located throughout the United States.

The data were most often gathered by mailed questionnaire from school superintendents or principals. The unit of analysis was the school system in almost all these investigations. A number of central findings have emerged from the education diffusion studies which may be summarized as follows.

1. Among the great variety of factors related to innovativeness (or "adaptability") among schools, the best single predictor of this dimension is educational cost per pupil. The wealth factor almost appears to be a necessary prerequisite for innovativeness among public schools.

2. A considerable "time lag" is required for the wide-

spread adoption of new educational ideas. ". . . The average American school lags 25 years behind the best practice" (Mort, 1946, pp. 199–200). Why is the diffusion of educational ideas so much slower than farm innovations or medical drugs? It may be because of the (1) absence of a scientific source of innovations in education, (2) lack of change agents to promote new educational ideas, and (3) lack of an economic incentive to adopt. Pelley (1948, pp. 170–171) stated, "Unfortunately, there seems to be no possible profit motive in being an educational innovator."

There is, of course, a wide range in the rate of adoption among educational ideas. For example, Allen (1956, pp. 56–83) compared the diffusion of driver training, an innovation promoted by safety groups and car dealers, with the idea of pupils studying their community. Sixty years were required for this idea to reach 90 per cent adoption among 168 United States schools while only 18 years were needed for driver training to reach this level of adoption.

3. The pattern of adoption of an educational idea over time approaches an S-shaped curve.[19] At first, only a few "pioneer" schools adopt the idea, then the majority decide the new idea is desirable, and finally the adopter curve levels off as the last remaining schools adopt.

4. An innovativeness scale (called a "time scale") was developed by Mort and Pierce (1947) that consisted of a number of new educational ideas. A scoring system was developed that gave a school greater numerical credit for earlier adoption of an idea. The Mort and Pierce "time scale" led to improved measures of innovativeness by later researchers in other traditions as well as in education. Rogers' (1958b) method of adopter categorization in rural sociology is directly based upon the Mort and Pierce (1947) method that was completed 11 years earlier.

The first nationwide diffusion study of any kind was com-

19. Studies supporting this statement are Farnsworth (1940), Mort and Cornell (1941), Cocking (1941), Barrington (1953), Lovos (1955), Adler (1955), and Allen (1956).

pleted in the education tradition by Cocking (1951). He sampled 1,200 United States schools regarding their adoption of seven educational ideas such a student work experiences, career conferences, popularized budgets, and radio workshops. He found no significant differences among regions of the United States as to their innovativeness in adopting these new ideas. More cosmopolite schools, located nearer to metropolitan cities, were found to be more innovative.

The extensive number of education diffusion studies at Columbia University makes one wonder why these 150 studies have gone relatively unnoticed. The lack of attention paid the Columbia education studies is characteristic both of other researchers in the education tradition and of those in other diffusion research traditions.

The convergence of the education tradition with other traditions has been somewhat aided in most recent years by several studies on resistances to the adoption of educational ideas.[20] These studies have typically been completed at institutions other than Columbia University. Eichholz (1961), for example, effected a convergence of the rural sociology with the education tradition in his analysis of the rejection of such audiovisual innovations as films, filmstrips, radio programs, and television shows for school purposes. Eichholz gathered data from 45 elementary school teachers in one city; it is significant that in his study the unit of analysis is the *teacher* rather than the school. Eichholz postulated a theory of rejection of new ideas, somewhat parallel (but opposite) to the adoption of innovations. Attempts empirically to test this theory of rejection were not completely successful.

Barton (1961) is currently conducting an investigation of the diffusion of educational methods for teaching retarded

20. Among these studies are those of Clendenen (1961) and Goldstein and others (1961) on the rejection of educational television viewing, Fox and others (1961), and McIntyre (1960) on resistances to audiovisual materials by college teachers. Another recent study of educational innovations is Haber's (1961) investigation of the spread of high school language laboratories.

children among school systems. He is a sociologist in Columbia University's Bureau of Applied Social Research. As such, the Barton study constitutes a convergence of the sociology traditions with the education tradition.

In summary, intratradition communication of education research far excelled intertradition communication with other diffusion traditions.

INDUSTRIAL

The industrial tradition of diffusion research includes researchers with a wider range of disciplinary backgrounds than in the case of other traditions. Economic historians, industrial economists, and industrial engineers are represented among those investigating the adoption of new industrial ideas. A strong economic orientation is evident throughout the industrial tradition, and the economics of innovation have probably been analyzed more thoroughly in the industrial tradition than in any other. The most common methodological approach used by those in the industrial tradition is the case study. This approach has been combined, however, with mathematical and statistical analyses in recent years. The data generally are obtained from secondary sources such as historical records. The industrial firm is most often the unit of analysis in this tradition.

Danhof (1949) described four adopter categories that he felt could be observed among industrial firms.

1. Innovators—the first firms to adopt a new idea.

2. Initiators—the firms who adopted the idea soon after the innovators.

3. Fabians—the firms who adopted the idea only after its utility was widely acknowledged in a particular industry.

4. Drones—the last firms to adopt new ideas.

Since Danhof's typology of four adopter categories was published, several researchers have attempted to determine empirically the characteristics of industrial firms associated with innovativeness. Carter and Williams (1957, p. 110) classified 130 English firms as to innovativeness, and then proceeded to determine the characteristics of the most "parochial" and the most progressive. A similar approach was used in a later study by the same authors (Carter and Williams, 1959) in an analysis of 50 English firms and by Sutherland (1959) in his investigation of 16 cotton-spinning companies. Particular emphasis was placed on the relationship of innovativeness to profitability by Enos (1958 and 1960), Mansfield (1960, 1961a, and 1961b), and Strassman (1959). The latter investigation utilized case studies of industrial innovations in the steel, textile, machine tool, and electric power industries to determine the effect of risk on innovative behavior.

The Carter and Williams (1959) study of the innovativeness of 50 English industrial firms is perhaps somewhat typical of the industrial diffusion tradition. Each firm was rated as to "technical progressiveness" on a ten-point scale. The researchers then proceeded to determine the characteristics of the most and least innovative firms. Factors found to be related to innovativeness included:

1. A favorable attitude toward science as evidenced by the status given scientists in the firm.

2. Cosmopoliteness as indicated by the worldwide travel of executives, and lack of secretiveness with plant visitors.

3. Adequate information sources as measured by subscriptions to scientific journals and degree of contact with universities.

4. A high growth rate for the firm.

5. Lack of "shop-floor resistance to innovation" as evidenced by the conservatism of foremen and union resistance.

Several of the industrial studies have been published in the same journal, the *Journal of Industrial Economics,* but there appears to be less awareness of other studies within the industrial tradition (as evidenced by cross-referencing) than in the case of other traditions. Perhaps this results from the greater variety of disciplinary backgrounds of the researchers, and from the fact that the research has been completed in both England and the United States. There has certainly been an academic isolation of the industrial tradition from other traditions. The first awareness by industrial diffusion researchers of other research traditions did not come until 1960 when Mansfield cited the rural sociology and medical sociology traditions.

MEDICAL SOCIOLOGY

The medical sociology tradition on the diffusion of innovations began somewhat later than the other major traditions. The innovations studied consisted of (1) either new drugs or techniques, where the adopters are doctors, or (2) polio vaccine, chest X rays, or other medical ideas, where the adopters are the public.

The medical sociology tradition really got under way in the 1950's,[21] about the same time that medical sociology began to become increasingly recognized as a field of sociological specialization.[22] One of the first studies of the diffusion of a medical drug was by Caplow (1952) and Caplow and Ray-

21. Earlier studies that might be classified in the medical sociology tradition are Miller's (1957) analysis of the adoption of smallpox inoculation in England and France, and Stern's (1927 and 1937) work on resistances to new medical developments. Neither the Stern nor the Miller study, however, seems to have influenced later investigations in the medical sociology tradition.

22. It is important to note that the early researchers in the medical sociology tradition did not identify themselves as "medical" sociologists.

mond (1954). They sought mainly to determine the degree of influence of opinion leaders in the diffusion of drugs among medical doctors. Their results were somewhat inconclusive.

The Columbia University Drug Study

Certainly the classic study in the medical sociology tradition is that by three sociologists, Elihu Katz, Herbert Menzel, and James Coleman, who were in Columbia University's Bureau of Applied Social Research. The significance of this investigation, hereafter referred to as the "drug study," is comparable to that of the Ryan and Gross analysis of hybrid seed corn in terms of its contributions to our knowledge of the diffusion of new ideas.

The roots from which the drug study grew can be traced to a series of discussions by staff members in the Bureau of Applied Social Research about areas of needed investigation.[23] One proposal by Elihu Katz involved sociometrically tracing the chains of personal influence which had resulted in some type of changed behavior. One of the Bureau's alumni was a director of market research for a large pharmaceutical firm, Charles Pfizer and Company, in New York. He approached the Bureau in 1954 about a study of medical doctors' readership of the Pfizer drug magazine. The existing Katz proposal for studying personal influence was adapted to the problem of how physicians decided to adopt new drugs.

The Pfizer Company provided a grant of about $40,000 to the Bureau for the study, which began in 1954. A pilot study of the spread of a new drug among 33 doctors in a New England town was carried out in May, 1954, and the results were reported by Menzel and Katz (1955).

The primary investigation was conducted, after methodo-

23. Much of the background material about the drug study comes from a private communication from Menzel (1960b).

logical techniques had been pretested in the pilot study, in four cities in Illinois in late 1954. Three of the sites selected had about 30,000 to 40,000 population, while the fourth was a city of about 110,000. The Illinois data were reported in Menzel and others (1959), Coleman and others (1957, 1959, and in press), Katz (1956, 1957, and 1961), Katz and Levin (1959), and Menzel (1957, 1959, and 1960a). The present discussion features data mainly from the four Illinois cities, rather than from the pilot study in New England.

The drug study analyzed the diffusion of a new antibiotic that appeared in late 1953. The innovation was referred to by the Bureau researchers in most of their published reports by a pseudonym, "gammanyn," except in one report (Katz, 1956, p. 189). Gammanyn had been tried at least once by 87 per cent of the doctors interviewed in the four Illinois communities within 15 months after its release. The respondents had been making extensive use of two closely related "miracle" drugs, belonging to the same antibiotic family as gammanyn. Thus, the new drug superceded an existing idea just as hybrid corn replaced open-pollinated seed.

Pharmaceutical companies retain a corps of salesmen called "detail men" who call on physicians to inform them about new drugs. The Pfizer Company, of course, hoped to learn from the Bureau study how doctors were influenced to purchase new products, and then to design their magazines and instruct their detail men accordingly. It is perhaps important to note that the sponsors of the drug study made little practical use of the results of the drug study and did not fully appreciate the sociological significance of their research investment.

It is, of course, the patient and not the doctor who pays for a costly new drug, although it is the doctor who makes the adoption decision. One of few similar decision situations occurs when a college teacher "adopts" a new textbook that his students actually purchase. The textbook salesman, like the detail man, does not make direct sales of his products, but tries to influence the teacher to adopt.

The Bureau sociologists interviewed 125 general practitioners, internists, and pediatricians in the four Illinois communities. These were 85 per cent of the doctors practicing in specialties where "the new drug was of major potential significance" (Coleman and others, 1957).

During the personal interview, each doctors was asked to name: (1) his three best friends among physicians; (2) the three or four physicians with whom he most often discussed cases or therapy; and (3) the colleagues whom he most frequently called when in need of special information or special advice on questions of drug therapy.

The 125 respondents sociometrically designated at least 103 additional doctors in other specialties in their cities, who were also interviewed. Whereas many of the findings from the drug study are based upon the sample of 125 physicians, the sociometric analyses of opinion leadership are based upon data from the total sample of 228 doctors,[24] which constituted 64 per cent of all doctors in active private practice in the four cities (Coleman and others, 1957).

Date of trial for each doctor was determined by means of an audit of prescriptions on file in pharmacies in the four communities studied. A three-day sampling period was selected for each of the 17 months following the introduction of gammanyn. All prescriptions on file for these three-day periods were examined (Katz, 1961). "Records were obtained from 64 of the 84 drugstores in the four cities. Of the remaining 20, only two had any significant pharmaceutical business" (Coleman and others, 1957).

One of the neat methodological twists of the drug study was the use of an *objective measure* of time of adoption from

24. There appears to be some ambiguity as to the total number of doctors interviewed. The sample size is variously reported as 228 by Coleman and others (1957), 216 by Katz (1956, p. 185), and 256 by Coleman and Menzel (1955, pp. 1–3). These differences have never been explained by the Bureau researchers, but may be the result of discarding certain interview schedules for various reasons such as incomplete data.

the written record of prescriptions. This is the only study, except Havens' (1962) analysis of the adoption of the bulk milk tank, where the researchers were not forced to depend upon recall-type data on innovativeness. There was, in fact, a marked tendency for most doctors to report themselves as having adopted the drug earlier than the prescription records indicated (Menzel, 1957).

But the drug study methodology, while eliminating one source of inaccuracy in adoption dates of gammanyn, introduced another. The three-day sampling period out of each month leaves something to be desired. What of the doctor who prescribed the drug on one of the 27 days each month not sampled, but did not prescribe it during the three days that were sampled? Nevertheless, the use of prescription records was probably a major improvement in accuracy over recall data. It is unfortunate that the researchers used only a three-day sample per month, but the volume of effort involved in a complete enumeration of prescriptions evidently prohibited a complete audit of the drug records.[25]

Another shortcoming of the drug study was the researchers' use of the date of *trial*, or first use of gammanyn, rather than the date of adoption, as a basic measure of innovativeness. In this regard, the drug study suffered a weakness similar to that of the hybrid corn investigation. The distribution of trial dates probably followed the distribution of adoption dates rather closely for gammanyn, but some imprecision in the measure of innovativeness is nevertheless introduced.[26]

Hawkins (1959a) criticized the drug study for its inadequate review of existing literature[27] in the drug diffusion field. The Bureau researchers certainly were not aware of

25. Another possible source of inaccuracy in adoption dates was eliminated by Coleman and others (in press) by correcting for seasonal variations in the amount of gammanynlike drugs.

26. Use of the date of trial as a measure of innovativeness is probably less accurate for the relatively earlier adopters than for the later adopters. We shall see in Chapter IV that the trial-adoption period for laggards is much shorter than for innovators.

27. Such as Caplow (1952) and Caplow and Raymond (1954).

other research traditions on diffusion nor of other studies in their own tradition at the time the gammanyn data were gathered. The latter is probably not too serious an omission, since the gammanyn study would not have been influenced much by knowledge of previous drug studies.

However, the drug study may have suffered somewhat in design and methodology through ignorance of other traditions. For instance, little attention was paid in the drug study to stages in the adoption process (Coleman and others, in press). The Bureau researchers make no secret of their surprise upon discovery of the hybrid seed study. Katz (1961) stated ". . . the drug study was completed only a few years ago without any real awareness of its many similarities to the study that had been undertaken by Ryan and Gross almost fifteen years before."

It is difficult to say exactly when the convergence of the drug study with other intellectual traditions occurred. The Bureau researchers certainly knew of the rural sociology tradition, and vice versa, by 1956 (Katz, 1956), but this awareness did not lead directly to much academic interchange between the two traditions for several years. One result of the convergence, as Katz and Levin (1959) pointed out, occurred for mass communications researchers, who had two inaccuracies inherent in their image of modern society. They (1) assumed that people were easily manipulated by mass media, and (2) perceived society as "an atomized mass of disconnected individuals." Both of these important inaccuracies have recently been recognized, Katz (1960) feels, through convergence of the mass communications researchers with studies in rural sociology.

The findings from the drug study with greatest significance to the present book are threefold:

1. The detailed sociometric data secured from the physicians allowed an analysis in depth of the patterns of influence through which gammanyn spread in the medical community. The relationship between opinion leadership (or "integration," as the Bureau researchers preferred to call

the number of sociometric choices received by a doctor) and innovativeness was established. The rather complete data on the positions of physicians in the social structure allowed one of the most sophisticated analyses yet completed of personal influence in the spread of new ideas.

2. The drug study also established the correlates of innovativeness for a type of respondent that had not previously been studied in this regard. Most of the variables related to innovativeness (such as cosmopoliteness, social status, opinion leadership, size of operation, and communication behavior) had already been thoroughly investigated for samples of farmers and public schools (see Chapter VI). Yet it was important to learn that these same relationships of innovativeness with other concepts held for physicians.

One factor related to innovativeness was whether a respondent was "profession-oriented" or "patient-oriented." The most salient reference group for the profession-oriented doctor was his local colleagues, while the patient-oriented physician placed greater importance on "the respect in which he is held by his own patients" (Coleman and others, 1957). The profession-oriented doctors first used gammanyn an average of 2.8 months sooner than the patient-oriented physicians.

3. The third major contribution of the drug study is the methodological technique of determining the date of doctors' first use of gammanyn from prescription records rather than from recall.

Later Studies in the Medical Sociology Tradition

Since the time of the Columbia University drug study, a number of analyses have been completed of public acceptance of medical ideas. Examples of these kinds of investigations are:

(1) studies of the acceptance of the Salk polio vaccine, completed by Deasy (1956), Glaser (1958), and Sills and Gill (1959); (2) Hochbaum (1960) and Yeracaris (1961), who analyzed the public use of X rays and other preventive health ideas;[28] (3) McNeil (1957), Gamson (1961 and in press), Davis (1959), and others, who studied why communities adopt or reject the fluoridation of water supplies to prevent tooth decay.

Most of the later studies in the medical sociology tradition have analyzed correlates of innovativeness, such as social status and scientific attitudes. These studies have probably added relatively little to the state of knowledge about the diffusion of ideas.

RELATIONSHIPS AMONG THE TRADITIONS

There has been a greater academic interchange among certain of the six major research traditions than among others. The relative isolation from other traditions of both the anthropolgy and the industrial traditions has already been noted. Figure 2-1 shows certain of the relationships among the six major traditions on the basis of references cited in written reports of research.[29] In general, a trend can be observed for researchers in earlier traditions to affect researchers in traditions that developed later.

28. A series of studies has been completed by rural sociologists on the adoption of health insurance (Lowry and Hay, 1957 and 1958; Hay and Lowry, 1957 and 1958; Belcher and Hay, 1959 and 1960; and Lowry and others, 1958).

29. The data from which these lines of convergence are drawn were obtained mainly from cited references and are supported in many cases by the author's personal communication with a number of diffusions researchers. The use of footnote references to trace convergences between traditions has also been utilized by Katz and Levin (1959).

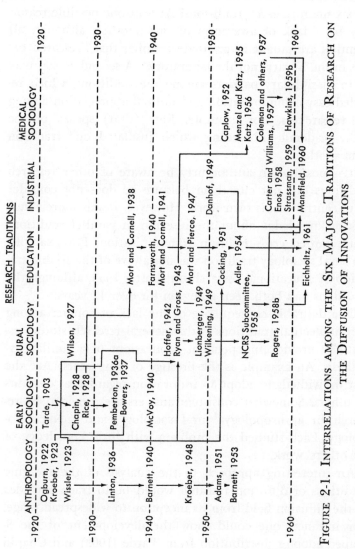

FIGURE 2-1. INTERRELATIONS AMONG THE SIX MAJOR TRADITIONS OF RESEARCH ON THE DIFFUSION OF INNOVATIONS

Only some of the major research studies are shown in this diagram for the sake of brevity. The arrows illustrate influences of one study upon another.

Why is there such a marked lack of communication among the six main research traditions? At least one possible reason may be a lack of awareness of one another, although all scientists are taught in graduate training that "research begins in the library, not the laboratory." A second reason may lie in disciplinary barriers among the traditions, which retarded easy communication and mutual appreciation among the researchers. For example, Katz (1961) speaks of the ". . . academic inbreeding which insulated one tradition from another."

It is possible an author may be aware of other research traditions but not cite them because he does not consider them central to his own work. However, it was more likely lack of knowledge about the research in parallel traditions that retarded cross-tradition communication. For example, the rural sociology tradition was not aware of the sizable tradition of educational research until after 1955, although the traditions had both been going on for over 17 years!

One desirable consequence of the lack of contact among the intellectual traditions is that several research studies essentially provide independent replications of a similar hypothesis. An example is the prestige of innovators: Are the first individuals to adopt an innovation regarded as deviants by others? Somewhat consistent answers are provided by research in anthropology, rural sociology, and medical sociology. Each studied the problem with little knowledge of the others' work.

An interesting approach to the analysis of the merging traditions of diffusion research would be to trace one idea in the diffusion field from its inception to widespread usage. For instance, one could show the development of the S-shaped adopter distribution from Tarde (1903) and Chapin (1928) through early sociology, rural sociology, education, and medical sociology. Or, one could trace such ideas as adopter categories, innovativeness scores, sociometric methods of locating opinion leaders, or the characteristics of innovations. To date, this type of analysis of the diffusion research traditions has not been completed.

SUMMARY

Six major traditions on the diffusion of innovations are described: anthropology, early sociology, rural sociology, education, industrial, and medical sociology. A *research tradition* is a series of research studies on a similar topic in which successive studies are influenced by preceding investigations. There has been a very inadequate diffusion of diffusion research findings among those researching the topic.

Each of the six major traditions is described in summary form in Table 2-1.

TABLE 2-1

A COMPARISON OF THE DIFFUSION RESEARCH TRADITIONS

Tradition	Main Disciplines Represented	Main Method of Data-Gathering and Analysis	Main Unit of Analysis	Major Types of Findings
1. Anthropology	Anthropology	Participant observer combined with descriptive analysis	Societies or tribes	How idea diffuses from one society to another; consequences of innovation
2. Early sociology	Sociology	Data from secondary sources, and a type of statistical analysis	Mainly communities, but also individuals	S-shaped adopter distribution; correlates of innovativeness

Tradition	Main Disciplines Represented	Main Method of Data-Gathering and Analysis	Main Unit of Analysis	Major Types of Findings
3. Rural sociology	Sociology	Personal interviews and statistical analysis	Individual farmers	Correlates of innovativeness; characteristics of ideas related to their rate of adoption; source of information at adoption process stages; S-shaped adopter distribution
4. Education	Education	Mailed questionnaires and statistical analysis	School systems	Correlates of innovativeness; S-shaped adopter distribution
5. Industrial	Industrial economists; Industrial historians; Industrial engineers	Case studies and statistical analysis	Industrial firms	Correlates of innovativeness
6. Medical sociology	Sociology; Public health	Personal interviews and statistical analysis	Individuals	Opinion leadership in diffusion; correlates of innovativeness

CHAPTER III

Culture, Norms, and Diffusion

If we know what a so-
ciety's culture is, including its particular system of values and attitudes,
we can predict with a fairly high degree of probability whether the
bulk of its members will welcome or resist a particular innovation.

RALPH LINTON, 1952, p. 74

The purpose of this chapter is to show
the importance of cultural values on the diffusion of new
ideas, to describe two ideal types of social system norms (traditional and modern), and to show the effect of a system's
norms on individual innovativeness.

IMPORTANCE OF CULTURE IN DIFFUSION

A norm is defined as the most frequently occurring pattern
of overt behavior for the members of a particular social system. Norms influence the diffusion of new ideas. A system's
norms can be a barrier to change, as was shown in the earlier
example of water-boiling in a Peruvian community. Cultural
resistances to new ideas are often found in food habits. In
India, for example, sacred cows roam the countryside while
millions of people are undernourished. Pork cannot be con-
sumed in Moslem countries. Polished rice is eaten in most of
Asia and the United States even though whole rice is more
nutritious. Food habits are generally imbedded deeply in a

society's traditions; they are affected directly by cultural
values.

Apodaca (1952, pp. 35–39) illustrated the importance of
a social system's norms in causing the discontinuance of an
innovation. An improved hybrid seed corn was introduced in
a Spanish-American farm community in New Mexico by
a county extension agent. Careful technical observations were
made to ensure the success of the innovation; local soils were
tested for their applicability in growing the new corn. The
change agent set up a demonstration plot near the village the
first year. The hybrid seed yielded three times the normal
harvest expected from the old varieties. The next year, half
of the farmers adopted the hybrid seed. But two years later
nearly all had returned to planting their original varieties.

Why did the village farmers discontinue the new idea? Because their wives did not like the hybrid. Corn was ground
to make tortillas, a flat corn bread indispensable to the local
diet. The hybrid corn had a strange flavor and did not "hang
together well" for tortillas. The norms of the social system
favored the old varieties rather than the hybrid. If the
county agents had considered local norms as well as local soil
conditions, perhaps he could have introduced a hybrid variety that would have resulted in good tortillas as well as
high yields.

Yet another illustration of the importance of cultural
values on the spread of new ideas comes from Vietnam. A few
years ago, when rice yields fell far short in that country,
U.S. technical assistance workers introduced the tilapia fish.
These fish multiply like rabbits, provide needed protein, and
are tasty eating. Lakes and farm ponds were stocked with
tilapia fish. All went well until Communist sympathizers
started a whispering campaign that the fish were poisonous.
Sick persons were fed tilapia and induced to spread the word
that the fish caused their sickness. A great deal of resistance
to the idea was developed. It took three years of whispering

back and forth before the tilapia fish were accepted as part of the local diet.

This example shows that the spread of innovations is not a simple matter of economic advantage, although economic factors may be important in many instances. Economic considerations are more likely of greater significance in modern societies than in traditional ones. One of the early studies in the rural sociology tradition emphasized this point. Pedersen (1951) compared the rate of adoption of farm ideas by Danish and Polish farmers in Wisconsin. The Polish farmers came from a background of subsistence farming; the Danish farmers were accustomed to producing for a world food market. The cultural values of the Danish farmers facilitated the adoption of new ideas, whereas the norms of the Polish community perpetuated the *status quo*.

One last illustration of the interrelatedness of culture and diffusion is provided by the Shoshoni Indians of Nevada (Harris, 1940). Cultural values influence not only the original adoption or rejection of an innovation but also how the new idea will be integrated into the existing way of life. The consequences of an innovation are at least partially determined by the culture. When horses were introduced into the Shoshoni culture, the Indians knew what to do with them. The Shoshonis had previous experience with horses; they had stolen horses from settlers for food. So, when Indian agents gave them horses for transportation, they readily accepted them. But they ate them.

TRADITIONAL AND MODERN NORMS

It is theoretically important to distinguish two ideal types of norms: traditional and modern. These two types of norms will be described, but first the reader should understand what is meant by "ideal types." *Ideal types* are conceptualizations that are based on observations of reality and designed to institute comparisons.[1] They do not necessarily exist empirically, but may be constructed by abstracting the characteristics of the behavior under analysis to a logical extreme. Empirical instances (in the present case, norms) are compared with the ideal types to see how closely the empirical cases approach the ideal types. The purpose of constructing ideal types is purely methodological. They provide tools for analysis and understanding of some dimension. Ideal types are "ideal" in the sense not that they describe what ought to be but that they logically accentuate some dimension of analysis. Ideal types could be constructed for the analysis of brothels as well as for the study of religion.

Since early times sociologists have conceptualized polar types. These ideal types include the *Gemeinschaft* and *Gesellschaft* of Toennies and Loomis, Durkheim's mechanical and organic solidarity, Weber's rational and traditional types, Hawley's commensalistic-symbiotic types, Merton's local and cosmopolitan, Sorokin's familistic and contractual, and the sacred and secular types of Becker. The ideal types of social system norms utilized here—traditional and modern—are based, at least in part, on the previous ideal typologies.[2]

A number of synonyms may be used to describe the modern cultural type; it may be said to be more innovative, more progressive, more developed, or more economically rational. The crucial dimension, in any case, is that individuals in social systems with modern norms view innovations more favorably

1. This definition is based primarily on that of Martindale (1959, p. 58).

2. The traditional and modern ideal types are based most directly on the work of Redfield (1930 and 1956), Weber (1947, pp. 115–116), Wolf (1955), and, particularly, Lerner (1958). Social system norms have been termed "high adoption" and "low adoption" by Marsh and Coleman (1954a) and Rahudkar (1960), and "traditional" and "progressive" by van den Ban (in press). The present author prefers the terms traditional and modern for social system norms, which are regarded as extremes on a continuum of innovativeness.

and are likely to adopt new ideas more rapidly than are members of traditional social systems. While the modernist welcomes change, the traditionalist resists the new.

In general terms, a social system with traditional norms is characterized by: (1) A less developed or complex technology. Subsistence agriculture is the most common occupation. (2) Literacy and education are at a relatively low level. Communication via word of mouth is more prevalent than by mass media. (3) Little communication by members of the social system with outsiders. Most individuals are localites rather than cosmopolites. (4) Lack of economic rationality. Primary group relationships such as friendliness and hospitality are highly valued as ends in themselves rather than as means to ends. (5) Lack of ability to empathize or see oneself in others' roles, particularly the roles of outsiders to the system. The traditional person does not meet new individuals, recognize new roles, or learn new social relationships involving himself as well as the modern individual does. Individuals in a traditional system usually play only one role, never learn other roles, and seldom learn how to learn them.

In comparison, a modern social system is typified by: (1) A developed technology with a complex division of labor. The individuals in the modern social system are more urban in occupation than those in the traditional system. Although a traditional social system may be industrialized, the type of industry would likely be cottage industries rather than large factories. (2) A high value on science and education. (3) Cosmopoliteness of social relationships. New ideas enter the social system freely from external sources, and members of the system interact often with outsiders. (4) Planning is careful and decisions are economically rational. The most effective means are used to reach desired ends. (5) Ability to empathize and see oneself in the other fellow's shoes.

In summary, the social system with modern norms is more technologically developed, cosmopolite, literate, rational, and empathetic. The traditional strategy of action was described

by von Neumann and Morganstern (1953, p. 88) in terms
of game theory. The traditional "player," instead of making a
decision as the necessity arises, makes up his mind in advance
for all possible contingencies. Thus the traditionalist ". . .
begins to play with a complete plan; a plan which specifies
what choice he will make in every possible situation, for
every possible actual information that he possesses. . . ." In
the traditional social system, the alternatives to be selected in
a choice situation are prescribed by the "authority of an
eternal yesterday" (Weber, 1958, p. 78).

There is one danger in thinking in terms of ideal cultural
types; the extent of differences in norms may be overempha-
sized. We may misjudge the size of the molehills. The traditional and modern ideal types are actually end points on an
innovativeness continuum.

Our discussion should not be interpreted to mean that
traditional norms are necessarily undesirable. In many cases,
tradition may lend stability to a social system where it is
undergoing rapid change and the danger of disorganization.

MEASURING THE
TRADITIONAL-MODERN DIMENSION

1. At the Individual Level

Traditional and modern social system norms have now
been described. It is possible to measure the location of
individuals on a continuum extending from one ideal type
to the other. The variety of techniques utilized to measure
the traditional-modern dimension at the individual level include:

1. Benvenuti's (1961) scale, composed of ten public issues. Each of the 484 farmers in a rapidly changing Netherlands community were asked their opinion of ten issues. Points were awarded for having an opinion about an issue, whether the opinion was "correct" or "incorrect." Thus, the degree to which an individual was involved in the society outside his community was used as the yardstick of modernism by Benvenuti. Some evidence of the validity of the Benvenuti scale was found.[3]

2. Lerner's (1958) modernism scale, indicating whether his respondents in Middle East countries had opinions or replied they "didn't know" to nine questions about public issues. The respondents were classified into three categories on the basis of their scale responses: moderns, transitionals, or traditionals. Lerner assumed that moderns should have the ability to empathize with outsiders' roles, and should thus have an opinion about nonlocal public issues.

3. Copp's (1956) index of the traditional-modern dimension among Kansas cattlemen, which was obtained by asking them what they felt were the determinants of success in farming. Responses were categorized as modern ("flexible") or traditional ("rigid"). Typical of traditional replies were "Hard work," "Keeping one's nose to the grindstone," and "Don't drive around too much."

4. Hobb's (1960) scale which indicated whether his sample

3. Benvenuti asked 25 judges in the community to describe a list of farmers who had scored extremely high or low on his modernism scale. The validity of the scale is suggested by the consistency with which the judges' descriptions of the respondents were in terms of their modernism or traditionalism. This interesting kind of validity check might be used in other studies.

It may have been implied in this chapter that the traditional-modern continuum is undimensional, but there is no research evidence that this is true. In fact, van den Ban's factor analyses of data from three Netherlands communities and of Bose's (1962) correlation matrix suggest that the traditional-modern dimension may be multidimensional.

of 315 Iowa farmers were "traditional work oriented" or "management oriented." He regarded a high value on work *per se* as one indication of traditionalism.[4]

Further insight into the location of individuals on a traditional-modern continuum is provided by a composite word picture of two Netherlands farmers who were respondents in Benvenuti's (1961) study.[5]

FARMER *M:* MODERN. The *M* family live on a larger-than-average-sized farm, but their modernism is owing to more than a higher social status alone. Farmer *M* is both busy and businesslike. It was necessary to make an interview appointment by telephone. He is a director of the local farmers' cooperative and active in several formal organizations in the community. Some disorder about the barn and yard was noticed; Mr. *M* explained this by saying, "One must disregard appearances and try to work as efficiently as one can."

Farmer *M* is about thirty-five. He graduated from an agricultural school, and has since had evening school training in agriculture. He inherited his farm from his father, who now lives in town. Mrs. *M*, dressed in an urban fashion, had just returned from a shopping trip when the interviewer called. The children are friendly and evidently accustomed to seeing

4. Several other researchers have measured specific dimensions of the traditional-modern dimension at the individual level. Examples are van den Ban (1956), Wichers (1956), Mendras (1958), van de Ven (1957), Harris (1956), Hill and others (1959), Katz (1961), Hoffer and Strangland (1958), Emery and Oeser (1958, p. 115), Ramsey and others (1959), Dean and others (1958), Bemiller (1960), van den Ban (in press), Bose (1962), Burdge (1961), and Klietsch (1961).

5. Adapted from *Farming in Cultural Change* by B. Benvenuti. Assen, The Netherlands: Royal Van Gorcum, Ltd., 1961, by permission of the publisher.

strangers in their house. The *M* family recently toured several other Netherlands provinces on excursions organized by a farmer organization. Vacations are taken to visit friends in other provinces or to relax at the seashore. None of *M*'s neighbor-farmers are included in their circle of personal friends. The *M* family visits in town with acquaintances who are not farmers. During the course of the interview, a neighbor dropped in to ask Farmer *M* for some advice on a hog-raising problem and it was evident that *M* is regarded by his neighbors as a progressive farmer.

Farmer *M* keeps accurate farm management accounts. He raises purebred hogs and serves as the local sales representative of a farm machinery company. He learns of new farm ideas from his wide traveling and from reading farm publications. *M* has regular contact with his extension agent about once a month plus frequent telephone conversations. At the end of the interview, while showing the interviewer to the door, Farmer *M* said, "When your study is finished, will I be able to secure the results?"

FARMER *T:* TRADITION. In many ways, the *T* farm family offers a contrast to the *M*'s. Farmer *T* is older, less educated, and his reference group is the local neighborhood rather than the greater society beyond. When asked whether their friends were neighbors or not, Mrs. *T* replied with a tone of voice that indicated, "Where on earth would one have friends, if not with one's neighbors?"

The farm buildings are in a state of disrepair and the farm is poorly equipped with machinery. No farm accounts are kept. Most of the interviewer's questions about farm management puzzled Mr. *T;* he had never thought of the subject before. When asked why he had an inefficient breed of dairy cows, Farmer *T* replied, "Well . . . we have always had them. They do quite all right for us."

Mr. *T* continually emphasized how hard he must work. No vacations are taken by the family and no guests or friends are received from town. The *T* children seemed shy, and huddled in a corner of the kitchen during the interview. The family is extended in nature; Mrs. *T*'s parents live with them and are influential in family decisions. The family reads no papers or magazines and are not interested in politics or organizations of any kind. Farmer *T* is opposed to the government's compulsory dairy sanitation measures: "It is the fault of all the government clerks nowadays. They just have to invent programs in order to keep their jobs." One detects a feeling of alienation on the part of Farmer *T*. He feels his community is changing too rapidly, and in directions that he cannot control.

The *T* family had difficulty in answering many of the interviewer's questions. Indifference is mixed with servility in responding to the queries. The first answer to almost every question is "yes." For example, when a traditional person was asked whether his parents were alive, he answered, "Yes, but they are both dead." Farmer *T* has few points of interest in the interview which mainly proceeds as a series of direct questions and short answers until the conclusion of the interview is finally reached.

The exact characteristics of modern and traditional individuals in other social systems obviously vary widely from these two case illustrations. Nevertheless, Farmer M typifies the modern ideal type described earlier in this chapter. Compared to Farmer *T*, he is more technologically competent, cosmopolite, educated, economically rational, and empathetic.

It is important to note that in *each* of the research studies[6]

6. Except Lerner (1958) where no measure of individual innovativeness was available. Klietsch (1961) found his sample of Minnesota dairy farmers contained traditional acceptors of bulk milk tanks as well as traditional rejectors. Klietsch defined traditionalism as the organization of choices around habituated means or goals. His traditional ac-

where an adequate measure of the traditional-modern dimension was available at the individual level, *innovativeness of individuals is related to a modern rather than a traditional orientation.*[7] One would certainly be surprised if individuals with a more modern orientation were not more innovative in their reception of new ideas. Nevertheless, it is reassuring to know that this generalization is supported so overwhelmingly by empirical investigation.

Not only are the more modern members of a social system more innovative than their more traditional peers, but there may be few social relationships between the moderns and the traditionals. This is illustrated by the van de Ven (1957) investigation of the diffusion of artificial dairy breeding in one Netherlands village. A few modern farmers pioneered in adopting the new idea, and their followers adopted soon after. But then the rate of adoption seemed to plateau as the majority of traditional farmers did not adopt. Van de Ven found there were almost no visiting relationships between the modern and the traditional farmers. It was as if each lived in a separate social system rather than in the same community.

2. For a Social System: Norms

The traditional-modern dimension has been measured not only at the individual level. Several attempts have also been made to measure the modernism or traditionalism of social system norms. The difficulty of measuring the traditionalism of norms, defined as the most frequently occurring

---

ceptors of bulk tanks, of course, adopted innovations in a habituated fashion. It is important to remember that traditional acceptance might be possible, even though rare, as well as traditional rejection.

7. The reader is reminded that innovativeness is defined as the degree to which an individual is relatively earlier to adopt new ideas than the other members of his social system.

patterns of overt behavior for the members of a particular social system, is probably greater than the measurement of traditionalism at the individual level.

Three different approaches to measuring social system norms on traditionalism-modernism have been reported:

1. One method is simply to average the innovativeness scores of the members of a social system. Then the relative traditionalism-modernism of one social system's norms can be compared with another's. Researchers who have utilized the *average innovativeness* method are Marsh and Coleman (1954a), van den Ban (1960b), Rahudkar (1960), and Rogers and Burdge (1962). One difficulty sometimes encountered with the average innovativeness method is that the same innovations are not equally applicable in all the social systems under study. Farmers in one community, for example, may not raise dairy cows, so dairying ideas cannot be utilized to measure the modernism of that community.

2. Another method of measuring social system norms is an *attitude-toward-innovators* type of measure. If the members of the social system view innovators favorably, the social system is assumed to have modern norms. For example, van den Ban (in press) asked farmers in three Netherlands communities, "What do people in this community think of the first farmers to adopt new farm ideas?" The percentage of respondents in each community who reported that innovators were viewed favorably was taken as the measure of traditional-modern norms.[8]

3. A third measure of system norms is *judges' ratings*. The judges should be acquainted with all the social systems under analysis, and able to rate them on the traditional-modern dimension in terms of their norms. This norm measure was used by Campbell and Holik (1960) in two Missouri

8. Other researchers who have used this type of measure of community norms are Campbell and Holik (1960) and Rogers and Burdge (1962).

farm communities, and by Rogers and Burdge (1962) in seven Ohio communities.[9]

Table 3-1 presents a comparison of the three measures of system norms in the seven Ohio communities. A high degree of similarity among the three measures suggests that almost any one of the three is equally valid.[10] Similar evidence is available from a reanalysis of the Campbell and Holik (1960) Missouri data, and from van den Ban (in press).[11]

None of these measures of social system norms is above methodological criticism.[12] It must be remembered, however, that in spite of the central position of norms in sociological writings, very few attempts have been made to measure them. Perhaps future research efforts might be directed toward developing improved measures of social system norms on traditionalism-modernism and on other dimensions.

Nevertheless, existing measures provide a rough indication of a system's norms. It is possible to say that the norms

9. The latter researchers found a high degree of agreement among the three judges whom they asked to rate the seven communities' norms as to traditionalism-modernism. Kendall's coefficient of concordance was +.67 which is significant at the 5 per cent level (Rogers and Burdge, 1962).

10. Spearman rank-order correlation was computed among the three norm measures by Rogers and Burdge (1962). The average-innovativeness measure correlated +.79 with the attitude-toward-innovators measure, and +.99 with the judges' norm ratings. The attitude-toward-innovators measure correlated +.79 with the judges' norm ratings.

11. In Prairie, the Missouri community with a modern norm, the average-innovativeness score was 52, and 64 per cent of the respondents viewed innovators favorably. In Ozark, the Missouri community with a traditional norm, similar figures were 32 and 56 per cent. Van den Ban (in press) found a high degree of agreement between the attitude-toward-innovators and average-innovativeness measures of community norms in a Netherlands study.

12. Yet a fourth measure of a social system's traditional-modern norms might be the rate of adoption for an innovation (or innovations) in the system. This measure is similar to, but not identical with, the measure computed by averaging individuals' innovativeness scores.

TABLE 3-1

COMPARISON OF THREE MEASURES OF SOCIAL
SYSTEM NORMS ON TRADITIONALISM-
MODERNISM USING DATA FROM
SEVEN OHIO FARM COMMUNITIES

Names of Seven Ohio Farm Communities	Average Innovativeness Scores of Farmers in Each County as a Measure of Community Norms*	Per Cent of Farmers in Each Community Viewing Innovators Favorably as a Measure of Community Norms*	Average Ratings by Three Judges as to Modernism of Community Norms*
Oak Grove	5.15	100	6.7
DeVola	4.92	67	6.3
Beverly	4.60	89	3.7
Reno	4.22	86	3.3
Lowell	3.95	56	3.3
Belpre	3.86	43	2.3
Hillgrowers	3.83	65	2.3

* A larger number indicates a more modern norm in the community.
Source: Rogers and Burdge, 1962.

of one social system are more traditional or more modern
than those of another system.

SOCIAL SYSTEM NORMS AND
INDIVIDUAL INNOVATIVENESS

Earlier in this chapter it was shown that norms have an
important influence on whether a new idea is adopted and
what the consequences of the innovation will be. In addition,
if social system norms on traditionalism-modernism are of
great significance, they should explain a portion of in-

dividual innovativeness that cannot be explained in any other way. In other words, the norms of a social system are expected to affect the behavior of members of the social system.[13] *An individual's innovativeness varies directly with the norms of his social system on innovativeness.*[14]

There are two research studies which support this latter statement:

1. Van den Ban (1960b) studied a sample of 903 Wisconsin farmers living in 47 townships. The norm on traditionalism-modernism for each township was computed by the average-innovativeness method. Such characteristics as a farmer's education, size of farm, and net worth were found to be positively related to individual innovativeness. But the township norms were even better predictors of innovativeness than were these social and economic characteristics. Van den Ban concluded that a farmer with a high level of education, on a large farm, and with a high net worth, but residing in a township with a traditional norm, adopted fewer farm innovations than if he farmed in a township where the norms were modern.

2. The second study is Rogers and Burdge's (1962) analysis of seven Ohio truck-growing communities. The community norms were found to statistically explain 20 per cent of the variation in farmers' innovativeness scores, in addition to that accounted for by four social characteristics.[15]

13. This later statement has been demonstrated in another area of sociological inquiry. Community and neighborhood norms on juvenile delinquency have considerable effect on the chances a youth will become delinquent (Reiss and Rhodes, 1961; Reckless and others, 1956; and Scarpitti and others, 1960). Jones (1960, p. 71) found that norms had a greater effect on the individual innovativeness of later than of earlier adopters.

14. When a system's norms are measured by the average-innovativeness method, it is possible that there may be some circularity in this statement, particularly if an individual's innovativeness score is included in computing the average for his system.

15. The Rogers and Burdge study is described in greater detail in Chapter X.

Not only do social system norms affect individual innovativeness, but they are also involved in two generalizations which will be discussed in detail in Chapter VIII.

1. The social system norms on innovativeness seem to determine, at least in part, the innovativeness of opinion leaders. The opinion leaders in modern social systems, several studies show, are mostly innovators and early adopters, but in traditional social systems the opinion leaders are less innovative.

2. Differences in innovativeness between pairs of individuals are a more important barrier to the flow of influence in a social system where the norms are modern than where they are traditional. For example, in a traditional system, a laggard might seek information from an early adopter, but in a modern system, the laggard would more likely talk to an individual only slightly more innovative than himself.

NEEDED RESEARCH

There has been relatively little research on the effect of social system norms on individual innovativeness in cultures outside of the United States,[16] where, in fact, normative differences may be relatively more important to consider. Perhaps generalizations about diffusion in "underdeveloped" countries are hazy because our research is relatively "underdeveloped" in these non-Western cultures. The lack of adequate findings from diffusion research in less developed countries is illustrated by the fact that only about 39 of the 465 studies (exclusive of the anthropology tradition) reviewed here had a locale in a less developed area. The 558,000 rural

16. One exception to this statement is rural sociological research in the Netherlands by van den Ban (1957b, 1958, 1960b, and in press) and Wichers (1956).

villages in India, for example, offers a promising laboratory for testing the effect of community norms on the diffusion of ideas. Research efforts might seek to determine norm-to-norm relationships (where social systems are the units of analysis), as well as the effect of norms on individual behavior.

One example of a norm-to-norm analysis is Armstrong's (1959) attempt to explain variations in farm innovativeness

TABLE 3-2

TYPES OF ANALYSES COMPLETED OR POSSIBLE BY DIFFUSION RESEARCHERS

	Dependent Variable *	*Independent Variable(s)* *	*Unit of Analysis*
Type 1.	Rate of adoption of an innovation in a social system	Characteristics of the innovation as perceived by members of the social system (e.g., complexity, divisibility, relative advantage)	Innovation
Type 2.	Innovativeness of individuals in a social system	Characteristics of individuals (e.g., cosmopoliteness, social status)	Individual
Type 3.	Innovativeness of individuals in a social system	Social system norms on traditionalism-modernism	Individual
Type 4.	Social system norms on traditionalism-modernism	Other norms and characteristics of social systems (e.g., cosmopoliteness, average income level)	Social System
Type 5.	Characteristics of the innovation as perceived by members of a social system (e.g., complexity, divisibility)	Innovativeness of individuals in a social system	Individual

* A dependent variable is the main factor investigated in a research study while the independent variables are those factors related to the dependent variable.

among Kentucky counties.[17] An average-innovativeness measure of norms was constructed for each county and correlated
with such county variables as degree of urbanization, farm
income level, and farm specialization. The attempt in this
type of research is to explain as much as possible of the variation in county norms on innovativeness, rather than the
variation in individuals' innovativeness.

Table 3-2 shows five different types of analyses by diffusion
researchers. Type 1 will be discussed in Chapter V, and Type
2 in Chapter VI. Types and 3 and 4 have been discussed in
the present chapter, but have received much less attention
than Types 2. Type 4 is the norm-to-norm type of analysis
discussed in this section of which the Armstrong (1959) study
is typical. Type 5 has not been studied, but needs to be.

Another area of needed research is the investigation of
how social system norms develop along modern or traditional
lines. This type of study might entail a historical approach,
or perhaps a long-term panel design. If norms are important
in affecting individual behavior, then it is essential to determine the process by which a social system's norms change.

To date there has been little integration of what is known
about the diffusion of innovations with present theories of
social change.[18] Such a convergence might result in increased fruitfulness for both fields.

17. Another norm-to-norm type of analysis is Rogers and Burdge
(1962) and yet another is in process under the direction of Professor
Milton Coughenour at the University of Kentucky. The innovativeness of neighborhood norms is being studied in relationship to sociometric integration of the neighborhoods and other variables.

18. The Dutch historian Romein (1937, pp. 9–64) proposed a theory
of social change called the "retarding lead," which states that a particular innovation is more likely to be adopted by members of a social
system if the system is relatively retarded in that particular aspect of
culture. Van den Ban (1957a) found that vocational agriculture training was adopted more rapidly by farmers in the sections of the Netherlands where subsistence farming prevailed. He suggested that Romein's
retarding lead theory may hold true if individuals feel a need for
change in some aspect of their culture that is relatively retarded.

SUMMARY

A norm is the most frequently occurring pattern of overt behavior for the members of a particular social system. *Ideal types* are conceptualizations that are based on observations of reality and designed to institute comparisons. Two ideal types of norms are distinguished, traditional and modern. A social system with modern norms is more technologically developed, cosmopolite, literate, rational, and empathetic. The traditional-modern dimension has been measured at both the individual level and for a social system. A common finding at the individual level is that innovativeness of individuals is related to a modern rather than a traditional orientation. Three types of measures of traditional-modern norms have been utilized by researchers: (1) average-innovativeness of the members of the social system, (2) attitude-toward-innovators, and (3) judges' ratings of norms. Community norms appear to explain variation in individuals' innovativeness not explained by other variables, such as social characteristics. An individual's innovativeness varies directly with the norm of his social system on innovativeness.

CHAPTER IV

The Adoption Process

The seeds of great discoveries are constantly floating around us, but they only take rest in minds well prepared to receive them.

WALTER B. CANNON, 1945, p. 76

The adoption process is the mental process through which an individual passes from first hearing about an innovation to final adoption. The adoption process should be distinguished from the diffusion process which is the spread of a new idea from its source of invention or creation to its ultimate users or adopters. A major difference between the diffusion process and the adoption process is that diffusion occurs among persons while adoption is an individual matter.

The purpose of this chapter is to show the similarity of the adoption process to learning and other types of decision-making, to present research on the existence of adoption stages, to describe the sources of information used by individuals at each adoption stage, and to analyze the adoption period.

LEARNING THEORY

The academic ancestry of sociological research on the adoption process can be traced from the learning theories of psychologists. *Learning* is defined by psychologists as the relatively enduring change in the response to stimulus.[1] The heart of most learning theories is the stimulus-response relationship. A stimulus is interpreted and causes a response in the individual. Continued reinforcement of this response by later stimuli results in a more or less permanent change in the individual's behavior; this is learning.

The process by which innovations are adopted by individuals is essentially a limited example of how any type of learning takes place.[2] In the adoption process, various stimuli about the innovation reach the individual from communication sources. Each ensuing communication about the innovation cumulates until the individual responds to these communications, and eventually adopts or rejects the innovation.

Learning occurs, of course, not only in the classroom but throughout the span of life. Thus, the process by which a fourth grader learns to multiply is generally similar to that of the medical doctor learning about a new drug or a school superintendent adopting a new educational idea.

DECISION-MAKING

The adoption process is one type of *decision-making*.[3] The adoption of an innovation requires a decision by an individ-

1. This definition of learning is based upon those of English and English (1958), Hilgard (1956, p. 3), and Wickens and Meyer (1955, p. 28).
2. An important question that receives little attention in the literature is the relationship between innovative behavior and creativity.
3. As March and Simon (1958, p. 177) have recognized, "The innovative processes . . . are closely related to the various intellective processes referred to by psychologists as 'problem-solving,' 'productive thinking,' 'creative thinking,' 'invention,' and the like."

ual. He must begin using a new idea and, in most cases, decide to cease using an idea that the innovation replaces. The adoption process is actually more complex than this statement implies; several interrelated decisions must be made during the adoption process.

Decision-making is the process by which an evaluation of the meaning and consequences of alternative lines of conduct is made. Johnson and Haver (1953, p. 8) listed the following steps in decision-making: (1) observing the problem, (2) making an analysis of it, (3) deciding the available courses of action, (4) taking one course, and (5) accepting the consequences of the decision.

Decision-making is thus a process that may be divided into a sequence of stages with a different type of activity occurring during each stage. Likewise, the way in which an individual adopts an innovation is viewed by most researchers as a process. Adoption of a new idea is a bundle of related events flowing through time; in short, it is a *process*.

Most of the human behavior studied by social scientists involves different types of decisions. Examples are consumer preferences, occupational choices,[4] industrial and farm management, migration patterns, and voting behavior. The types of decision-making investigated in these studies have generally involved the choice of one course of action from an existing list of alternatives. In the case of the adoption of an innovation, however, the individual is selecting a *new* alternative over those previously existent.

In summary, the adoption process is one type of decision-making. It is a special type of decision-making, however, with some attributes not found in other kinds of situations.

---

4. Bealer and Fliegel (1961) argued that studies (1) of rural youth migration decisions, and (2) of farmers' adoption decisions are essentially similar in a sociological sense. ". . . educational and occupational alternatives, although we do not normally label them as innovations, are new to a young person in a choice situation(s) in much the same sense as are items of technological diffusion."

ADOPTION AS A PROCESS

The adoption process may be arbitrarily broken down into stages for conceptual purposes. This breakdown is (1) consistent with the nature of the phenomena, (2) congruent with previous research findings, and (3) potentially useful for practical applications. It should be pointed out that there are not necessarily *only* five stages in the adoption process.[5] It is simply that at the present time there seem to be five main functions involved in the adoption process, and each of these is assigned to a stage. The number of stages in the process is selected primarily on the basis of ease of conceptualization. Either more or fewer stages might be postulated in the adoption process, but further subdivision needs to be pursued only if the fruitfulness of the analysis is enhanced.

Sill (1957, p. 17) provided a homey explanation of why the adoption process can be viewed as composed of stages. Raising an eyebrow looks like several still pictures on stopped movie film but, when projected, it looks like a gesture. Which is it then? The answer would seem to be both. It all depends on one's point of reference. Raising an eyebrow may be regarded as an act or as a series of acts.

Development of the Concept

At this point, it may be fruitful to trace briefly the conceptual development of the adoption process. Ryan and Gross (1943) were probably the first to recognize that the adoption of a new idea consisted of stages. They distinguished between "awareness" of hybrid seed corn, "conviction" of its usefulness, trial "acceptance," and "complete adoption"

5. The five stages in the adoption process, which will shortly be described in detail, are awareness, interest, evaluation, trial, and adoption.

of the innovation. Pedersen (1951) also suggested that a sequence of events leads to adoption.

However, it was Wilkening (1952, p. 16) who first pointed out that an individual's decision to adopt an innovation was a *process* composed of stages or steps. Wilkening (1953, p. 9) described the adoption of an innovation as ". . . a process composed of learning, deciding, and acting over a period of time. The adoption of a specific practice is not the result of a single decision to act but of a series of actions and thought decisions." Wilkening proceeded to list four adoption stages: awareness, obtaining information, conviction and trial, and adoption. These stages, with slightly different titles, were highly publicized by a committee of rural sociologists in their widely distributed bulletin, *How Farm People Accept New Ideas* (NCRS Subcommittee, 1955, pp. 3–6). Their five-stage adoption process is basically the same, even if not in exact terminology, as described here.

Two research studies have been designed primarily to determine whether the concept of a five-stage adoption process is empirically valid. Both Beal and others (1957) and Copp and others (1958) concluded that the concept of stages is valid.[6] These studies will be discussed in greater detail later in this chapter.

There is not complete agreement as to the number of stages in the adoption process, although there is general consensus on the existence of stages, and that adoption is seldom an "impulse" decision. Ryan and Gross (1943) utilized four stages, as did Wilkening (1953, p. 9). The North Central Rural Sociology Subcommittee (1955, pp. 3–6) described five adoption stages after a review of the literature available in 1954. Beal and others (1957) and Copp and others (1958) utilized five stages in their investigations. However, Emery

6. There is no adequate research evidence that the stages concept is valid when an innovation is adopted by a group decision such as by a school board rather than by an individual. One of few researches on this point is the Burns and Stalker (1961) case studies of how new ideas were accepted in Scottish and English electronics firms.

and Oeser (1958, p. 3) and Wilkening (1956) utilized a three-stage[7] process, while Lavidge and Steiner (1961) postulated six stages.

The development of the adoption process concept can be traced almost entirely in the rural sociology tradition of research. Holmberg (1960), however, utilized the concept of a seven-stage adoption process in his Cornell University anthropology courses.[8] The first stage in his process of "individual cultural change" is availability of the innovation to the individual. His middle five stages are similar to those of the rural sociologists: awareness, interest, trial, evaluation,[9] and adoption. Holmberg's seventh stage is integration of the innovation into the individual's routine.

STAGES IN THE ADOPTION PROCESS

Five stages are utilized in this book: (1) awareness, (2) interest, (3) evaluation, (4) trial, and (5) adoption. The type of behavior occurring at each stage is described, as well as the main funtcion that each stage fulfills in the adoption process.

1. Awareness Stage

At the *awareness* stage the individual is exposed to the innovation but lacks complete information about it.[10] The in-

7. Wilkening may have utilized this three-stage process only for operational purposes as he had postulated a four-stage process three years earlier.

8. Others outside of the rural sociology tradition who have used adoption stages are Lavidge and Steiner (1961) in marketing and Brim (1954) in an analysis of the adoption of child-rearing ideas by mothers.

9. Holmerg (1960) conceptualized the trial stage as preceding the evaluation stage.

10. Some other authors have termed the awareness stage "exposure" (Emery and Oeser, 1958).

dividual is aware of the innovation, but is not yet motivated to seek further information. The primary function of the awareness stage is to initiate the sequence of later stages that lead to eventual adoption or rejection of the innovation.

Most researchers have implicitly conceptualized the awareness stage as a random or nonpurposive occurrence. An individual often becomes aware of an innovation quite by accident; he cannot seek out an innovation which he does not know exists.[11] Hassinger (1959), however, has recently criticized the assumption of nonpurposiveness of the awareness stage. He argues that awareness must be initiated by the individual and is not a passive act. Hassinger points out that information about new ideas often does not create awareness, even though the individual may be exposed to this information, unless the individual has a problem or a need that the innovation promises to solve.

Perhaps one is faced with a chicken-and-egg type of question. Does a need precede awareness of an innovation or does awareness of a new idea create a need for that innovation? The available research studies do not yet provide a clear answer to this question, but tentative evidence suggests the latter is more common.

2. Interest Stage

At the *interest* stage the individual becomes interested in the new idea and seeks additional information about it. The individual favors the innovation in a general way, but he has not yet judged its utility in terms of his own situation. The function of the interest stage is mainly to increase the individual's information about the innovation. The cognitive or "knowing" component of behavior is involved at the in-

11. As Coleman and others (in press) concluded, "The earliest information about a new drug seldom comes from a source which the physicians have to seek out themselves."

terest stage (Lavidge and Steiner, 1961). The individual is more psychologically involved with the innovation at the interest stage than at the awareness stage. Previously, the individual listened or read about the innovation; at the interest stage he actively seeks information about the idea. His behavior is now definitely purposive, rather than nonpurposive. His personality and values, as well as the norms of his social system, may affect *where* he seeks information, as well as how he *interprets* this information about the innovation.[12]

The interest stage has been referred to as the "information" stage by Beal and others (1957), as the "knowledge" step by Lavidge and Steiner (1961), and as the "interest-information" stage by the North Central Rural Sociology Subcommittee (1961).[13]

3. Evaluation Stage

At the *evaluation* stage the individual mentally applies the innovation to his present and anticipated future situation, and then decides whether or not to try it. A sort of "mental trial" occurs at the evaluation stage. If the individual feels the advantages of the innovation outweigh the disadvantages, he will decide to try the innovation. The trial itself, however, is conceptually distinct from the decision to try the new idea. The evaluation stage is probably least distinct of the five adoption stages and empirically one of the most difficult about which to question respondents.[14]

12. Rahim (1961, p. 36) found that Pakistani farmers did not have negative attitudes toward innovations (that they later rejected) until the interest stage.

13. The interest stage is also essentially similar to the "search processes" described by March and Simon (1958, p. 178) in problem-solving.

14. Different types of evaluation occur at each stage in the adoption process, of course, but the decision to try the new idea occurs, by definition, only at the evaluation stage.

The innovation carries a subjective risk to the individual. He is unsure of its results, and for this reason a reinforcement effect is needed at the evaluation stage to convince the individual that his thinking is on the right path. Information and advice from peers is likely to be sought at this point. Mass communications transmit messages that are too general to provide reinforcement to the individual at the evaluation stage.

Other research workers have termed the evaluation stage "application" (Beal and others, 1957; Beal and Rogers, 1960, p. 20), "acceptance" (Copp and others, 1958), "evaluation-application-decision" (NCRS Subcommittee, 1961), and "conviction" (Rogers and Yost, 1960, p. 21; Rogers and Pitzer, 1960).[15] All these terms imply that an affective component of behavior, a favorable or unfavorable feeling toward the idea, is involved at the evaluation stage (Lavidge and Steiner, 1961).

4. Trial Stage

At the *trial* stage the individual uses the innovation on a small scale in order to determine its utility in his own situation. The main function of the trial stage is to demonstrate the new idea in the individual's own situation and determine its usefulness for possible complete adoption. It is thus a validity test or "dry run"; the decision to use the idea on a trial basis was made at the evaluation stage. The individual may seek specific information about the method of using the innovation at the trial stage.

Most persons will not adopt an innovation without trying

15. The evaluation stage, and to some extent the trial stage also, is essentially similar to the "screening processes" described by March and Simon (1958, p. 178) in problem-solving, and to the "liking" and "preference" steps of Lavidge and Steiner (1961).

it first on a probationary basis.[16] Ryan and Gross (1943) found that however clearly the advantages of hybrid corn had been demonstrated by community experience, most farmers insisted upon personal experimentation before they would adopt the innovation completely. Even the last Iowa farmers to adopt the innovation, although often surrounded by neighbors successfully using hybrid seed, planted only a portion of their acreage in hybrid seed during their first year. Likewise, Strassman (1959, p. 219) found that industrial innovations during the nineteenth century were usually developed first on the smallest possible scale in order to demonstrate their utility.

While rejection of the innovation may occur at any stage in the adoption process, it sometimes happens when the results of the trial stage are misinterpreted. An example comes from the author's research interview with an Iowa farmer who had recently applied nitrogen fertilizer to a portion of his field.

Yah, I put 100 pounds to the acre on about half of the oats field. I got 10 more bushels to the acre than my neighbors and figured it was a pretty good thing. Made the clover grow like crazy. But the first rainy September morning that I turned my milk cows out on that clover, two of them swelled up and died. You can't tell me that fertilizer ain't poison.

The farmer blamed the bloating of his cattle on an irrelevant cause, namely to what he considered the toxic properties of fertilizer, rather than to the actual cause, wet clover. As a consequence, he rejected the practice of fertilizing his crops. Incidentally, later interviews with this farmer's neighbors disclosed they were not using fertilizer. Several referred to the experience of the farmer whose cattle had bloated.

Most individuals probably judge trial results more accurately than the farmer in this illustration. In any event, the results of the trial are very important in the adoption-rejection decision.

16. Some ideas, of course, are more difficult to divide for trial than are others.

5. Adoption Stage

At the *adoption* stage the individual decides to continue the full use[17] of the innovation. The main functions of the adoption stage are consideration of the trial results and the decision to ratify sustained use of the innovation. Adoption implies continued use of the innovation in the future. The connative or motivational component of behavior is involved at the adoption (and trial) stage (Lavidge and Steiner, 1961).

ADOPTION OF HOME CANNING IN A GEORGIA COUNTY: A CASE ILLUSTRATION[18]

This case example illustrates how one individual adopted a new idea, home canning. Parenthetical remarks indicating stages in the adoption process are bracketed. The case illustrates the importance of personal influences from peers in convincing individuals to adopt new ideas.

The Canning Campaign

In Greene County, Georgia, as is the case throughout the cotton plantation areas of the South, most of the tenant families had a diet of fat-back meat, corn meal, and sorghum molasses. In the early 1940's, over 500 low-income farm families in Greene County were led to can an average of nearly 500 quarts of food per person per year.

17. By "full use" is meant 100 per cent utilization of the idea by the individual. An example is the farmer cited in Chapter I who planted his total corn acreage in hybrid seed in 1938.

18. Adapted from Raper and Tappan (1943), "Never Too Old to Learn New Tricks: The Canning Program in Greene County, Georgia," in *Applied Anthropology*, 2:3–11, 1943, by permission of the publisher.

The home-canning campaign began in 1939 in Greene County. [The social system in the present case is the county.] Over 500 farm families received loans and supervision from the Farm Security Administration, a government agricultural agency. Most of these families were farm tenants, and had canned only an average of 12 quarts per family prior to 1939. [The culture included little previous experience with the new idea.] They increased their canning to an average of 225 quarts in 1939, to 350 in 1940, to 386 in 1941, and to 499 in 1942. How they raised their average from a dozen quarts to half a thousand per family in four years can best be told from inside the county.

The Case of Lula McCommons

Lula McCommons, a Negro mother of seven children, did not believe in canning. [The individual is already aware of canning, but lacks information about its advantages.] She had always gone to the store for something to eat when she could; when she could not, she and her family got along somehow. Lula had never canned over eight or nine quarts, as "I ain't ever had any more jars, and where can I get the stuff to can?" [The individual secures additional information at the interest stage.] When she was told how many she was expected to can, she said, "It ain't any use to tell you I kin can that much. I don't lie. I can't." Every method of persuasion was used. The FSA supervisors [change agents] appealed to her husband. Mary, her twelve-year-old girl, was asked to help. All promised to do what they could, but no canning was done. Lula and Mary were invited down the road to the home of one of the best canners, and were left there to talk for over an hour. [The individual is exposed to personal influences from peers at the evaluation stage.]

A few days later, Lula began to can. She agreed to put up 75 quarts. [A small-scale trial is planned.] She attended church the next Sunday, and between Sunday school and preaching, the women were all talking about "how many" and "what" they had canned. Lula said: "I just told myself that if old Mary Rooth and all them others could can all them quarts, I could too. So I just told old Satan to git behind me, for I was a goin' to can everything I could git my hands on." And, she did. She canned 675 quarts that year. [The individual has now reached full-scale, continued adoption.] The next year she canned nearly 800 quarts.

The Results

One unexpected consequence of the canning campaign was the element of prestige that soon came to be associated with canned food. In fact, many families kept their jars on display in the parlor or guest room or on shelves around the kitchen. Some families, in their zeal to use all of their jars, filled them with sweet potatoes, pumpkins, turnips, and other foods readily stored without canning. [Individuals used the innovation differently from what was anticipated; this is an example of overadoption.] Many people were so proud of their canned goods the first year that they would not open their jars. The FSA supervisors realized then that they had to teach the families to use the food they had canned. [Some of the consequences of the innovation were unanticipated.]

DISCONTINUANCES

An innovation may be rejected at any stage in the adoption process.[19] *Rejection* is a decision not to adopt an innovation.

19. It is possible to reject an innovation at the awareness stage (by forgetting about it), interest, evaluation, or trial stage. Rejection of an idea may be temporary, just as adoption may be. A discontinuance, by definition, can occur only after the adoption process is completed.

The individual may decide at the evaluation stage that the innovation will not apply to his situation and mentally reject the idea. Or, the innovation may be rejected at the trial stage, where the individual decides that the rewards expected from adoption will not outweigh the cost and effort of doing so. Rejection may occur for less rational reasons; an example is the previous illustration of the farmer whose cattle bloated and who influenced his neighbors to reject the fertilization of oats.

Rejection of an innovation can also occur after adoption. This behavior is called a "discontinuance." A *discontinuance* is a decision to cease use of an innovation after previously adopting.

Several research studies have investigated discontinuances, but many of these have labeled this behavior by some other term. Few of these investigations were specifically designed to study discontinuances; often the "discovery" of discontinuances was "serendipitous."[20] While Chapin (1928, pp. 369–371) did not utilize the term, he found a number of U.S. cities "abandoned" the commission form of government and the city manager plan from 1912 to 1923. There were almost as many cities abandoning the innovations during certain years as there were adopting these ideas.

The following studies[21] show the diversity of behavior in which discontinuances have been found:

1. An investigation of North Carolina farmers found over 20 per cent had discontinued the use of hybrid corn (Wilkening. 1952, p. 32).

2. Adler (1955, pp. 49–82) found discontinuances in the case of 16 of the 33 educational innovations he investigated among 170 public schools.

3. A study of 4,326 families in India (Indian Planning

20. A *serendipitous* finding is one that is chanced upon by the researcher.

21. Other studies reporting discontinuances that are not listed here are Wilkening and Santopolo (1952, p. 19), Allen (1956, p. 28), Sheppard (1960a, pp. 18–19), and Coughenour (1961).

Commission Programme Evaluation Organization, 1958) disclosed discontinuance rates ranging from 97 per cent for a Japanese method of rice cultivation to less than one per cent for compost fertilizer.

4. Eichholz (1961) found that discontinuances were more common than 11 other types of rejection in his study of rejected audio-visual innovations by 45 elementary teachers in five public schools.

5. Silverman and Bailey (1961) found about half as many discontinuances as adoptions over a three-year period by 107 Mississippi farmers.

Probably the most comprehensive investigation of discontinuances was completed by Johnson and van den Ban (1959). They partly eliminated one of the major problems involved in studying discontinuances, that of inaccurate respondent recall, by gathering data from 176 Wisconsin[22] farmers both in 1952 and again in 1957. During the five-year period, the 176 respondents made 266 adoptions of 17 innovations studied and 255 discontinuances. It should be pointed out that these farmers were also adopting other innovations (other than the 17 studied in 1952 and in 1957) during this time period. Nevertheless, the Wisconsin data indicate that a surprising number of discontinuances occur over a relatively short time period. Few of the Wisconsin discontinuances were caused by supersedence of a superior innovation replacing a previously adopted idea.

One of the most significant findings by Johnson and van den Ban (1959) was that the relatively later adopters had twice as many discontinuances as the earlier adopters. Previous researchers had assumed that later adopters were relatively less innovative because they did not adopt or were relatively slow to adopt innovations. The Johnson and van den Ban evidence suggests the later adopters may adopt, but then discontinue at a later point in time.

22. Van den Ban was at the University of Wisconsin in 1958–1959 while on leave from the University of Wageningen, Netherlands.

To summarize, the frequency of discontinued innovations is not rare. Many researchers have reported discontinuances even though few were looking for them. The extent of discontinuances seems to vary with the nature of the idea and with the characteristics (particularly the innovativeness) of the individuals adopting. Findings reported by Adler (1955), Johnson and van den Ban (1959), and Silverman and Bailey (1961) support the generalization that *relatively later adopters are more likely to discontinue innovations than are earlier adopters.* Later adopters have lower incomes; their lack of resources may either prevent adoption of ideas or cause discontinuances because the ideas do not fit their limited financial position.

There may be both rational and irrational discontinuances just as there are both rational and irrational adoption decisions (Chapter V). Rationality is the use of the most effective means to reach a given end. An example of an irrational discontinuance is an unsatisfactory experience with an innovation because the idea was not fully understood. This type of discontinuance is probably more likely to occur among later adopters than among earlier adopters. Laggards have less education and more traditional values, both of which might be expected to cause discontinuances.

The author learned of one Netherlands laggard who adopted hay tripods upon the recommendation of a neighbor. However, he used the tripods incorrectly, the results were unsatisfactory, and he discontinued the innovation after one year. Often, a relatively later adopter may adopt a new idea but not the related ideas that must accompany it to achieve successful results. Such a case is the farmer, described by Silverman and Bailey (1961), who adopted thicker planting of corn but not the related ideas of fertilization and hybrid seed. His corn yields were even lower than if he had adopted none of the three ideas.

Any innovation, once it is adopted by an individual, is in

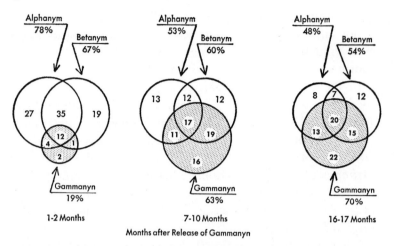

FIGURE 4-1. GRADUAL SUPERSEDENCE OF TWO EXISTING
DRUGS BY A NEW DRUG, GAMMANYN

These data show the percentage of medical doctors in four Illinois communities who had adopted a new drug, gammanyn, 1–2, 7–10, and 16–17 months after its release. The rapid rise in the adoption of gammanyn did not mean that its predecessors, alphanym and betanym, were completely dropped from use. Thus, only 22 per cent of the physicians were using gammanyn exclusively as late as 16–17 months after its introduction, while 48 per cent were using gammanyn plus another drug. The new drug was an addition to the drugs many doctors were using rather than a substitute. Only slowly did supersedence of existing drugs occur as gammanyn replaced them.

Source: Coleman and others (1959). Used by permission.

danger of being superseded by later ideas that replace it.[23] Figure 4-1 shows how gammanyn gradually superseded two existing drugs among Illinois physicians. In a rapidly chang-

23. Diffusion research studies have emphasized the new idea being adopted rather than the old idea being superseded. Of course, not all innovations may entail a direct substitution for an existing idea, but certainly most do. Dr. Saxon Graham (1961), a medical sociologist in Buffalo, is currently investigating the discontinuance of smoking. He views this discontinuance as a new idea that the individual adopts as the result of various group influences.

ing culture, one is constantly faced with a new stock of innovations. One result is necessarily a high rate of rational discontinuances.

The Innovation-Use Tree

One recent method of analyzing discontinuances over a period of time is the "innovation-use tree." The innovation-use tree is a historical description of shifts between adoption and discontinuance of ideas over a period of time.

Coughenour (1961) secured data from a sample of 111 Kentucky farmers in 1950, 1955, and 1960 as to their adoption or nonadoption of 13 farm innovations. The pooled 1,162 adoption-rejection decisions (13 innovations times 111 farmers minus the ideas that did not apply to certain farms) were the units of analysis. Figure 4-2 shows the innovation-use tree that resulted. A general tendency may be observed for farmers to continue either rejection or adoption of innovations from one five-year period to another. Past behavior appears to be a fairly effective predictor of future behavior.

A number of discontinuances occurred over the ten-year period from 1950 to 1960. They numbered about 18 per cent of the 1,162 decisions by 1960, and this is certainly an underestimate because the data were gathered only at five year intervals. Figure 4-2 shows 35 cases where a farmer switched from adoption to discontinuance and back again to "readoption." Coughenour (1961) suggested several new concepts if innovation-use trees are to be used such as "first-order discontinuances" (the discontinuances in 1955) and "second-order discontinuances" (those occurring for the first time in 1960).

The innovation-use tree is a valuable method of presenting the total panorama of adoption and rejection over a time

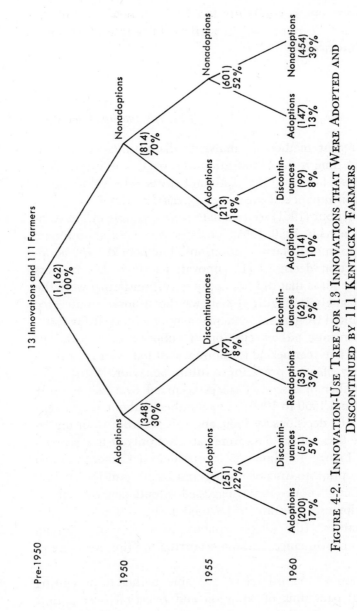

Pre-1950   13 Innovations and 111 Farmers

(1,162)
100%

1950   Adoptions   Nonadoptions

(348)   (814)
30%   70%

1955   Adoptions Discontinuances   Adoptions Nonadoptions

(251)   (97)   (213)   (601)
22%   8%   18%   52%

1960 Adoptions Discontin- Readoptions Discontin- Adoptions Discontin- Adoptions Nonadoptions
                 uances   uances   uances

(200)   (51)   (35)   (62)   (114)   (99)   (147)   (454)
17%   5%   3%   5%   10%   8%   13%   39%

FIGURE 4-2. INNOVATION-USE TREE FOR 13 INNOVATIONS THAT WERE ADOPTED AND DISCONTINUED BY 111 KENTUCKY FARMERS

Source: Redrawn from Coughenour (1961). Used by permission.

period. It is possible, of course, that the extent of disenchantment with an idea might be predicted, just as the rate of adoption of an innovation might be estimated in advance. Future studies might seek to show whether the cumulative percentage of discontinuance is an S-shaped curve, as is the rate of adoption.

ARE THERE ADOPTION STAGES?

Five stages or steps in the adoption process have been theoretically postulated. What evidence is available that these stages actually exist?

Before answering this question, it should be pointed out that a definite answer is extremely difficult to provide. Researchers can probe only indirectly the mental processes of individuals who adopt an innovation.[24] Nevertheless, there is evidence that the concept of stages in the adoption process is valid. Two major investigations of the validity of the stages concept came to the same conclusion (Beal and others, 1957; Copp and others, 1958). Four main types of evidence are available.[25]

1. INTERVIEWER'S OPINIONS. In an Iowa study of the adoption of two farm innovations utilizing a

24. This retrospective probing of how a decision was made and the influences bearing upon the decision is known as "reconstruction" or "reason analysis," a methodology described by Lazarsfeld and Rosenberg (1955).

25. Certain of the ideas contained in the remainder of this section previously appeared in Beal and others (1957). "Validity of the Concept of Stages in the Adoption Process," in *Rural Sociology*, 22: 166–168, 1957, by permission of the publisher.

relatively unstructured interview approach, Beal and Rogers (1960) found that most of the respondents recognized that they went through a series of stages as they moved from awareness to adoption. They realized they had received information from different sources, and seemed to have little trouble recalling the time at which they were aware, tried, and adopted the innovations. The respondents were forced to answer specific questions; thus it might be argued that the idea of the stages was "forced." However, if the stages were not meaningful to the respondents, they would have stated so, refused to answer, given "don't know" answers, or suggested other stages or actions taken. There were very few "don't know" or "I don't remember" responses.

2. Skipped Stages. The adoption stages should be such that most individuals go through each of the five stages for each innovation. Rogers and Beal (1960) found only 20 stages were skipped out of the possible 1,170 stages (for two farm innovations adopted by 129 and 104 respondents, respectively). The trial stage was skipped most often, and particularly by later adopters. The fact that only a few respondents reported skipping any stages provides some evidence that the stages concept is valid.

3. Different Information Sources. It is quite possible for an individual to use the same sources of information, perhaps in different ways, at several stages in the adoption process. However, if respondents reported different sources of information at each stage, this would indicate some differentiation of the stages.

Beal and Rogers (1960) found that all their respondents reported different information sources for two innovations at the trial-and-adoption stages. Less differentiation of information sources was found at the awareness-and-interest stages and the evaluation-and-trial stages. Least difference was found at the interest-and-evaluation stages where only 43 per cent of the adopters of one innovation and 53 per cent of the adopters of the other innovation reported different information sources. There are many other research studies, reviewed elsewhere in this book, that also indicate a differentiation of information sources at different stages in the adoption process.

4. DIFFERENT TIME. A logical question could be raised about the validity of the stages concept if individuals reported they adopted on impulse—that they became aware of an innovation and adopted immediately.[26] Beal and Rogers (1960) found that none of their 148 respondents reported adopting in this fashion. Instead, 73 per cent of the adopters of one innovation and 63 per cent of the adopters of the other innovation reported different years for awareness and trial. Respondents were less likely to report different dates for trial and adoption, 14 and 25 per cent, respectively, but perhaps this was because the innovations could be easily tried and adopted in the same year. Most individuals seem to require a period of time, that can often be measured in years, to pass through the adoption process. This provides some indication that adoption behavior is a *process* and one that may contain stages.

To summarize the present evidence, there seems support for the validity of the adoption stages concept, but the find-

26. It must be pointed out that whether adoption occurs on impulse depends in part on the characteristics of the innovation. Perhaps an innovation that is very low in cost and extremely simple in nature could be adopted on impulse. Even an impulse decision may be an intensely compressed adoption process.

ings are not conclusive.[27] There is very little evidence as to exactly how many stages there are in the adoption process. Nevertheless, until more evidence is available, it seems conceptually clear and practically sound to utilize the five-stage adoption process described in this book.

SOURCES OF INFORMATION BY STAGES

Many research studies have attempted to determine the relative importance of various information sources at different stages in the adoption process.[28] Two different generalizations will be presented in this section about the sources of information utilized at stages in the adoption process.

1. Personal Versus Impersonal Communications

Personal communications involve a direct face-to-face exchange between the communicator and receiver (Rogers and Beal, 1958a). The terms "personal sources of information" and "personal influence" are used somewhat interchangeably, although it is recognized that this is not completely consistent

27. The study by Copp and others (1958) with data from 175 Pennsylvania farmers also concluded that the concept of the adoption process is valid. Mason (1961) analyzed data from about 150 Oregon farmers to show that some evaluation and information-seeking occurred *after* the adoption stage. Nevertheless, Mason's data generally support the concept of an adoption process composed of stages, although his analysis suggests that the stages (except for awareness and adoption) may not always occur in the same time sequence for all individuals.

28. One methodological difficulty in all these studies is the unknown ability of respondents to accurately recall the sequence of information sources leading to their decisions. It must be cautioned that there is no assurance that farmers, physicians, or housewives have this ability.

with their literal meanings. Communication is the way in which influence is spread.[29] *Impersonal* communications do not involve a direct face-to-face exchange between the communicator and communicatee. Impersonal communications nearly always are spread via a mass communications medium. They function mainly as rapid, one-way, efficient dispensers of information. Mass communications are most effective at calling various decision alternatives to the initial attention of individuals. Because of their "mass" nature they cannot be beamed at a specialized or local audience. In short, impersonal information sources are best able to create awareness of an idea.[30]

A generalization supported by many studies is that *impersonal information sources are most important at the awareness stage, and personal sources are most important at the evaluation stage in the adoption process.*[31] People would

29. This definition is generally consistent with that of Hovland (1953, p. 182), who defined communication as the process by which an individual transmits stimuli to modify the behavior of other individuals.

30. Studies of the diffusion of major news events such as the launching of Sputnik, President Eisenhower's heart attack, and Alaskan statehood (for example, Deutschmann and Danielson, 1960), show that about five out of six persons hear about the event from the mass media within a short time of its occurance. The mass media are important transmitters of awareness-type information.

31. Research studies supporting this generalization are Wilkening (1956), Copp and others (1958), Rogers and Beal (1958a), Rogers and Pitzer (1960), Beal and Rogers (1960, p. 8), Beal and Rogers (1957), Rahim (1961, p. 43), van den Ban (in press), and Wilkening (1952b, p. 16). Several research workers (Wilkening, 1950a; Coughenour, 1960; and Lionberger, 1955) have utilized a classification of information sources on the basis of whether they are (1) "institutionalized," such as government agencies, or (2) "noninstitutionalized," such as peers. This classification is essentially similar to the present one where noninstitutionalized sources are equivalent to personal communications.

Although a direct test of the present generalization is not available in the medical drug study because information sources by adoption stages were not determined in a method allowing comparison, there is some evidence that personal communications were most important at the evaluation stage (Katz, 1961).

rather believe people than facts at the evaluation stage (Boddewyn, 1961). Reasons for the differential importance of personal and impersonal sources in the adoption process have been suggested by Wilkening (1952b, pp. 14–15; and 1956) and Rogers and Beal (1958a). Personal communication is most important at the evaluation stage, where mental judgment of the innovation is made, because:

1. Personal communication allows a two-way exchange of ideas. The communicatee may secure clarification or additional information about the innovation from the communicator.

2. Personal communication is likely to influence behavior as well as transfer ideas. In most cases, persons who interact have similar values and attitudes and may be important reference groups to one another. Mass communications seldom affect decisions directly, although they may operate through an intervening variable of group interaction to cause changes in behavior.[32]

3. Greater accessibility and credibility may be cited as reasons for the importance of personal information sources at the evaluation stage. When the source is well known, it is more likely to be regarded as trustworthy.

4. Personal contact may have greater effectiveness in the face of resistance or apathy on the part of the communicatee.[33] Impersonal information sources can usually be more easily avoided or ignored than personal ones. An example of this point comes from a sociometric study of Missouri farmers by Lionberger (1955, p. 32). He found the "nonreceptive farmers" (who opposed most farm innovations) readily sought information and advice from farmers who, in turn, were highly receptive to innovations. Lionberger concluded, "It is

32. The implicit objective of most mass advertising runs counter to this statement. However, the author has seen little adequate evidence that mass advertising directly causes changes in human behavior.

33. A study by McKain and others (1958, p. 2) of a campaign to increase the milk consumption of older persons indicates that personal influence from a change agent was particularly effective in securing adoption of an idea among lower-status persons.

thus obvious that interpersonal sources provide low-resistance avenues for farm information which is not accepted when coming from the more direct institutionalized agencies.[34]

Regarding the relative importance of personal and impersonal communications at each stage in the adoption of 2,4-D weed spray, data were obtained by Beal and Rogers (1960, p. 6) from 148 Iowa farmers. The percentage of respondents mentioning a personal information source (such as neighbors, friends, and relatives) increases from 37 per cent at the awareness stage, to 50 per cent at the interest stage, and 63 per cent at the evaluation stage; however, this percentage then decreases to 50 per cent at the trial stage. Experience with the innovation gained at the trial stage was reported as the most important information source by 95 per cent of the respondents at the adoption stage. Impersonal sources (such as farm magazines and bulletins) are more important than personal sources only at the awareness stage for 2,4-D weed spray.

Generally similar patterns in the importance of personal and impersonal communications in the adoption process are shown in data obtained from 175 Pennsylvania farmers by Copp and others (1958). These indicate a rather consistent trend for personal information sources to increase in relative importance from the awareness stage to the evaluation stage. Personal communications then fall off in importance at the trial stage.

Sill (1958) found that if the probability of adoption is to be maximized, information sources must be utilized in an ideal time sequence. In an investigation of 175 Pennsylvania farmers, Copp and others (1958, p. 70) found, "A temporal sequence is involved in agricultural communication in that messages are sent out through media directed to awareness, then to groups and finally to individuals. A farmer upsetting this sequence in any way prejudices progress at some point in

34. The high degree of communication between nonreceptive and receptive farmers in this community may not be true in other communities with more traditional norms (van den Ban, 1961a).

the adoption process." The greatest "thrust" from the awareness stage was provided by mass media, from the evaluation and trial stages by group influences, and into the adoption stage by individual experiences with the trial. Use of an information source inappropriate to a given adoption stage was associated with later adoption.

2. Cosmopoliteness of Information Sources

A second generalization about information sources by adoption stage also needs to be discussed. *Cosmopoliteness* is the degree to which an individual's orientation is external to a particular social system. Not only do individuals range along a cosmopoliteness-localiteness dimension, but information sources may also be classified as to their degree of cosmopoliteness (Campbell, 1959). Cosmopolite information about innovations comes from outside of the social system, while other information about new ideas reaches the individual from sources inside of the social system.

Cosmopolite information sources are most important at the awareness stage, and localite information sources are most important at the evaluation stage. This generalization is supported by the findings of Wilkening and others (1960) and by the data reanalyzed in Figure 4-3. The original data were gathered from 148 Iowa farm housewives by Beal and Rogers (1957a) and were reanalyzed on the basis of the cosmopoliteness dimension using a classification system suggested by Campbell (1959) and Leuthold (1960b). It should be cautioned that there is probably a relationship between the cosmopoliteness-localiteness and personal-impersonal nature of information sources. Personal sources are often more localite than cosmopolite. Nevertheless, the two classifications of information sources are conceptually distinct.

The findings of both Ryan and Gross (1943) and Katz

Per Cent of All Information Sources

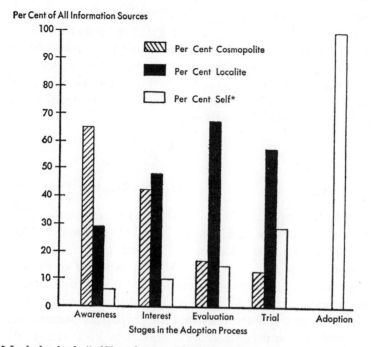

* Includes both "self" and some "don't know" answers.

FIGURE 4-3. IMPORTANCE OF COSMOPOLITE AND LOCALITE
SOURCES OF INFORMATION AT EACH STAGE IN THE
ADOPTION OF "MIRACLE" FABRICS BY
IOWA HOUSEWIVES

Data were obtained from 148 farm housewives residing in one Iowa community as to their sources of information in adopting "miracle" fabrics. The sources were classified as (1) cosmopolite, or outside of the community, or (2) localite, or inside of the community. It can be seen that cosmopolite sources are most important at the awareness stage, and localite sources play their greatest role at the evaluation stage.

Source: A reanalysis of data reported by Beal and Rogers (1957a).

(1961) suggest that cosmopolite communications are more important for the first members of a social system to learn of a new idea. Information about innovations usually emanates from sources external to the system, so this statement seems reasonable. Once the idea gains adherents in the system, localite sources are widely available to persons who are relatively later in hearing about the idea. The hybrid corn investigation also indicates that farmers who became aware of the idea relatively late were more likely to learn of the innovation from personal sources.

The Exposure-Adoption Proposition

A basic proposition tested in several research studies (Hoffer, 1942; Emery and Oeser, 1958; Coughenour, 1960b; Rahudkar, 1961; and Lackey and Larson, 1961) is that adoption of a new idea varies directly with exposure to the new idea. The results of past studies indicate this relationship between exposure and adoption is generally very high. Perhaps this is because, in a sense, all that the proposition states is that awareness must precede adoption of a new idea. Hence, the only real contribution of these findings to the present chapter is further validity for the concept of stages in the adoption process.

Cautions

This section on sources of information by adoption stages should be concluded with two cautions:

1. The present analyses ignore the effect of (1) the characteristics of the innovation,[35] and (2) the adopter category of

35. For example, mass media might be relatively unimportant in the case of the diffusion of birth control methods because these media are prohibited by some state laws from carrying this type of news. Likewise, the importance of friends as an information source might be particularly low in the case of underarm deodorants.

the respondents, on the information sources utilized. Wilkening (1950a) found wide differences in information sources used at each adoption stage on the basis of the innovations studied. In Chapter VI, several generalizations will be listed about differences in information sources on the basis of adopter category. However, in this chapter these differences by adopter category are ignored.

2. In the studies reviewed, the questions asked to determine information sources directed the responses mainly to *external* sources (Beal, 1958). Could not the individual's own past experience or his deductions from known information be considered a source of information? The implicit assumption of most past research on this topic is that information sources in the adoption process are external to the individual. It should be cautioned that this is not necessarily so.[36]

THE ADOPTION PERIOD[37]

The *adoption period* is the length of time required for an individual to pass through the adoption process from awareness to adoption. The time elapsing from awareness of an innovation to adoption for an individual is measured in days, months, or years. The adoption period is thus a gestation period in which a new idea is fermenting in the individual's mind.

Many change agents wish to speed up the process by which innovations are adopted. One method is to more adequately communicate information about new ideas so awareness is

36. Hildebrand and Partenheimer (1958) have argued this same point; they call nonexternal information sources "noncommunicative sources."

37. Certain of the ideas contained in this section appeared previously in Rogers (1961a), "The Adoption Period," in *Rural Sociology,* 26: 77–82, 1961, by permission of the publisher.

Table 4-1

LENGTH OF THE ADOPTION PERIOD FOR CERTAIN INNOVATIONS

Innovation	Average Length of Adoption Period (in years)	Per Cent Adopted	Respondents	Research Study
1. Hybrid seed corn	9.0	99	259 Iowa farmers	Gross, 1942, p. 57
2. Contour farming for soil conservation	5.0	—	110 Illinois farmers	Coleman, 1946
3. Improved pasture	8.0	94	100 N. Carolina farmers	Wilkening and Santopolo, 1952, p. 29
4. Growing alfalfa	5.0	26	100 N. Carolina farmers	Wilkening and Santopolo, 1952, p. 29
5. Ten farm innovations	3.7	—	493 Virginia farmers	Dimit, 1954, p. 50
6. Antibiotic swine supplements	1.6	71	148 Iowa farmers	Beal and Rogers, 1960, p. 10
7. 2,4-D weed spray	2.1	87	148 Iowa farmers	Beal and Rogers, 1960, p. 10
8. "Miracle" fabrics	1.6	91	148 Iowa farm homemakers	Rogers, 1955
9. 2,4-D weed spray	1.3	78	104 Ohio farmers	Rogers, 1957c
10. Warfarin rat poison	0.8	78	104 Ohio farmers	Rogers, 1957c
11. "Miracle" fabrics	0.5	79	88 Ohio farm homemakers	Rogers, 1957c

12. Stilbestrol	2.1	77	44 Ohio county extension agents*	Rogers and Yost, 1960, p. 25
13. Bulk milk tanks	2.4	89	44 Ohio county extension agents*	Rogers and Yost, 1960, p. 25
14. Irrigation	4.5	1	105 Ohio farmers using irrigation	Rogers and Pitzer, 1960, p. 33
15. Line sowing of paddy	2.5	59	63 Pakistani farmers	Rahim, 1961, p. 32
16. Insecticides	2.2	22	63 Pakistani farmers	Rahim, 1961, p. 32
17. Fertilizers	3.8	57	63 Pakistani farmers	Rahim, 1961, p. 32
18. Revised Standard Version of the Bible	3.4	27	117 Iowa church members	Koontz, 1958
19. Language laboratories	2	1	51 U.S. high school	Haber, 1961

* Note: County extension agents become aware of an innovation much as farmers do, but "adoption" for county extension agents amounts to recommending the innovation to farmers in their county.

created at an earlier date. Another method is to shorten the amount of time required for adoption after an individual is once aware of a new idea. *There is little evidence that lack of knowledge about innovations actually delays their adoption* (Wilkening and Santopolo, 1952, p. 31; and Coleman, 1946). Nonadopters are often aware of an innovation but are not motivated to try out and adopt it. Ryan and Gross (1943) reported that almost all of the Iowa farmers in their study heard about hybrid seed corn before more than a handful were planting it. "It is evident that . . . isolation from knowledge was not a determining factor in late adoption for many operators" (Ryan and Gross, 1950, p. 679).

Table 4-1 shows the average length of the adoption period for a number of innovations. Innovations with certain characteristics are generally adopted more quickly. For example, innovations that are relatively simple in nature, divisible for trial, and compatible with previous experiences may have a shorter adoption period than innovations without these characteristics. The main dimension of analysis in the present discussion, however, is individual differences in length of the adoption period, rather than differences in adoption periods among various innovations.

Rates of Awareness and Adoption

The adoption period for 2,4-D weed spray is illustrated in Figure 4-6 with data originally obtained by Beal and Rogers (1960, p. 8). It can be observed that *awareness occurs at a more rapid rate than does adoption*. For example, there are 1.7 years between 10 per cent awareness and 10 per cent adoption, but 3.1 years between 92 per cent awareness and 92 per cent adoption.

Why is there a range in years in the reported dates of awareness in Figure 4-4? Impersonal communications are

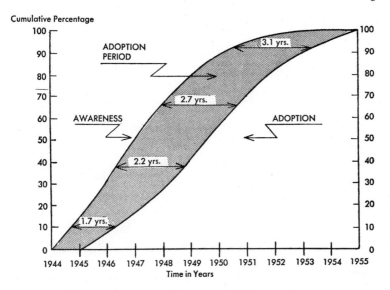

FIGURE 4-4. ADOPTION PERIOD FOR IOWA FARMERS ADOPTING
2,4-D WEED SPRAY BY YEAR

The shaded area in this figure illustrates the aggregate adoption period between awareness and adoption of 2,4-D weed spray. Awareness proceeds at a more rapid rate than does adoption. This suggests that relatively later adopters have a longer average adoption period than do earlier adopters. For example, there are 1.7 years between 10 per cent awareness and 10 per cent adoption, but 3.1 years between 92 per cent awareness and 92 per cent adoption.

Source: A reanalysis of data originally gathered by Beal and Rogers (1960, p. 8). Used by permission.

most important at the awareness stage, and the "mass" nature of these sources suggests that all members of a social system should become aware of a new idea at the same time. Then why is there a seven-year range in reported times of awareness in Figure 4-4? The answer probably lies in the social-psychological processes of selectivity. *Selective exposure* is the tendency for individuals to expose themselves to commu-

TABLE 4-2

LENGTH OF THE ADOPTION PERIOD
BY ADOPTER CATEGORY

LENGTH OF ADOPTION PERIOD (IN YEARS)

Adopter Category	2,4-D Spray in Iowa[a]	Antibiotics in Iowa[a]	2,4-D Spray in Ohio	"Miracle" Fabrics in Iowa[d]
Innovators	0.40	1.50[b]		0
			0.20	
Early adopters	0.55	0.55		0.61
Early majority	1.14	0.79	1.20	1.70
Late majority	2.34	1.52	2.14	1.49
Laggards	4.65	4.12	5.09[c]	2.71

[a] Data come from interviews with 148 Iowa farmers (Beal and Rogers, 1960, p. 14). Used by permission.

[b] The innovators of antibiotics constitute an exception to the otherwise consistent trend for adoption periods to increase in length from innovators to laggards. One reason may be the extremely small number of antibiotics innovators (only three).

[c] This category of "laggards" actually included some nonadopters in Ohio of 2,4-D spray. Source: Unpublished data from 104 farmers (Rogers, 1957c).

[d] Source: Unpublished data from 148 farm homemakers (Rogers, 1955).

nications that agree with their existing opinions. Even though a stimulus may be presented to a total audience, only certain individuals will receive it. Their reception or nonreception depends upon such factors as their past experiences, social values, mental set, and state of knowledge. The way in which an individual perceives a new idea and whether or not he retains knowledge of it also depends upon his opinions and attitudes.[38] Thus, a farmer may drive his car past 100 miles of hybrid corn but still not "see" or be aware of hybrid corn (Beal, 1958). Hassinger (1959) may be correct in claiming that the awareness stage has been viewed by researchers in too passive a light. In summary, the selectivity processes are prob-

38. A more detailed description of selective exposure, selective perception, and selective retention is contained in Chapter VIII.

ably one reason why all members of a social system do not become aware of a new idea at the same time.

Length of the Adoption Period by Adopter Category

The first individuals to adopt innovations require a shorter adoption period than do relatively later adopters. Table 4-2 shows the adoption period is consistently longer in years for each adopter category from innovators (the first to adopt) to laggards (the last to adopt).[39] This suggests that the first individuals to adopt a new idea do so, not only because they become aware of the practice sooner than their neighbors but also because they require fewer years to move from awareness to adoption. Innovators perhaps gain part of their innovative position (relative to later adopters) by learning about innovations at an earlier time, but the present data also suggest that innovators are the first to adopt because they require a shorter adoption period.

Why do innovators require a shorter adoption period? Research studies show that innovators have more favorable attitudes toward new ideas and less resistance to change must be overcome by communications about the ideas. Innovators may have shorter adoption periods because they use more technically accurate sources of information such as direct contact with scientists, and because they place more credibility in these sources than the average individual. Innovators may also possess a type of mental ability that enables them to deal with abstractions. An innovator must be able to conceptualize relatively abstract information about new ideas and apply this new information to his own situation.

39. Similar evidence for this generalization has been reported by Wilkening and Santopolo (1952, p. 31), Rogers and Yost (1960, p. 28), Ryan (1948), and Petrini (1953, p. 71). Lazarsfeld and other (1944, p. 53) found a similar type of evidence in the case of voting decisions. Haber's (1961) findings, however, do not support the generalization.

Later adopters can observe the results of innovations by earlier adopters and may not require this mental ability.

Awareness-to-Trial and Trial-to-Adoption Periods

The adoption period is the length of time required for an individual to pass through the adoption process from awareness to adoption of an innovation. Research workers have been successful in isolating two distinct time periods[40] that compose the total adoption period: (1) the *awareness-to-trial* period—the length of time required for an individual to progress from awareness-to-trial of an innovation, and (2) the *trial-to-adoption* period—the length of time required for an individual to go from trial-to-adoption of an innovation.

Evidence from several investigations supports the generalization that for most innovations *the awareness-to-trial period is longer than the trial-to-adoption period*. For example: (1) 5.5 years were required for the awareness-to-trial period for hybrid seed corn and 3.3 years for the trial-to-adoption period (Gross, 1942, pp. 58–59). (2) The awareness-to-trial period was 1.58 years for 2,4-D weed spray, and the trial-to-adoption period was 0.48 years (Beal and Rogers, 1960, p. 10). (3) 1.43 years were required for the awareness-to-trial period for antibiotic swine feed supplement, compared to 0.18 years for the trial-to-adoption period for the same innovation (Beal and Rogers, 1960, p. 10). (4) Dimit (1954, p. 50) found a total adoption period that averaged 3.7 years for 11 farm innovations; the trial-to-adoption period ranged from 1.35 to 2.06

40. It is entirely possible that a research worker might also be able to isolate and measure awareness-to-interest, interest-to-evaluation, and evaluation-to-trial periods. It is the author's personal experience with farmers in research interviews that they can much more easily recall their time of adoption, trial, and awareness (in about that order) than they can recall their dates of interest or evaluation of an innovation. In fact, the evaluation stage may not occur at one definite point in time in the case of certain innovations.

years for the 11 innovations. Dimit concluded there was a longer period of years between awareness and trial than between trial and adoption of an innovation.

The research evidence suggests that the adoption stage directly follows the trial stage. Thus, efforts to encourage the trial of innovations may act to speed up the adoption process. Klonglan and others (1960) studied the effect of a free trial of a new weed spray offered to Midwestern farmers by an agricultural chemical company. They estimated that the free trial speeded up the adoption process for the weed spray as much as one year for these farmers.

Awareness-to-Trial and Trial-to-Adoption
Periods by Adopter Category

Earlier it was generalized that earlier adopters require a shorter adoption period than later adopters. Breaking down the adoption period into two subperiods, awareness-to-trial and trial-to-adoption, offers a further insight into this generalization.

Two more-detailed generalizations are now suggested.

1. *The awareness-to-trial period is shorter for relatively earlier adopters than for later adopters.* This statement is consistent with the generalization about the length of the adoption period for adopter categories. Figure 4-5 shows that the innovators and early adopters of hybrid seed corn required an awareness-to-trial period of 1.6 years while the laggards required 9.5 years.[41] In fact, the average laggard was not

41. It should be pointed out that the hybrid seed corn adopters were not classified into the five adopter categories proposed in the present book. Gross (1942, p. 42) used four adopter categories: the "A" group, 8.9 per cent; B's, 27.8 per cent; C's, 56.0 per cent; and D's, 7.3 per cent. This would mean that A's were mostly innovators and early adopters, B's mostly early majority, C's mostly late majority, and D's mostly laggards.

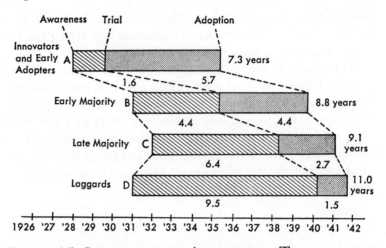

FIGURE 4-5. LENGTH OF THE AWARENESS-TO-TRIAL AND THE
TRIAL-TO-ADOPTION PERIOD FOR HYBRID SEED
CORN BY ADOPTER CATEGORY

Innovators and early adopters have a much shorter awareness-to-trial
period (1.6 years) than do laggards (9.5 years). These relatively earlier
adopters became *aware* of the innovation only a few years sooner than the
relatively later adopters, but they moved much more quickly to the *trial*
stage (in this case, first planting hybrid seed) after becoming aware.

Innovators and early adopters have a longer average trial-to-adoption
period (5.7 years), shown as a solid bar above, than do laggards (1.5
years). These first adopters take a relatively greater risk in adopting,
so they initially plant a smaller percentage of their acreage in hybrid
seed. More years are required for them to go from first planting the
seed (trial) to 100 per cent adoption.

The total awareness-to-adoption period is relatively shorter for
the innovators and early adopters (7.3 years) than for any other adopter
category including the laggards (11.0 years). In this study the innovators and early adopters reached 100 per cent adoption 6.7 years
sooner than the laggards; 3 of these 6.7 years were owing to earlier
awareness of the innovation, and 3.7 years were owing to a shorter
awareness-to-adoption period. It should be cautioned that the four
adopter categories shown here were classified by Gross (1942, p. 42)
on the basis of time of *trial* rather than the more usual time of *adoption*.

Source: A reanalysis of data from Gross (1942, pp. 58–59). Used
by permission.

aware of hybrid seed (1931) until after the average innovator
and early adopter had tried the innovation (before 1930).

2. *The trial-to-adoption period is longer for relatively
earlier adopters than for later adopters.* At first glance, this
generalization seems inconsistent with those about the total
adoption period and the awareness-to-trial period. For, compared to the later adopters, the earlier adopters require *more
years* to pass from trial to adoption! However, there is no
real inconsistency between these generalizations.

Since first adopters take a relatively greater risk in adopting
the innovation (at the time they adopt), they initially plant
a smaller percentage of their acreage in hybrid seed. The
innovators and early adopters have no precedent to follow;
they are creating the precedent for later adopters. Because of
this greater subjective risk, the relatively earlier adopters require a longer trial-adoption period than do later adopters.
More years are required for earlier adopters to go from first
planting the seed (trial) to 100 per cent adoption. Figure 4-5
shows that innovators and early adopters have a longer
average trial-to-adoption period (5.7 years) than do the laggards (1.5 years).

Since the awareness-to-trial period is longer than the trial-
to-adoption period, the total adoption period is relatively
shorter for the earlier adopters (7.3 years in Figure 4-5) than
for any other adopter category including the laggards (11.0
years). Thus, the innovators and early adopters of hybrid
seed had a longer trial-to-adoption period (5.7 years) than the
laggards (1.5 years), but this was more than overcome in the
total adoption period by the innovators' and early adopters'
shorter awareness-to-trial period (1.6 years to 9.5 years for
the laggards).

Similar evidence to that described here for hybrid seed is
provided by Ryan (1948) in his study of the same innovation
in Iowa, "As would be expected, the operators adopting late
tended to come more rapidly to 100 per cent planting. . . .
However, the actual date at which complete adoption was

reached tended to be earlier for those who started the adoption process early."

It should be cautioned that the generalizations about the awareness-to-trial period and the trial-to-adoption period by adopter category are based almost entirely upon one innovation, hybrid seed corn, and may not hold for other innovations.[42]

Adoption on the Installment Plan

Not only do earlier adopters require a longer trial-to-adoption period than later adopters, but they also try innovations more tentatively. Earlier adopting physicians used smaller prescriptions of gammanyn on their first trial (Katz, 1961). These data, as well as those from two hybrid corn investigations, are shown in Table 4-3. The generalization derived from these data is that *earlier adopters try innovations on a smaller scale than later adopters.*[43] Innovators, as compared to laggards, take more installments to go from trial to adoption and they try the new idea with a smaller first installment.[44]

Haber's (1961) study of the adoption of language laboratories among U.S. high schools supports the present generali-

42. Another shortcoming of the present generalizations is the dependence upon recall-type data. Katz (1961) inferred from his data that there may have been a tendency for his doctor-respodents to report inaccurately a later date for awareness of a new drug and an earlier date for adoption so that the adoption period appeared shorter than in actuality.

43. Another study supporting this generalization is Rogers and Pitzer (1960, p. 28) who found that earlier adopters of irrigation in Ohio were more likely to try it on a small scale the first year.

44. Innovators may be caught with a larger stock of the superseded idea (farm machines, drugs, or industrial equipment) on hand at the time of adoption of the new idea than laggards, and this may partly explain why laggards require a longer trial-to-adoption period.

TABLE 4-3

EARLIER ADOPTERS TRY INNOVATIONS ON A SMALLER SCALE THAN LATER ADOPTERS*

Year of Trial of Hybrid Corn by 257 Iowa Farmers[a]	Per Cent of Corn Acreage in Hybrid During First Year	Year of Trial of Hybrid Corn by 433 Iowa Farmers[b]	Per Cent of Corn Acreage in Hybrid During First Year	Date of Trial of Gammanyn by 125 Physicians[c]	Number of Drug Prescriptions During Three-Day Period
Before 1936	13	Before 1935	19	First two months after release	1.5
1936-37	19	1935-36	27	Third and fourth month	2.0
1938	25	1937	28	Fifth and sixth month	2.7
After 1938	42	After 1937	44	Seventh and eighth month	2.6

* It should be cautioned that innovativeness was measured in terms of time of first *trial* in the three studies included in this table, rather than time of *adoption*.

[a] *Source:* A reanalysis of Ryan and Gross's (1943) data.

[b] *Source:* A reanalysis of Ryan's (1948) data.

[c] *Source:* Katz (1961).

zation. He concluded: "It is almost as if those that know how to use [the innovation] also know that it needs extensive testing. Those who have never used it rush in where the proverbial angels fear to tread."

In spite of the widely publicized tests by manufacturers of new products, individuals hesitate to adopt an innovation until it has been proved by their own cautious trials (Katz, 1961). No farmer in the Iowa hybrid corn study reported planting all of his acreage to hybrid in his first year of trial. Even the experiences of earlier adopting peers are not enough to convince the later adopters, who still reveal some degree of tentativeness in their partial trial of new ideas.

Further research is needed on the adoption period. The eventual goal of this endeavor might be recommendations to change agents as to how they may shorten the length of the adoption process and, hence, of the diffusion process.

The Adoption Period in the Diffusion Process

While the adoption process is the mental process through which an individual passes from first hearing about an idea to final adoption, the diffusion process is the spread of a new idea from its source of invention or creation to its ultimate adopters or users.

The length of the diffusion process (the "diffusion period") is measured from the date the first individual is aware of the innovation until it has reached complete adoption in a given social system.[45] The diffusion period required for an audience to reach complete adoption is, at least partly, a function of the length of the adoption period for individual adopters. This is probably not a linear function. An innovation with a relatively short adoption period (on the average)

45. Rapoport (1956, p. 49) refers to the diffusion period as "public time" required for diffusion to occur, and the adoption period as "private time."

will likely have a relatively short diffusion period. As the adoption period becomes longer (in the case of other innovations), the diffusion period will likely become proportionately longer. Efforts to derive empirically the nature of the "adoption period—diffusion period" relationship should be a priority item for future research.

SUMMARY

The *adoption process* is the mental process through which an individual passes from first hearing about an innovation to final adoption. This process by which innovations are adopted by individuals is one example of how any type of learning takes place.

The adoption process is conceptualized in five stages or steps: awareness, interest, evaluation, trial, and adoption. At the *awareness* stage the individual is exposed to the innovation but lacks complete information about it. He then becomes interested in the innovation and seeks information about it at the *interest* stage. At the *evaluation* stage the individual mentally applies the innovation to his present and anticipated future situation, and then decides whether or not to try it. The individual uses the innovation on a small scale in order to determine its utility in his own situation at the *trial* stage. At the *adoption* stage the individual decides to continue the full use of the innovation. Evidence from research studies indicates the conception of adoption stages is probably valid.

An innovation may be rejected at any stage in the adoption process. A *discontinuance* is a decision to cease use of an innovation after previously adopting. Relatively later adopters are more likely to discontinue innovations than are earlier adopters.

Personal communications involve a direct face-to-face exchange between the communicator and communicatee. Impersonal information sources are most important at the awareness stage, and personal sources are most important at the evaluation stage in the adoption process. Cosmopolite information sources are most important at the awareness stage, and localite information sources are most important at the evaluation stage.

The *adoption period* is the length of time required for an individual to pass through the adoption process from awareness to adoption. Awareness occurs at a more rapid rate than does adoption in a social system. There is little evidence that lack of knowledge about innovations actually delays their adoption.

The first individuals to adopt innovations require a shorter adoption period than do relatively later adopters. The portion of the adoption period from awareness to trial is longer than from trial to adoption. The awareness-to-trial period is shorter for relatively earlier adopters than for later adopters; however, the trial-to-adoption period is longer for relatively earlier adopters than for later adopters. Earlier adopters try innovations on a smaller scale than later adopters.

CHAPTER V

Characteristics of the Innovation

The reception given to a new idea is not so fortuitous and unpredictable as it sometimes appears to be. The character of the idea is itself an important determinant.

HOMER G. BARNETT, 1953, p. 313

Among the members of a social system, some innovations diffuse from first introduction to widespread use in a few years. Other innovations require fifty years. What characteristics of innovations affect the rate at which they diffuse and are adopted?

The purpose of this chapter is to suggest a list of characteristics by which any innovation may be described, to show how individuals' perceptions of these characteristics may be utilized in predicting rate of adoption, and to analyze cases of overadoption. Generally speaking, there have been fewer research studies designed to probe these points than to answer other major questions presented in this book. Out of necessity, the statements here are more hypothetical in nature and have fewer empirical claims to support them.

Past research has focused upon the diffusion and adoption of new ideas, but not upon the innovations themselves. Researchers have tended to regard all innovations as equivalent units from the viewpoint of analysis.[1] This is an oversimplification, and a dangerous one. One evidence that all innovations are not equivalent units is that some new products fail

1. One exception to this statement is Menzel (1960a).

while others succeed. A New York industrial design concern reported its research indicates that 23 of every 26 new products introduced by industry fail. The high casualty rate of new products is also underscored by a large advertising agency that reports that of every 25 products that are test-marketed, only one succeeds. The U.S. Department of Commerce estimates that 90 per cent of all new products fail within four years of their release.

Many companies try to predict the rate of adoption of an innovation before it is marketed on a full-scale basis.[2] The following example illustrates one of these failures. The case of the pill that failed points out some of the difficulties involved in predicting rate of adoption even after extensive consumer tests.

THE PILL THAT FAILED[3]

The story of Analoze, a combination pain killer and stomach sweetener, provides evidence that even if consumer tests are favorable, a new product may fail. The business executives who conceived the pill were impressed by the fact that Americans were gulping record quantities of analgesics (pain killers). Since this was true, they reasoned, wouldn't an analgesic that could be taken without water have a ready market? Mindful of the success of antacid pills, they later decided to make Analoze a combination tablet.

The company's laboratories came up with the desired product, a cherry-flavored combination tablet. Working with a large New York advertising firm, the manufacturer submitted

2. Fount and Woodlock (1960) attempted to predict the market success of new grocery products at an early point in the diffusion process.

3. Adapted from Schorr (1961), "The Mistakes: Many New Products Fail Despite Careful Planning, Publicity" in the *Wall Street Journal*, April 5, 1961, pp. 1, 22, by permission of the publisher.

samples of Analoze and competing products to a consumer panel. The verdict: Panel members overwhelmingly preferred Analoze.

The advertising copywriters then developed ads boosting Analoze as the combination analgesic-antacid that "works without water." Tests showed the ads had strong impact. The package was well designed and the price was right. Backed by heavy advertising outlays, Analoze moved into test markets—Denver, Memphis, Phoenix, and Omaha. Dealers were enthusiastic and prospects appeared bright. The sales reports began to trickle in. Despite all the careful preparations, the public was buying only small quantities of Analoze. Weeks went by with no improvement, and the manufacturer glumly withdrew Analoze from the test markets.

After months of post-mortem probing, it was concluded that the fatal flaw was the "works without water" feature. Headache sufferers unconsciously associate water with a cure, and consequently had no confidence in a tablet that dissolved in the mouth.

Conclusions

This illustration shows that consumers did not perceive the new product as compatible with their existing values on the importance of water as part of a headache cure. The characteristics of an innovation have a great deal to do with its rate of adoption. It is the characteristic of a new product not as seen by experts but as perceived by the potential adopters that really matters. This point was emphasized by Wassen (1960), who utilized several case examples to show that "The ease or difficulty of introduction [of ideas] . . . depend basically on the nature of the 'new' in the new product—the new as the customer views the bundle of services he perceives in the newborn."

CHARACTERISTICS OF INNOVATIONS

It matters little whether or not an innovation has a great degree of advantage over the idea it is replacing. What does matter is whether the individual perceives the relative advantage of the innovation.[4] Likewise, it is the potential adopter's perceptions of the compatibility, complexity, divisibility, and communicability of the innovation that affect its rate of adoption.[5]

In this section, five different characteristics of innovations will be described. Each of these five is somewhat interrelated with the other four, but they are conceptually distinct. Selection of these five characteristics is based on past writings and research, as well as a desire for maximum generality. What is needed is a comprehensive set of characteristics of innovations which are as mutually exclusive and as universally relevant as possible. The five characteristics of innovations utilized are (1) relative advantage, (2) compatibility, (3) complexity, (4) divisibility, and (5) communicability.

1. Relative Advantage

↙ Relative advantage is the degree to which an innovation is superior to ideas it supersedes. The degree of relative advan-

4. Tucker (1961) found that 12 agricultural change agents did not perceive the characteristics of 13 farm innovations differently from 12 farmers residing in the same county. Kivlin (1960) found similar evidence in a Pennsylvania study. There is no other research evidence, however, on whether certain categories, say innovators, perceive innovations differently from others, say laggards, but it is reasonable to expect differential perceptions. This is the type of analysis designated as Type 5 in Table 3-2.

5. The unit of adoption for an idea, whether an individual decision or a group decision, also affects the idea's rate of adoption (as pointed out in Chapter I).

tage is often expressed in economic profitability, but the relative advantage dimension may be measured in other ways.[6] For instance, one of the major advantages of 2,4-D weed spray over previous methods of farm weed control was a reduction in unpleasant labor requirements rather than a direct financial gain from higher crop yields.

The relative advantage of a new idea may be emphasized by a *crisis*. Wilkening (1953, p. 13) investigated the effect of a climatic crisis on the adoption of grass silage by Wisconsin farmers. The per cent who had adopted grass silage went from 16 per cent in 1950 to 48 per cent in 1951. Rain and cool weather in 1951 made the curing of hay difficult and many farmers turned to grass silage. Had not the relative advantage of the new idea been sufficiently demonstrated before 1951, the weather would not have had such an effect that year.

In a somewhat similar fashion, the threat of the Berlin problem to world peace in 1961 hastened the construction of fallout shelters in the U.S. Research studies confirm the generalization that *a crisis emphasizes the relative advantage of an innovation and affects its rate of adoption.* For example: Mulford (1959) concluded that an economic crisis speeded the rate of adoption of industrial development commissions by Iowa communities. Sutherland (1959) showed that a cotton spinning innovation was adopted more quickly by English firms because of the labor shortage in World War II. Bertrand (1951) found that the crisis of unionized farm laborers and wartime labor shortages aided the rate of adoption of farm mechanization in Louisiana.

Two other studies show that a decisive event may *retard* the rate of adoption of an innovation. However, the members of a social system made up for lost ground as soon as the crisis was past. Adler (1955, p. 27) found that depressions and

6. The nature of the innovation may determine what specific type of relative advantage (e.g., economic or social) is important to adopters (Wilkening and Johnson, 1961).

wars retarded the adoption of educational innovations, but that the school systems he studied accelerated their rate of adoption as soon as the crises were past. Pemberton (1937) found a similar case in his analysis of memberships in a national parent-teacher organization. World War I and the Depression caused a lag in adoption behind a theoretical normal curve, but the members of the social system made up for lost ground once the crises were past.

The relative advantage of an innovation may also be emphasized by a strong promotional effort by change agents (Wilkening, 1952b, p. 36). For instance, Ross (1952) attempted to determine reasons for the relatively rapid adoption of driver education programs by high schools. Fifteen years are normally required for an educational innovation to be adopted by the first 3 per cent of the public schools in the U.S. However, 87 per cent of the school systems in Ross's study adopted driver training in the first 15 years. Why was driver education adopted so rapidly? Promotion by car dealers (who often loaned cars without cost for driver training), insurance companies, and the AAA helped emphasize the relative advantage of the new idea. Of course, another fact was the need for driver education which had been called to national attention by high accident rates. The seriousness of the need for an innovation is an indication of the relative advantage of the new idea.

In summary, the relative advantage of an innovation is a matter of perception. *The relative advantage of a new idea, as perceived by members of a social system, affects its rate of adoption.*

2. Compatibility

✗ *Compatibility* is the degree to which an innovation is consistent with existing values and past experiences of the adopters. An idea that is not compatible with the cultural norms of a social system will not be adopted so rapidly as an idea that is compatible. Compatibility ensures greater security to the potential adopter and makes the new idea more meaningful to him. One example of a noncompatible idea is birth control techniques in countries where the religion discourages this idea. The lack of compatibility of beef production in India with cultural values prevents the adoption of this innovation.

An innovation may be compatible not only with cultural values but also with previously adopted ideas. Compatibility of an innovation with a preceding idea that is evaluated unfavorably may retard its rate of adoption. Thus, compatibility may either speed up or retard the adoption rate. Old ideas are the main tools with which new ideas can be assessed. One cannot deal with an innovation except on the basis of the familiar and the old-fashioned. The rate of adoption of a new idea is affected by the old idea that it supersedes. Obviously, however, if a new idea were completely congruent with existing practice, there would be no innovation.

There are several investigations which show that *the compatibility of a new idea, as perceived by members of a social system, affects its rate of adoption.*

Graham (1956) found that only 24 per cent of his upper-class respondents adopted television, compared with 72 per cent of the lower class. Canasta was accepted by 72 per cent of the upper class, but only 12 per cent of the lower class. Upper-class and lower-class values on types of recreation were found to explain these differences in rates of adoption. The compatibility of the innovation with social class values partly determined its speed of adoption.[7]

Yeracaris (1961) found that the acceptance of tuberculosis testing was ". . . a direct function of the degree to which the

7. Similar evidence for the adoption of educational television is presented by Geiger and Sokol (1960, p. 39).

innovational characteristics are compatible with the health practices, attitudes and values of the respondents. . . ."

Hawley (1946) sought to determine why the Rio Grande pueblo Indians accepted the Catholic religion while the western pueblo Indians rejected it forcefully, killed the priests, and burned the missions. Hawley concluded that Catholicism was more compatible with the eastern pueblo culture, which is more patriarchal and father-dominated.

Santopolo (1961) reported the difficulty encountered by Kentucky county agents in convincing farmers to switch from tobacco-growing to pickle-raising. Even though the latter crop was more profitable, it was not adopted because cucumbers were perceived by farmers as a feminine type of enterprise. On the other hand, raising tobacco was prestigious.

In one section of Southern Germany, the average farm has become fragmented to about 75 "postage stamp" plots through land inheritance customs. Government change agencies consolidated these parcels of land, and redistributed them to the owners so that each farm was in one large plot. Farm mechanization and improved efficiency were expected to result. But farmers' attitudes toward their larger fields had not been changed. As a result, the author encountered some German farmers who divided their newly consolidated farms into 75 small plots! Their seeding and fertilization rates, they claimed, were on the basis of the tiny plots and they resisted consolidation efforts. The idea of land consolidation was incompatible with their cultural values, and unless these values were changed, the new idea could not be forced upon them by government agencies. The case is similar to the problem of urban slum dwellers in the U.S. who are relocated in new apartment buildings without efforts to change their values and teach them how to use their new facilities.

McCorkle (1961) sought to determine why chiropractic, a form of healing by manual adjustment of the spine, was so popular in rural Iowa. He concluded that chiropractic satisfies needs not well covered by orthodox medicine, and it fits well into the value system of the rural Iowan. Chiropractic offers to put him in order rapidly so that he may return to work. It is cheap in cost and does not require hospitalization. The 1,000 chiropractic practitioners in Iowa are evidence that the idea is compatible with rural Iowa culture.

Parish (1954) found that Australian farmers adopted mechanical innovations more rapidly than nonmechanical innovations. Prundeanu and Zwerman (1958) found that soil conservation practices that were mainly production-increasing and required a minimum of maintenance (for example, tiling) were adopted more quickly by New York farmers than such conservation practices as terracing and contouring. Farmers' values tend to be more compatible with mechanical innovations and with those that increase production.[8]

Innovations are seldom viewed singularly by individuals. They may be perceived as an interrelated bundle or *complex* of new ideas. The adoption of one new idea may "trigger" the adoption of several others. For example, a farmer who purchases a tractor may, as a result, also adopt an entire line of new farm equipment that attaches to the tractor frame. Of course, it is possible that the farmer may have purchased the tractor in order to adopt the related equipment. But the result is the same. An entire complex of new ideas is adopted rather than each innovation singly.

One of the few investigations of a complex of new ideas is Silverman and Bailey's (1961) analysis of the adoption of three corn-growing innovations by 107 Mississippi farmers. The three ideas (fertilization, hybrid seed, and thick planting) were functionally interrelated in such a way that adoption of the latter innovation without concurrent use of the other two ideas resulted in lower corn yields than if none of the ideas were used. Most farmers either adopted all three of

8. Similar evidence was provided by Lionberger (1960, p. 25).

the ideas or none of them, but 8 per cent used unsuccessful combinations. Silverman and Bailey suggested the need for change agents to show more farmers the interrelationships among the three ideas in the corn-growing complex.

Some merchandisers offer "tie-in" sales, a technique that recognizes the high degree of compatibility among several new products. A new clothes washer may be offered to housewives as a package deal along with a clothes dryer. Some marketing schemes "hook-on" an unwanted product to a compatible innovation that possesses a high degree of relative advantage. The term "rice Christians" conveys this tie-in of two ideas. The term has come to be widely employed beyond the field of religion to denote persons who accept a nuisance, religion, in order to get an essential, rice (Barnett, 1953, p. 363).

There is need to analyze complexes of innovations in future research, to study ideas in an evolutionary sequence, and to determine the degree of compatibility perceived by individuals among interrelated ideas.

3. Complexity

Complexity is the degree to which an innovation is relatively difficult to understand and use. Any new idea may be classified on the complexity-simplicity continuum. Some innovations are clear in their meaning to members of a social system, others are not. Although the research evidence is far from conclusive, the generalization is suggested that *the complexity of an innovation, as perceived by members of a social system, affects its rate of adoption.*

Kivlin (1960) found that the complexity of farm innovations was more highly related (in a negative direction) to their rate of adoption than any other characteristic of the innovations except relative advantage.

Graham (1956) sought to determine why canasta and television diffused at different adoption rates in the upper and lower classes. He concluded that one reason was the difference in complexity of the two ideas. Canasta had to be learned through detailed personal explanation from other card players. Its procedures were complex and difficult to master. Television, however, appeared to be a relatively "simple" idea that required only the ability to turn a knob.

4. Divisibility

Divisibility is the degree to which an innovation may be tried on a limited basis. New ideas that can be tried on the installment plan will generally be adopted more rapidly than innovations that are not divisible. Some ideas that cannot be divided for small-scale trial may be subjected to a trial over time. An example is the Ohio farmer who tried a new feed on his entire dairy herd for one week. He then compared milk production with that of previous weeks. Nevertheless, some innovations are more difficult than others to divide for trial. Examples of take-it-or-leave-it innovations are bulk milk tanks, home air conditioners, and driver training education in a school system. A generalization is suggested, in spite of its lack of wide evidence, that *the divisibility of an innovation, as perceived by members of a social system, affects its rate of adoption.*[9]

There is evidence from several investigations[10] *that relatively earlier adopters may perceive divisibilty as more important than later adopters.* Laggards move from initial trial

9. Kivlin (1960) found a correlation between divisibility and rate of adoption for 43 farm innovations that was not significant but in the expected direction.
10. These studies include Gross (1942, pp. 58–59), Ryan (1948), and Katz (1961).

to full-scale use more rapidly than do innovators and early adopters. The more innovative individuals have no precedent to follow while the later adopters are surrounded by peers who have already adopted the innovation. These peers may act as a "psychological trial" for the later adopters; divisibility of a new idea is hence of less significance for them.

5. Communicability

Communicability is the degree to which the results of an innovation may be diffused to others. The results of some ideas are easily observed and communicated to others, while some innovations are difficult to describe to others. *The communicability of an innovation, as perceived by members of a social system, affects its rate of adoption.* One illustration of this generalization is the case of pre-emergent weed-killers that are sprayed on a field before the weeds emerge from the soil. The rate of adoption of this idea has been slow by Midwestern farmers, in spite of its relative advantage, because there are no dead weeds which the farmer can show his neighbors.

Hruschka (1961) rated farm innovations into four categories of "observability" in an investigation of the role of demonstration farmers in diffusing new ideas in German villages. The ideas which were rated as more communicable diffused more readily from the demonstration farmers to surrounding villagers. For example, more villagers were aware of a new haymaking technique than of keeping farm records.

Erasmus (1961, p. 23) shows that the visibility of an innovation is particularly important in affecting its rate of adoption in a less developed, preliterate society. In 1951, for example, the Point Four program in Bolivia introduced Cuban Yellow Corn in one town. Within two years the local demand for the seed far exceeded the supply. The farmers were mostly illiterate, but were convinced to adopt by the spectacular results of the new seed, which often tripled corn yields. The results of adoption were so highly visible and widely discussed that a more scientific comparison of the new idea with existing varieties was not necessary to convince the local villagers.

Menzel (1960a) hypothesized that the amount of out-of-town communication would be more highly related to the adoption of gammanyn (an easily communicable idea) than to the adoption of modern patient-management (a relatively difficult idea to communicate). Menzel's findings did not provide much support for his hypothesis, but his work is suggestive of future research attention.

Ogburn's (1922) cultural lag theory fits into the present discussion of communicability. Ogburn claimed that material innovations diffused and were adopted more readily than nonmaterial ideas. Linton (1936, pp. 337–338) pointed out that one reason for this cultural lag (of nonmaterial behind material innovations) is greater visibility and communicability of material ideas. He stated, "The material techniques and their products are probably the only elements of culture which can be completely communicated, and it is significant that it is usually these elements which are accepted most readily. . . ." The culture lag theory of Ogburn has fallen into academic disrepute in recent years. In fact, Boskoff (1957, p. 296) labeled the distinction between material and nonmaterial ideas as a theoretical *cul de sac* and recommends a hasty exit.

Other Characteristics of Innovations

The five characteristics of innovations just described are by no means the only ones that have been used by diffusion researchers. Thirty-nine different terms have been used, and they may be subsumed under the five general characteristics utilized in the present book.

Further research will certainly be necessary before the five characteristics of innovations described in this section can be accepted as the five most important characteristics in affecting the rate of adoption.[11] At the present time relative advantage, compatibility, complexity, divisibility, and communicability should properly be regarded only as potentially useful tools for the analysis of the characteristics of new ideas.

CHARACTERISTICS AND RATE OF ADOPTION

Which of the characteristics of innovations are most important in influencing their rate of adoption? Several research studies provide a partial answer to this question.

Rate of adoption is the relative speed with which an innovation is adopted by the members of a social system. Rate of adoption is usually measured by the length of time required for a certain percentage of the members of a social system to adopt an innovation.[12]

11. Obviously, variables other than these five characteristics might affect the rate of adoption of innovations.
12. A variety of specific measures of rate of adoption have been used by researchers, although all these measures are based on the length of time required to reach a certain level of adoption. Kivlin (1960, p. 28) used the annual per cent of adoption during the eight years of most rapid growth in adoption. Tucker's (1961) measure was the number of years from 5 per cent adoption to 20 per cent adoption. Mansfield (1961a) and Havens and Rogers (1961b) measured rate of adoption by dividing the number of individuals adopting in a given year by the number yet to adopt that year. Griliches (1957) measured rate of adoption by the slope of the adopter distribution. Adler (1955) utilized a "vitality index" to operationalize this dimension which also took discontinuances into account.

Kivlin (1960) probably completed the most adequate study on the relationship of characteristics of innovations to their rate of adoption. He asked 20 judges to rate 11 characteristics of 43 farm innovations. The judges were farmers and agricultural change agents in a Pennsylvania county.[13] Data on the rate of adoption of these 43 farm ideas were secured from 299 of the farmers in the same county.

Kivlin found highest correlations between rate of adoption and (1) relative advantage, (2) complexity, and (3) compatibility. No significant relationship was found between rate of adoption and divisibility. The combined effect of the characteristics of innovations explained only 51 per cent of the variation in the rate of adoption of the 43 farm innovations. None of the characteristics alone explained more than 16 per cent of the variation in rate of adoption. Incidentally, Kivlin found either low or negative intercorrelations among four[14] characteristics of innovations (divisibility, compatibility, complexity, and advantage) which suggests they may be relatively independent of one another.

Tucker (1961) utilized Kivlin's methodology in a study with data from one Ohio county. He found divisibility, compatibility, complexity, and relative advantage were not significantly related to rate of adoption although the relationships were all in the expected direction.

Mansfield (1961a) explained about 50 per cent of the vari-

A measure of the rate of awareness might be computed for a social system to measure the relative speed with which members of a system are aware of a new idea. There is no research completed to date that uses the rate of awareness as a dimension of analysis.

13. Kivlin's (1960) and Tucker's (1961) research designs both called for pooling or averaging the ratings of characteristics of innovations. Wilkening (1961, p. 58) found that Australian farmers perceived the relative advantage of an innovation differently, depending on their personal characteristics. Perceptions of an innovation probably vary on the basis of the individual's education, innovativeness, etc.

14. Kivlin (1960) did not measure the fifth characteristic, communicability.

ation in the rate of adoption of 12 innovations in the coal, steel, brewing, and railroad industries. He related rate of adoption to (1) a measure of profitability, and (2) a measure of the extent of interaction with other firms about the innovation.[15]

Profitability Versus Compatibility: A Controversy[16]

A controversy has raged as to the relative importance of profitability (one dimension of relative advantage) versus compatibility in explaining the rate of adoption of innovations. *Profitability* is the difference between economic returns resulting from adoption of an innovation and the innovation's economic cost. Griliches (1957) explained about 60 per cent of the variation in rate of adoption of hybrid corn (measured by the slope of the S-shaped adopter distribution), on the basis of profitability. Griliches utilized aggregate data from U.S. crop reporting districts and states in his analysis, and made no particular claim that similar results would obtain when *individual* farmers were used as the unit of analysis.

Brandner and Straus (1959) investigated the relationship of (1) compatibility, and (2) profitability, to rate of adoption. They found that hybrid sorghum was adopted more rapidly,

15. Krug (1961) completed a rather ingenious analysis of the rate of adoption of ten farm ideas in Wisconsin to (1) characteristics of the innovations, and (2) the extent and type of farm magazine coverage accorded the ideas. However, no strong associations were found between rate of adoption and the characteristics of the innovations, as rated by judges.

16. Many of the ideas in this and the following section come from Havens and Rogers (1961b) "Adoption of Hybrid Corn: Profitability and the Interaction Effect" in *Rural Sociology*, 26: 409–414, 1961, by permission of the publisher.

as measured by per cent of adoption in the first year of release of the seed, in areas where it was similar to an existing innovation like hybrid corn than in areas where it was more profitable. Brandner (1960, p. 65) concluded that ". . . the power of hybrid-corn culture outpulls by far, in the early stages of adoption, economic incentives."

Griliches (1960a) retorted that *both* profitability and compatibility were key variables in the adoption of hybrid sorghum. Griliches (1960b) stated: "When uncertainty and the fact that the spread of knowledge is not instantaneous are taken into account, it appears that American farmers have behaved, on the whole, in a fashion consistent with the idea of profit maximization. Where the evidence appears to indicate the contrary, I predict a closer examination of the relevant economic variables will show that the change was not as profitable as it appeared."

In regard to sociological variables, Griliches (1957) stated:

It is my belief that in the long run, and cross-sectionally, these variables tend to cancel themselves out, leaving the economic variables as the major determinants of the pattern of technological change. This does not imply that the "sociological" variables are not important if one wants to know which *individual* will be first or last to adopt a particular technique, only that these factors do not vary widely cross-sectionally.

Wilkening (1952b, p. 5) reflected the sociological view of the importance of economic factors in explaining rate of adoption.[17]

The acceptance of improved farming practices is determined largely by economic considerations yet, if economic considerations were the only basis of acceptance, improved practices would be adopted as rapidly as their economic advantages were demonstrated. But, not only is there a considerable lapse of time be-

17. Further evidence that it is incorrect to assume that the rate of adoption of innovations is entirely explained by economic behavior is provided by Wilkening and Johnson (1961) and a number of other investigations.

tween initial acquaintance and adoption of a practice, but those who would benefit most from improved practices are frequently the last to adopt them.

The Interaction Effect

A controversy exists between the relative importance of "economic" and "sociological" variables in explaining the rate of adoption of innovations. To review the controversy, economists have claimed that the rate of adoption of innovations can be explained by such economic variables as profitability, while sociologists claim rate of adoption can be explained by sociological variables such as compatibility. Most innovations must be economically profitable for them to receive consideration by most individuals. But one of the most important variables affecting rate of adoption, after the prior consideration of economic profitability is fulfilled, is the amount and nature of interaction related to the new idea. The *interaction effect* is the process through which individuals in a social system who have adopted an innovation influence those who have not yet adopted.

Since the controversy mentioned has, in part, been concerned with the rate of adoption of hybrid corn, data are here reanalyzed from the initial study on the diffusion of hybrid seed corn by Gross (1942).[18] Gross presented data that permit determination of (1) the rate of adoption per year, (2) the per cent of farmers adopting hybrid corn annually from 1927 to 1939, and (3) the year-to-year profitability of hybrid corn.

Profitability, one dimension of relative advantage, is the difference between economic returns resulting from adop-

18. The present reanalysis of the Gross (1942) data do not allow a test of the main controversy between profitability and compatibility in explaining the rate of adoption, because Gross's data do not allow a measure of compatibility.

tion of an innovation and the innovation's economic cost. Year-to-year profitability was determined by Gross's (1942) formula.[19]

Rate of adoption was determined by the following formula so that it would be independent of per cent of total adoption.

$$\text{Rate of Adoption} = \frac{\text{Number adopting in a given year}}{\text{Number yet to adopt that year}}$$

For example, the rate of adoption in 1938 is .86 when 47 farmers adopted and only 55 were left to adopt.[20]

The interaction effect may be measured by the cumulative per cent of farmers who have adopted hybrid seed corn by year. This is a measure of the proportion of a farmer's neighbors who have adopted at any one point in time. It is obvious from the S-shaped adopter distribution that the more people who adopt a new idea, the steeper the curve becomes, and as more individuals adopt, the greater should be the interaction effect on the remaining nonadopters. For example, Gross (1942) interviewed 259 Iowa farmers; by 1939, 240 of his respondents had adopted hybrid seed. Therefore, the per cent of adoption for 1939 is 92.6 per cent. There is certainly greater likelihood that a member of a social system will discuss an innovation when 93 per cent of his peers have adopted

19. Gross utilized the formula, $P = (P_c \times 1) - \dfrac{(P_s - V_o)}{A}$.

Where: P = Profitability per acre when hybrid seed is used; P_c = Price of corn on the market; I = Increase in yield when hybrid seed is used per acre (six bushels was used as a constant); P_s = Price per bushel of hybrid seed; V_o = Value of open-pollinated seed per bushel; A = Acres planted by one bushel of corn (seven acres).

20. The formula supplies a rate of adoption on a yearly basis; however, it yields a value quite similar to the one presented by Griliches (1957) for the adoption of hybrid seed corn in Iowa. The availability of hybrid seed did not retard its diffusion. Gross (1942, p. 43) stated, "Not one operator indicated any problem in obtaining hybrid seed after he had initially heard of it." If this were not so, the present measure of rate of of adoption might simply reflect the availability of the innovation.

than when only 10 per cent have adopted (as was the case for hybrid corn adopters in 1933).[21]

Thus, a crude measure of the interaction effect is the total per cent of adoption in a social system.[22]

The effect of interaction upon rate of adoption may be observed graphically in Figure 5-1. It is apparent that rate of adoption is not related to profitability, but is related to the interaction effect as measured by the cumulative per cent of adoption. Statistical measures of association and tests of significance confirm this statement.[23]

The present findings indicate that profitability is not significantly related to rate of adoption on a year-to-year basis with the individual farmer as the unit of analysis. Griliches' contention that profitability explains the rate of adoption is not supported on a year-to-year basis. Profitability, as any other item of information about an innovation, must be diffused. The idea of profitability probably is more difficult to perceive than some other characteristics of the innovation such as divisibility. What really determines the rate of adoption of an innovation is the adopter's *perception* of profit-

21. This statement assumes, of course, that interpersonal interaction is the most important type of communication in convincing the individual to adopt the idea. This assumption is truer for later adopters than for earlier adopters.

22. A similar measure of the interaction effect was used by Coleman and others (1957) and Dodd (1950, 1953, and 1955).

23. The Spearman rank order coefficient of correlation was utilized to determine the relationship between profitability, rate of adoption, and cumulative per cent of adoption. Rho is $-.194$ between profitability and rate of adoption which is less than the .456 required for significance at the 5 per cent level when N is 13. Therefore, it can be concluded that profitability is not significantly related to rate of adoption. However, rho between rate of adoption and the cumulative per cent of adoption is $+.911$ which is greater than the .645 required for significance at the one per cent level when N is 13. Therefore, rate of adoption is significantly related to the interactive effect, as measured by the cumulative per cent of total adoption. See Griliches (1962) and Rogers and Havens (1962b) for a further discussion of these findings.

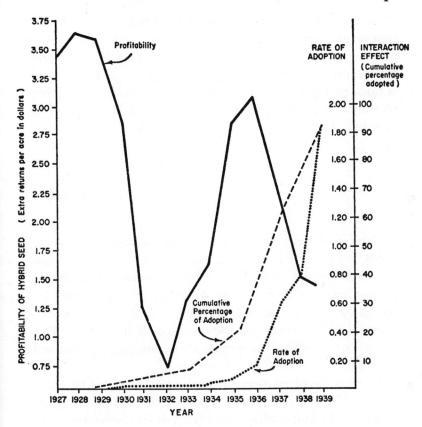

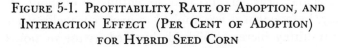

FIGURE 5-1. PROFITABILITY, RATE OF ADOPTION, AND
INTERACTION EFFECT (PER CENT OF ADOPTION)
FOR HYBRID SEED CORN

Data come from 259 Iowa farmers regarding their adoption of hybrid corn. This chart shows that profitability is not related to rate of adoption, but that the interaction effect is. This finding suggests it is not objective profitability but rather the adopter's perception of profitability that determines rate of adoption.

Source: A reanalysis of data from Gross (1942) by Havens and Rogers (1961b). Used by permission.

ability and not objective profitability. There is a vast tradition of social-psychological research which indicates the importance of group interaction in determining the selectivity of perception including perceptions of profitability. Thus, it is through interaction with others that individuals in a system internalize the relative advantage of an idea, as well as its other characteristics.

OVERADOPTION

Many past researchers have implicitly assumed that to adopt innovations is desirable behavior and to reject innovations is less desirable. In *all* cases, this may not be true.

Most past research on the diffusion of innovations investigated either rational adopters, or irrational underadopters, or else compared the two types of individuals. Few studies are available on irrational overadopters or rational rejectors.[24]

An example of irrational overadoption occurred throughout the Midwest in 1949 and 1950. A chemical weed-killer, 2,4-D, had been introduced in 1946, and its results were very spectacular. Farmers became so enthusiastic about 2,4-D spray, in fact, that it was applied to many cornfields whether the resulting increase in yields justified its use or not. Observers estimate that millions of dollars were lost through overadoption of the weed spray until later years when farm-

24. One might speculate why more research has not been completed on overadoption. Perhaps it is because of the greater usefulness of underadoption studies or the interests of the research sponsors. Of course, there are some ideas that cannot be overadopted. Wilkening (1958a) is evidently one of the first researchers to indicate the possibility of overadoption.

ers learned how to use it more wisely. Overadoption often results from insufficient knowledge; overadopters perceive the innovation as a panacea, as was the case in the Georgia home canning campaign described in Chapter IV.

It is often difficult to determine whether or not an individual *should* or *should not* adopt the innovation. The criterion of rationality is not easily measurable. The classification can sometimes be made by an expert on the innovation under study.[25] Often, the classification is made on the basis of economic criteria. In one sense, most individuals perceive their actions to be rational. Through lack of knowledge or inaccurate perceptions, the individual's evaluation of an innovation does not agree with the expert's. The main concern is with objective rationality in the present case, rather than with "subjective" rationality as perceived by the individual.

Research Studies

Most studies of irrational overadoption are concerned with farm innovations. A number of "agricultural crazes" have swept U.S. agriculture, such as the "Merino sheep mania," silkworms and Chinese mulberry trees, Belgian mammoth bullocks, Rohan potatoes, China tree corn, and Silver foxes. In more recent times, such noneconomic practices as "Canadian oats," fraudulent livestock mineral salts, and one-gallon-to-the-acre liquid fertilizers have been widely purchased by American farmers.

Even among modern farmers, the widespread adoption of

25. Homans (1961, p. 80) favors this measure of irrationality, "Behavior is irrational if an outside observer thinks that its reward is not good for a man in the long run."

noneconomic innovations is often found. Toussaint and Stone (1960) studied a sample of the several thousand North Carolina farmers who had purchased self-propelled tobacco harvesters, which were recommended by economists only if they could be used to full capacity. No farmers were found who used the machine on enough acres to be as economical as if they had harvested by hand methods. Toussaint and Stone emphasized the importance of noneconomic reasons for adopting the harvester.

Brandner and Straus (1959) found that hybrid sorghums were planted on 28 per cent of the sorghum acreage in northeastern Kansas the first year they were available, in spite of the fact this innovation was *not* recommended by the Kansas Agricultural Experiment Station or Extension Service.

Probably the most adequate analysis of overadoption was a novel study by Goldstein and Eichhorn (1961) of the adoption of four-row corn planters by 398 Indiana farmers. Agricultural economists at Purdue University stated that farmers with 60 acres of corn or less could not economically justify a four-row corn planter. The following portion of respondents were found in each of the four "types": rational adopters, 37 per cent; irrational underadopters, 19 per cent; irrational overadopters, 11 per cent; rational rejectors, 33 per cent.

It can be seen that in the case of the four-row corn planter, there were more underadopters than overadopters. The two rational types of individuals outnumbered the two irrational types. A further analysis by Goldstein (1959) indicated the rational types differed from the irrational types in amount of education and in lack of traditional beliefs. Thus, education is one factor that leads to more rational and discriminating decision-making in the adoption-rejection decision.

It is often difficult to find, for purposes of a research study, an innovation that is irrational for all individuals. For example, in the Goldstein and Eichhorn (1961) study, it is entirely possible that special circumstances might economically justify that an irrational underadopter reject the idea. This sticky problem of securing a universally irrational innovation was solved by Francis (1960). He surveyed the 88 adopters of grass incubators, an innovation that is universally not recommended to all farmers by scientists on the basis of economic and nutritional grounds.

The grass incubator costs several thousand dollars and is manufactured by several U.S. companies. It is a small air-conditioned room in which grain is sprouted and grown to a height of about six inches. The whole plant is then fed to livestock. The grass incubator is not recommended to farmers by either agricultural economists or animal nutritionists in the USDA, state experiment stations, or extension services.

All of Francis' (1960) respondents were irrational overadopters. Their characteristics and communication behavior marked them as quite different from the typical U.S. farmer. They were more affluent, more traditional, and more specialized. The grass incubator owners tended to have little communication contact with government agricultural change agents. Few were innovators of recommended farm ideas. Francis' findings suggest that county extension agents may be more effective at preventing the adoption of nonrecommended innovations than in promoting the adoption of recommended ideas.

It is entirely possible, of course, for a change agent to push his constituents into overadoption in some cases. An example is the fertilizer dealer who wishes to increase sales even past the point where farmers are purchasing economic amounts of fertilizer. One observer has suggested that this may be a reason why farmers place little credibility in salesmen.

There is certainly need for further investigation of overadoption, and of the role of change agents in causing or preventing overadoption.

SUMMARY

One important ingredient of the diffusion and adoption processes is the innovation itself. The characteristics of the innovation, as perceived by the individuals in a social system, affect its rate of adoption. Five characteristics of innovations are utilized in the present book (1) relative advantage, (2) compatibility, (3) complexity, (4) divisibility, and (5) communicability.

Relative advantage is the degree to which an innovation is superior to the ideas it supersedes. Crises may emphasize the relative advantage of an innovation and affect its rate of adoption. A crisis may retard or accelerate the rate of adoption. Profitability, the difference between economic returns resulting from adoption of an innovation and the innovation's economic cost, is one dimension of relative advantage.

Compatibility is the degree to which an innovation is consistent with existing values and past experiences of the adopters. *Complexity* is the degree to which an innovation is relatively difficult to understand and use. *Divisibility* is the degree to which an innovation may be tried on a limited basis. Relatively earlier adopters may perceive divisibility as more important than later adopters. *Communicability* is the degree to which the results of an innovation may be diffused to others.

The *rate of adoption* is the relative speed with which an innovation is adopted by members of a social system. The rate of adoption of new ideas is affected by the interaction effect, the process through which individuals in a social system who have adopted an innovation influence those who have not yet adopted. It is through interaction that individuals in a system internalize the relative advantage of an idea, as well as its other characteristics.

It should not be assumed that the adoption of all innovations is necessarily desirable. Overadoption occurs when an individual adopts a new idea under conditions when experts would consider him irrational to do so. *Rationality* is the use of the most effective means to reach a given end.

CHAPTER VI

Adopter Categories[1]

> At present, advice to farmers cannot be adjusted on a scientific basis to meet the needs of individual farmers. We need a classification system which ensures [that] farmers . . . classified in the same category each react in the same predictable way to an opportunity to introduce a new technique of production. . . . One group of farmers would adopt an innovation; one would try, but fail; other groups would not do it. . . .
>
> D. B. WILLIAMS, 1958

It is obvious that all individuals do not adopt an innovation at the same time. Rather, individuals adopt along a time continuum and may be classified into adopter categories on this basis. So far, the emphasis has largely been upon adoption by a "typical" farmer, doctor, or other respondent. In this chapter, the emphasis is upon differences between the earlier and later adopters of new ideas.

Adopter categories are the classifications of individuals within a social system on the basis of innovativeness. Titles for adopter categories are almost as numerous as adoption researchers themselves, ranging from "pioneers" (Ross, 1958, p. 31) and "progressists" (Chaparro, 1955) to "parochials" (Carter and Williams, 1957, p. 110) and "drones" (Danhof, 1949, pp. 20–24). The variety of names proposed for adopter categories emphasizes the need for standardization of both

1. With Rabel J. Burdge, Pennsylvania State University. Certain of the materials utilized in this chapter come from Rogers (1958b). Used by permission.

nomenclature and method of classification. The lack of standard adopter categories has made the comparison of similar research findings more difficult.

The purpose of this chapter is to suggest one standard method of adopter categorization, and to demonstrate the usefulness of this categorization system with findings from research studies. Discussion will be primarily devoted to the normality of adopter distributions, adopter categories as ideal types, and the characteristics of adopter categories.

Need for Standardization

Unfortunately, a search of the literature discloses few research workers who were concerned with the development of standard criteria by which to classify adopters of innovations into categories. As a means of easy reference, various titles have been widely used for categories of adopters. For example, the North Central Regional Rural Sociology Subcommittee (1955) proposed the titles, in decreasing order of innovativeness, of "innovators," "community adoption leaders," "local adoption leaders," and "later adopters." Gross (1942) utilized letters of the alphabet (A, B, C, and D) to label his four adopter categories. These and other titles for adopter categories are presented in Table 6-1. The titles are arranged in two sections, one representing titles given to relatively earlier adopters and the other listing the titles given to relatively later adopters.

Research on the diffusion of innovations is of little utility unless it can be communicated in a meaningful and accurate manner. How is a reader to draw precise conclusions from a body of literature that uses the variety of terms listed in Table 6-1? The need for greater standardization is apparent.

TABLE 6-1

TITLES USED FOR ADOPTER CATEGORIES BY VARIOUS RESEARCHERS

Titles for Relatively Earlier Adopters

1. *Innovators** (Danhof, 1949; NCRS Subcommittee, 1955; Chaparro, 1955; Enos, 1958; Mueller, 1958; Rogers, 1958b; Katz, 1961; Larson, 1962; Coleman and others, in press).

   Advance Scouts (Katz and Menzel, 1955)

   Lighthouses (Cocking, 1951, p. 75)

   Earliest Acceptors (Gross, 1942)

   Pioneers (Mort and Pierce, 1947; Ryan and Gross, 1950, p. 687; Katz and Menzel, 1955; Ross, 1958; Katz, 1961; Mansfield, 1960)

   Progressists (Chaparro, 1955)

   Non-Parochials, Non-Adoptives (Carter and Williams, 1957)

   Experimentals (Caplow, 1952)

   Cultural *Avant-garde* (Benvenuti, 1961)

2. *Early Adopters** (Rogers, 1958b; Olson, 1959b; Katz, 1961; Lionberger, 1960, p. 38; Jones, 1960; Larson, 1962; Cohen, 1962; Dennis, 1961b)

   Spark Plugs (Ross, 1958)

   Community Adoption Leaders (NCRS Subcommittee, 1955)

   Local Adoption Leaders (NCRS Subcommittee, 1955)

   High-Adopters (Straus, 1960)

   Technical Leaders (Mansfield, 1960)

   Leaders (Mort and Cornell, 1941, p. 77)

3. *Early Majority** (Rogers, 1958b; Olson, 1959b)

   Imitators (Danhof, 1949)

   Early Followers (Mort and Cornell, 1941, p. 77; Mort and Pierce, 1947; Ross, 1958)

   Relatively Early Acceptors (Gross, 1942)

   Adoptives (Carter and Williams, 1957)

TABLE 6-1 (cont.)

TITLES USED FOR ADOPTER CATEGORIES BY VARIOUS RESEARCHERS

Titles for Relatively Later Adopters

4. *Late Majority** (Rogers, 1958b; Olson, 1959b)

Relatively Late Acceptors (Gross, 1942)

Technical Follower (Mansfield, 1960)

Conservatives (Caplow, 1952: Chaparro, 1955)

Skeptics (Lionberger, 1960, p. 66)

Fabians (Danhof, 1949)

Neutrals (Caplow, 1952)

Late Followers (Mort and Cornell, 1941, p. 77; Mort and Pierce, 1947; Ross, 1958)

Latest Acceptors (Gross, 1942)

5. *Laggards** (Mort and Cornell, 1941, p. 77; Mort and Pierce, 1947; Ryan and Gross, 1950, p. 687; Enos, 1958; Rogers, 1958b; Sutherland, 1959; Mansfield, 1960)

Parochials (Carter and Williams, 1957)

Diehards (Katz and Menzel, 1955)

Drones (Danhof, 1949)

Low Adopters (Straus, 1960)

Later Adopters (NCRS Subcommittee, 1955; Lionberger, 1960, p. 39)

Late Adopters (Katz, 1961; Olson, 1959b; Jones, 1960; Dennis, 1961b)

Traditionalists (Chaparro, 1955)

* Each of the five adopter categories utilized in the present book is italicized and used as a heading. In order to prevent this table from becoming more cumbersome, the approximately twenty publications by Rogers or by Beal utilizing these five adopter categories are not listed.

NORMAL ADOPTER DISTRIBUTIONS

A general finding of past research is that the adoption of an innovation follows a bell-shaped curve when plotted over time. This type of distribution is essentially "S"-shaped when plotted on a cumulative basis. The present section will (1) provide evidence that adopter distributions are normal, (2) discuss possible reasons for this normality, and (3) suggest useful implications for the categorization of adopters.

Why Are Adopter Distributions Normal?

Perhaps an inquiry might be raised at this point as to why adopter distributions are expected to approach a normal shape.

1. EARLY SOCIOLOGISTS. Several early sociologists observed that the adoption of new ideas followed a bell-shaped pattern. However, few of these theorists were concerned with actually determining whether or not their observations were correct. Tarde (1903) described the process by which individuals imitated the actions and thoughts of others. He noted that the use of an innovation shows ". . . a slow advance in the beginning, followed by rapid and uniformly accelerated progress, followed again by progress that continues to slacken until it finally stops."

Chapin (1928) was probably the first scholar to use the idea of the S-shaped adopter curve, although he termed it a "growth curve" and did not use the word "S-curve." Chapin (1928, pp. 213–214) studied the diffusion and adoption of the city manager form of government, and concluded that his data showed ". . . a period of growth, a period of greatest extension of the idea, followed by a period of falling off of diffusion." Chapin's S-curve of adoption was later tested by Gilfillian (1935) with data on shipping inventions, by Pemberton (1936a) with data on the adoption by states of postage stamps and compulsory school attendance laws, by Davis (1941) with data on cotton machinery patents, and by Ryan and Gross (1943) with data on the adoption of hybrid corn. Each of these analyses found adopter distributions to be normal or to closely approach normality.[2]

2. LEARNING CURVES. Research by psychologists indicates that individuals learn a new skill, bit of knowledge, or set of facts through a learning process that, when plotted over time, follows a normal curve (Hilgard, 1956, p. 361). When an individual is confronted with a new situation in the psychologist's laboratory, the individual makes many errors at the beginning, but after a series of trials, the errors decrease until learning capacity has been reached. When plotted, these data yield a curve of increasing gains at first and later become a curve of decreasing gains until learning capacity is reached. The gain in learning per trial is proportional to (1) the product of the amount already learned, and (2) the amount remaining to be learned before the limit of learning is reached (Hilgard, 1956, p. 371). Psychologists feel that some self-limiting growth process may underlie learning. It should be pointed out, however, that the S-shaped learning curve was not selected by psychologists because of any formal learning theory, but simply because it resulted from learning experiments.

From the viewpoint of the present book, the learning curve

2. These researchers (with the exception of Ryan and Gross, 1943) did not apply statistical tests for normality.

is another reason to expect adopter distributions to be normal.[3] If one substitutes a social system for the individual in the learning curve, it seems reasonable that experience with the innovation is gained as each successive member in the social system adopts it. Each adoption in the social system is, in a sense, equivalent to a learning trial by an individual.

              3. INTERACTION EFFECT. Another reason for expecting normal adopter distributions is the interaction effect. The *interaction effect* is the process through which individuals in a social system who have adopted an innovation influence those who have not yet adopted.[4] Adoption of a new idea is the product of human interaction. If one considers the hypothetical case of the introduction of an innovation in a social system, there are theoretical grounds for expecting the number of adoptions over time to be normally distributed. If the first adopter of the innovation discusses it with two other members of the social system, and these two adopters each pass the new idea along to two peers, the resulting distribution follows a binomial expansion. This mathematical function follows a normal shape when plotted.[5]

    Of course, several of the assumptions underlying this hypothetical example are seldom found in reality. For instance, members of a social system do not have completely

    3. It has generally been found that many human traits are normally distributed, whether the trait is a physical characteristic such as height or a behavioral trait such as the learning of information. Hence, a variable such as degree of innovativeness might be expected to be normally distributed also.

    4. A more detailed discussion of the interaction effect is found in Chapter VIII.

    5. The reasoning why the interaction effect results in a normal adopter distribution is discussed by Dodd (1953) and Hagerstrand (1960).

free access to interact with one another. Status barriers and geographical location affect interaction patterns. The interaction effect begins to level off after half of the individuals in a social system have adopted because each new adopter finds it increasingly difficult to tell the new idea to a peer who has not yet adopted.

Sheppard (1960a, p. 20) recognized that the interaction effect was a possible reason for the S-shaped adopter distributions he obtained in a study of 446 English farmers "... influences affecting each farmer accumulate, and . . . this accelerates the adoption process." In one sense, adoption of an innovation may be viewed as conformity to group pressures which become more intense as a higher per cent of adoption is reached for a particular innovation in a socal system.

In summary, there are several reasons[6] why adopter distributions are expected to be normal:

1. The writings of early sociologists who observed that the adoption of new ideas tended to follow an S-shaped distribution.

2. Psychologists' learning curves are normal. If one extends the individual learning curve to the case of a social system, experience with the innovation is gained as each successive individual in the system adopts. Thus, a normal adopter distribution might be expected.

3. The interaction effect is the process through which adopters of an innovation influence those members of their social system who have not yet adopted. The group pressures for adoption thus become more intense as the number of adopters in a social system increases.

---

6. There are at least two other possible reasons for normal adopter distributions. A "decay" function may operate in the later stages of diffusion through discontinuances of the innovation. Individuals who discontinue thus cause the adopter curve to level off. A second possible reason for normal adopter distributions is that recall of adoption dates is so inaccurate that the responses are normally patterned even though actual dates of adoption are not. There is little direct support for these two possible reasons in the research completed to date.

TABLE 6-2

NORMALITY OF ADOPTER DISTRIBUTIONS

Innovation	Number of Adopters	Percentage of Adoption Completed	Normality of Adopter Distribution	Research Study
1. 2,4-D weed spray (all adopters)	129	87	Normal	Beal and Rogers, 1960
2. 2,4-D weed spray (beginning farmers excluded)‡	112	87	Normal	Beal and Rogers, 1960
3. Antibiotics (all adopters)	105	89	Not normal†	Beal and Rogers, 1960
4. Antibiotics (beginning farmers excluded)‡	95	89	Not normal*	Beal and Rogers, 1960
5. Hybrid corn (Iowa)	433	100	Not normal†	Ryan, 1948
6. Hybrid corn (Virginia)	642	100	Not normal†	Dimit, 1954
7. 2,4-D weed spray (Ohio)	80	76	Normal	Rogers, 1957c
8. Warfarin rat poison (Ohio)	82	78	Normal	Rogers, 1957c

9. Adoption-of-farm-innovations scores (Iowa)	148	—	Normal	Rogers, 1958b
10. Adoption-of-farm-innovations scores (Ohio)	104	—	Normal	Rogers, 1958b

* Deviation from normality is significant at the 5 per cent level of significance.

† Deviation from normality is significant at the one per cent level of significance.

‡ Ryan and Gross (1943) eliminated from their analysis of hybrid seed corn adopters the 64 farmers who had "started farming since the practice began its spread." Presumably these researchers discarded data from all farm operators who began farming either after the date at which the first respondent became aware of the practice (1924) or first adopted the practice (1927). In the present case, only the farmers who had begun farming after they were aware of the practice were eliminated from the analysis. If they began farming after they became aware of the practice, their actual adoption date might have been postponed because they could not adopt the practice until they began farming. There were 17 of these beginning farmers who were eliminated from the 2,4-D spray adopter distribution, and 10 beginning farmers were eliminated from the antibiotics adopter distribution.

Source: Rogers, 1958b. Used by permission.

Testing Adopter Distributions for Normality

A general finding of past investigations is that *adopter distributions follow a bell-shaped curve over time and approach normality*. There are useful implications of this generalization for a standard method of adopter categorization.

Eight adopter distributions tested[7] by Rogers (1958b) were bell-shaped and all approached normality, although half of those tested were found to deviate significantly from normality (Table 6–2). Four additional studies appear in the literature on the normality of adopter distributions. None of these analyses utilized the most precise statistical tools for determining normality, but each found that adopter distributions approached normality.

1. Ryan and Goss (1943) found the distribution of dates of first use of hybrid corn was nearly normal.

2. Griliches (1957) studied the adopter distributions for hybrid corn for each of the important corn states. He used crop reporting information from the USDA Field Crops Statistics Branch. Hybrid corn adopter distributions closely followed the logistic curve, which is very similar to the normal curve over the usual range of data.

3. Rahim (1961, p. 63) concluded that the adopter distributions for three farm innovations in a Pakistani village were normal, although he did not statistically test for normality.

4. Mansfield (1961a) studied twelve major innovations in the coal, steel, brewing, and railroad industries. He found that ". . . the growth in the number of users of an innovation can be approximated by a logistic curve."

Most adopter distributions closely approach normality and many are normal.[8] Further research is needed to determine

7. The adopter distributions were tested for normality by means of the Smirnov test. This goodness-of-fit test is a nonparametric statistical method by which the probability that an actual distribution may have been drawn from a normal distribution can be determined.

8. No claim is made, however, that adopter distributions for all innovations are necessarily normal. Sorokin (1959, p. 634) has attacked

specifically why some adopter curves are normal and some are not.

A METHOD OF ADOPTER CATEGORIZATION

Two problems face the researcher seeking to develop a standard method of adopter categorization: (1) how many adopter categories should be conceptualized, and (2) what portion of the total audience should be included in each category?

Innovativeness is a *continuous* dimension in that individuals adopt a new idea at different times. Partitioning this continuum into categories should be viewed as a conceptual device. The case is similar to that of the continuum of social status and the categories of social classes. Usefulness of these categorizations comes from the ease with which the concept of innovativeness may be understood. Each adopter of an innovation in a social system could be described, but this would be a tedious task. It is much easier to describe the members of a social system when grouped in categories. Adopter categories are essentially a shorthand notation for describing individuals.

The criterion for adopter categorization is innovativeness, which is the degree to which an individual is relatively earlier to adopt new ideas than other members of his social system. Thus, it is plain that innovativeness is a "relative" concept. One has either more or less innovativeness than others in a

such a claim: "The convincing logical considerations as well as the factual tests do not give any basis for a belief in the existence of any 'normal' or even typical curve of diffusion or diffusion rate for all cultural values in all circumstances. Such a 'normal' curve is but a myth." I prefer to disagree with Sorokin, as do most diffusion researchers. The normal adopter distribution is useful if viewed as an "ideal type" that provides a standard from which statistical goodness-of-fit can be computed.

social system. It is essential to specify the social system whose members one is classifying on the basis of their innovativeness.

Two methods of adopter classification on the basis of innovativeness have been utilized in past research.

1. JUDGES' RATINGS. Chaparro (1955) asked a number of judges in one Costa Rican community to classify 96 plantation owners into four adopter categories.[9] This method of adopter categorization, although a time-saver, should be used with caution unless representative judges can be secured who can accurately judge their fellow members. A similar use of judges has been made in social stratification studies. One difficulty is that the social class structure has largely been judged through upper-class eyes, and there is evidence the judge's position in a social structure affects his view of that structure.

2. TIME OF ADOPTION. Most diffusion researchers have classified adopters into categories on the basis of the relative time at which they adopt an innovation or innovations. Respondents are usually asked to recall the date at which they adopted these innovations.[10]

9. Van den Ban (1957b) has also used judges' ratings in several studies in the Netherlands. He reports correlations of about +.50 to +.60 between this measure of innovativeness and farmers' scores on innovativeness scales (van den Ban, 1961b). The judges are county extension agents who are relatively well acquainted with the farmers they are rating as to innovativeness.

10. This recall may be inaccurate for some individuals. In one study medical doctors' date of adoption of a new drug was secured from druggists' prescription records. When these adoption dates were compared with those recalled by the doctors, it was found that the interview statements made the doctors appear more up-to-date (Menzel,

Before considering exact methods of adopter categorization, it is important to list the characteristics that a series of categories should ideally possess. Jahoda and others (1951, p. 264) proposed that a set of categories should be (1) *exhaustive* in order that all respondents may be classified, (2) *mutually exclusive* so that a given respondent cannot ordinarily be placed in more than one category, and (3) derived from one *classificatory principle*.

In a number of empirical cases just reviewed, adopter distributions were either normal or closely approached normality. The normal distribution has two parameters, the mean $(\bar{x})$ and the standard deviation (σ), which may be used to divide the distribution into five portions. These five areas under the normal curve are labeled as innovators, early adopters, early majority, late majority, and laggards. These categories and the approximate percentage of the adopters that are included in each category are located on a normal frequency distribution in Figure 6-1. If this distribution were plotted on a cumulative basis, it would approach an "S" shape.

The area lying to the left of the mean year of adoption minus two standard deviations $(\bar{x} - 2\sigma)$ includes the first 2.5 per cent of the individuals to adopt a new idea, the "innovators" (Figure 6-1). Put another way, innovators adopt a new idea before 97.5 per cent of the members of a social system. The next 13.5 per cent of the adopters are included between $\bar{x} - \sigma$ and $\bar{x} - 2\sigma$ and are labeled "early adopters." At the mean year of adoption minus one standard deviation $(\bar{x} - \sigma)$, a point of inflection occurs[11] (Anderson and Bancroft, 1952, p. 25). At this point, adoption ceases to increase

---

1957). On the other hand, Havens (1962) found that Ohio dairy farmers were quite accurate in reporting their date of adoption of bulk milk tanks. Havens checked the adoption dates with records of the farmers' milk purchasers.

11. A point of inflection occurs at any point on a curve where the curvature changes direction.

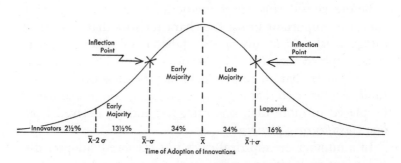

FIGURE 6-1. ADOPTER CATEGORIZATION ON THE BASIS OF
RELATIVE TIME OF ADOPTION OF INNOVATIONS

The innovativeness dimension, as measured by the time at which an
individual adopts an innovation or innovations, is continuous. However, this variable may be partitioned into five adopter categories by
laying off standard deviations from the average time of adoption.

Source: Rogers (1958b). Used by permission.

at an increasing rate and begins to increase at a decreasing
rate (and level off). Between this inflection point and the
mean year of adoption, 34 per cent of the adopters are included in the "early majority" category.

Between the mean and the other inflection point (at $\chi +
\sigma$), where adoption begins to decrease at a decreasing rate, are
included 34 per cent of the adopters labeled as "late majority." The last 16 per cent of the individuals to adopt a
new idea (to the right of the inflection point at $\overline{\chi} + \sigma$) are
labeled "laggards.[12] The two parameters of the normal distribution could be used to divide a continuous variable into
any number of categories. The five categories used in the

12. It must also be recognized that for innovations which do not
reach 100 per cent adoption, there will be a sixth category of "nonadopters." The problem of nonadopters will be discussed later in this
section.

present case are an arbitrary number, but are one suggested standardization.

Standard Scores

The foregoing method of adopter categorization is essentially on the basis of "standard scores.[13] A standard score is computed by subtracting the mean $(\bar{x})$ from an observation (X_1) and dividing by the standard deviation (σ) of the distribution. Where z represents a standard score, the formula may be expressed as:

$$z = \frac{X_1 - \bar{x}}{\sigma}$$

For example, School A adopted a driver training program in 1948. The mean year of adoption is 1950 and the standard deviation of the adoption dates for driver training programs is 4 years. The standard innovativeness score for School A is 1948 minus 1950 divided by 4 which equals —0.5. This would place School A in the early majority category (Figure 6-1). School A adopted one-half standard deviation sooner than the average school.

A standard score is a "relative" type of score which, in effect, expresses the individual's position in relation to other members of a distribution. For example, an individual's year of adoption of an innovation, when expressed in standard

13. The use of standard scores as a means of classifying the adopters of a new idea was first utilized by Mort and Pierce (1947). These authors divided school systems that adopted new ideas into three categories (pioneer schools, early followers, and late followers) on the basis of the time of their adoption of educational innovations.

Categorization of a sample of Appalachian Southerners into four social classes on the basis of standard scores was completed by Ford (1960). He classified 16 per cent of his respondents in the upper class, 34 per cent in the upper middle class, 34 per cent in the lower middle class, and 16 per cent in the lower class.

score form, indicates the individual's relative position in the distribution of adoption dates (of the other members of the social system).

An advantage of standard scores is that the measuring unit is "pure," or free from the original unit of measure. For example, the time of adoption of an educational innovation, such as driver training, may be mathematically compared with a widely different idea, such as using visual aids. This advantage is important when constructing a composite adoption-of-innovations score composed of many innovations. It is possible to add, subtract, or place weightings on each adoption item when it is expressed in standard units, even though the intervals of time in which the adoption of each innovation took place may vary.

The finding that some adopter distributions deviate from normality does not rule out the method of standard scores. Even in a skewed distribution, the use of standard scores may be utilized (with discretion) as the transformation of the raw data into standard score form tends to shape the distribution toward normality. In addition, little change is made in the number of cases appearing at different standard deviation units from the mean even when there is some departure from a normal distribution (Wert and others, 1954, p. 56).

Difficulties

It should be pointed out that there are at least two difficulties with the proposed method of categorization:

1. NONSYMMETRY. Why are there three adopter categories on one side of the mean year of adoption (Figure 6-1), and only two categories on the other? One reason for not breaking the laggards into two categories is the general lack of differentiation that has been found in past

research between "early laggards" and "late laggards." Laggards appear to be a fairly homogeneous category (athough this point needs further research attention).

Another method of achieving symmetry is to combine innovators and early adopters into one category. Their characteristics, however, mark them as two rather distinct categories. There are often "breaks" or changes in the direction of a trend between the innovators and early adopters.[14]

. 2. INCOMPLETE ADOPTION. An innovation is probably never completely adopted (1) as discontinuances occur, and (2) as new members continually enter the social system and adopt innovations. Then how does one categorize nonadopters? The proposed five-category system is not completely exhaustive. Certain respondents cannot be classified in one of the five categories until almost complete adoption, when the parameters of the distribution can be accurately estimated.

The problem of nonadoption cannot be completely solved if only one innovation is used as the criterion for categorization. However, if a series of innovations is combined by means of an innovativeness scale to form a composite measure of innovativeness, the nonadoptions can be weighted and the problem eliminated.[15]

14. In fact, the highest degree of homogeneity among adjacent adopter categories is between the early majority and late majority, as might be expected. Justification for two categories, however, lies in the 68 per cent of the audience that would be included in a "majority" category if the two categories were combined.

Van den Ban (1961b) prefers to use quartiles as adopter categories, particularly if the sample size is small. This procedure essentially pools the innovators and early adopters.

15. Another problem with the present system of adopter categorization is how to classify the individuals who enter a social system after an innovation being studied was introduced. These individuals could not have adopted relatively early because they were not members of the social system in the early stages of diffusion (Jones, 1960). This problem can be minimized, although not solved, by (1) including only re-

Innovativeness Scales

Evidence has been presented that adoption of a single innovation over time approaches normality. It then follows that the distribution of scores on an adoption-of-innovations scale, composed of the adoption of numerous innovations, will also approach normality. Table 6-2 shows that the adoption-of-innovations scores in two different studies (Rogers, 1958b) were normally distributed. This finding allows one to categorize adopters on the basis of innovativeness scores, thus eliminating the problem of nonadopters encountered in the case of a single innovation.

Rogers and Rogers (1961) reviewed 26 different studies by rural sociologists that attempted to measure the general dimension of innovativeness with an adoption-of-innovations scale. Following are four aspects of these scales considered by Rogers and Rogers.

1. VALIDITY. The degree to which a scale measures the desired dimension. Using construct validity, judges' ratings, and self-images as indications of validity, Rogers and Rogers (1961) found (in three Ohio farmer studies utilizing innovativeness scales) considerable evidence that adoption-of-innovations scales are a valid measure of the more general concept of innovativeness.[16]

---

cent ideas in the innovativeness scale, and (2) scoring those innovations as inapplicable if the individual entered the system after he was aware of them.

16. Almost all researchers who have constructed adoption-of-innovations scales have regarded them as a measure of innovativeness. One exception is Pederson (1951), who utilized the adoption of new ideas as a measure of the adjustment of Danish and Polish immigrants to U.S. dairy farming. In the present book, "innovativeness" scales and "adoption-of-innovation" scales are used interchangeably.

2. RELIABILITY. The degree to which a scale consistently measures the same dimension over time. Using split-half and test-retest methods of determining reliability, Rogers and Rogers (1961) tested innovativeness scales used in educational and farm diffusion studies. They concluded that innovativeness scales are reliable.

3. INTERNAL CONSISTENCY. The degree to which a scale's items are interrelated. Item-to-total-score correlations and intercorrelations of scale items provide researchers with a method to determine internal consistency. Most innovativeness scale items used by researchers have been found to be interrelated, although not as highly as might be desired.

4. UNDIMENSIONALITY. The degree to which a scale measures a single dimension. The Guttman, factor analysis, and cluster analysis methods of determining undimensionality did not yield clear-cut evidence that adoption-of-innovations scales measure a single dimension.

In general there is positive evidence of the validity, reliability, and internal consistency of innovativeness scales, while convincing evidence of undimensionality is not apparent. Rogers and Rogers (1961) suggested the improvement of innovativeness scalse by including more items in these scales.

Three principles of categorization were suggested earlier in this section. Innovativeness as a criterion for adopter categorization fulfills each of these requirements. The five adopter categories are exhaustive (except for nonadopters), mutually exclusive, and are derived from one classificatory principle. The proposed method of adopter categorization may have utility, not only in future research studies, but also in reanalyzing past studies using other methods of adopter categorization.

ADOPTER CATEGORIES AS IDEAL TYPES: SALIENT VALUES

The five adopter categories set forth in this chapter are ideal types. Ideal types are conceptualizations that are based on observations of reality and designed to institute comparisons. The traditional and modern norms described in Chapter III are ideal types. The function of ideal types is to guide research efforts and serve as a framework for the synthesis of research findings.

Actually, there are no pronounced "breaks" in the innovativeness continuum among each of the five categories. The case is similar to that of social classes on the continuum of social status.[17] Ideal types have also performed important functions in several other areas of sociology.[18]

Ideal types are not simply an average of all the observations about each adopter category. Exceptions must be found from the ideal types. If no exceptions or deviations are located, ideal types would not be necessary (Becker, 1940, p. 28). Ideal types are based on abstractions from empirical cases and are intended as a guide for theoretical formulations and empirical investigations. However, they are not a substitute for these investigations.

The next section includes a thumbnail sketch of the subcultural values of each category, and will be followed by more detailed generalizations.

17. Kahl (1957, pp. 184–220) makes use of the ideal type approach in setting forth five social classes. The format presented by Kahl is followed at some points in this section.
18. A number of these ideal types were listed in Chapter III.

1. Innovators: Venturesome

Observers have noted that venturesomeness is almost an obsession with innovators. They are eager to try new ideas. This interest leads them out of a local circle of peers and into more cosmopolite social relationships. Communication patterns and friendship among a clique of innovators are common, even though the geographical distance between the innovators may be great. They travel in a circle of venturesomeness, like circuit riders who spread new ideas as their gospel. Being an innovator has several prerequisites. They include control of substantial financial resources to absorb the loss of an unprofitable innovation, and the ability to understand and apply complex technical knowledge.

The major value of the innovator is venturesomeness. He must desire the hazardous, the rash, the daring, and the risking. The innovator also must be willing to accept an occasional debacle when one of the new ideas he adopts proves unsuccessful.

2. Early Adopters: Respect

Early adopters are a more integrated part of the local social system than are innovators. While innovators are cosmopolites, early adopters are localites. This adopter category, more than any other, has the greatest degree of opinion leadership in most social systems. Potential adopters look to them for advice and information about the innovation. The early adopter is considered by many as "the man to check with" before using a new idea. This adopter category is generally sought by change agents as a local missionary for speeding the diffusion process. Because early adopters are not "too far" ahead of the average individual in innovativeness, they serve as a role-model for many other members of a social system.[19] The early adopter is respected by his peers. He is the embodiment of successful and discrete use of new ideas. And the early adopter knows that he must continue to earn this esteem of his colleagues if his position in the social structure is to be maintained.

3. Early Majority: Deliberate

The early majority adopt new ideas just before the average member of a social system. Participation by the early majority in activities with their peers is high, but leadership positions are rarely held. The early majority's unique position between the very early and the relatively late to adopt, makes them an important link in the process of legitimizing innovations.

The early majority may deliberate for some time before completely adopting a new idea. Their adoption period is relatively longer than the innovator's and early adopter's. "Be not the last to lay the old aside, nor the first by which the new is tried," might be the motto of the early majority. They follow with deliberate willingness in adopting innovations, but seldom lead.

4. Late Majority: Skeptical

The late majority adopt new ideas just after the average member of a social system. Adoption may be both an economic necessity and the answer to increasing social pressures. Innovations are approached with a cautious air, and the late majority do not adopt until a majority of others in their

19. It will be pointed out in Chapter VIII that the degree of opinion leadership possessed by each adopter category depends, in part, on the social system's norms on innovativeness.

systems have done so. The weight of public opinion must definitely favor the innovation before the late majority are convinced. They can be convinced of the utility of new ideas, but the pressure of peers is necessary to motivate adoption.

5. Laggards: Tradition ♪

Laggards are the last to adopt an innovation. They possess almost no opinion leadership. Laggards are the most localite of all adopter categories, and many are near-isolates. The point of reference for the laggard is the past. Decisions are usually made in terms of what has been done in previous generations. The individual interacts primarily with others who have traditional values. When laggards finally adopt an innovation, it may already be superseded by another more recent idea which the innovators are using. Laggards tend to be frankly suspicious of innovations, innovators, and change agents. Their advanced age and tradition-direction slows the adoption process to a crawl. Adoption lags far behind awareness of the idea. Alienation from a too-fast-moving world is apparent in much of the laggard's outlook. While most individuals in a social system are looking to the road of change ahead, the laggard has his attention fixed on the rear-view mirror.

CHARACTERISTICS OF ADOPTER CATEGORIES

A myriad of research studies[20] are concerned with locating a battery of concepts related to innovativeness. Similar meth-

20. In fact, there are so many studies (over 60) that the characteristics of adopter categories must at some points be distilled in a general way and the proliferation of studies not cited for each statement.

ods of adopter categorization were not utilized in all these research studies. Comparison of research results on adopter categories is thus further complicated. Fortunately, most researchers utilized some measure of innovativeness, and many correlated innovativeness with generally similar variables. Research findings on the characteristics of adopter categories are summarized under the following headings (1) personal characteristics, (2) communication behavior, and (3) social relationships.[21]

Personal Characteristics

A number of the more important and well-researched characteristics of adopter categories will be presented in the form of generalizations.

1. AGE. *Earlier Adopters Are Younger in Age Than Later Adopters.* While there is not unanimous support for this generalization from the available research studies, Gross (1942), Jones (1960), Coleman and others (in press), Lionberger and Coughenour (1957), Rahudkar (1961), Lowry and others (1958), Rogers (1961b), Beal and Rogers (1960), and Rogers and Burdge (1961 and 1962) found younger age associated with innovativeness. However, ten research studies found no significant relationship between age and innovativeness, and three studies (Hoffer and Stangland, 1958; Beal and Rogers, 1960; and Sheppard, 1960a) found *older* age associated with innovativeness. Per-

21. The most extensive research on the characteristics of adopter categories has been done with farmer respondents. Caution should be exercised in extending the subsequent generalizations to other types of adopter categories until the present statements have been more fully validated in further research.

TABLE 6-3

AVERAGE AGE OF RESPONDENTS BOTH AT TIME OF ADOPTION OF HYBRID CORN AND AT TIME OF INTERVIEW BY ADOPTER CATEGORY

Gross's Adopter Categories	Number of Respondents	Average Age at Time of Interview (1941)	Average Year of Adoption of Hybrid Corn	Average Age at Time of Adoption of Hybrid Corn*
A—Earliest Acceptors	23	48.2 ⎤	1930	37.2 ⎤
B—Relatively early acceptors	72	49.7 ⎦ −10.8	1935	43.7 ⎦ −20.8
C—Relatively late acceptors	145	50.3 ⎤	1938	47.3 ⎤
D—Latest acceptors	19	59.0 ⎦	1940	58.0 ⎦
Total	259			

* When age at adoption is computed for each adopter category, much wider differences in age between adopter categories are found than between age at time of the interview. The age difference between earliest and latest adopters is 20.8 years at the time of adoption and 10.8 at time of interview. The above evidence may in part explain the inconsistent findings in past studies regarding age and innovativeness, as these studies used age at the time of interview.

Source: A reanalysis of the Gross (1942) data on the adoption of hybrid corn by Iowa farmers.

haps one solution to the inconsistency of these past research findings is suggested by Table 6-3. A reanalysis of Gross's (1942) original data from the Iowa hybrid seed corn study demonstrates there are wider differences in age between adopter categories when age at time of *adoption* of hybrid seed is used, than when age at the time of *interview* is computed.

The general evidence seems to indicate that innovators are younger than laggards. There are adequate theoretical grounds for expecting the younger members of a social system to be more innovative. The socialization of personality occurs mainly in very early life. In a rapidly changing culture, this means that younger people learn a more modern set of cultural values than do older people, who were socialized in an earlier era (Davis, 1940). The young are less conditioned by the older culture; hence, they are more innovative.[22]

2. SOCIAL STATUS. *Earlier Adopters Have Higher Social Status Than Later Adopters.*[23] It must be pointed out that the exact relationship between innovativeness and social status, while generally positive, may depend in part on the characteristics of the innovation under analysis. For example, Graham (1954 and 1956) found the upper class

22. This type of argument could lead one to expect that years of experience in a field such as farming would be more closely associated (negatively) with innovativeness than is age, a point which Dr. D. Sheppard has suggested in private communication.

23. Research studies which support this statement are Lionberger and Coughenour (1957), Rogers and Burdge (1961 and 1962), Rogers (1961b), Jones (1960), Chaparro (1956), Photiadis (1961), Marsh and Coleman (1955b), Fliegel (1956), Copp (1956), Belcher (1958), van den Ban (1957b), Sizer and Porter (1960), Rogers (1958a), Lowry and others (1958), Kreitlow and Duncan (1956), and Yerocaris (1961).

adopted canasta more rapidly, but the lower class adopted television more quickly. Thus, social class values attached to the innovation may affect the relationship between innovativeness and social status.

Some researchers have correlated education, one dimension of social status, with innovativeness. In fact, each of the 18 research studies listed previously that related social status indexes to innovativeness also found that education was related to innovativeness. Hoffer and Stangland (1958), Rahim (1961), Straus (1960a), Hobbs (1960), Coughenour (1960b), Rogers and Pitzer (1960), and Sheppard (1960a) also found education related positively to innovativeness.

3. FINANCIAL POSITION. *Earlier Adopters Have a More Favorable Financial Position Than Later Adopters.* Affluence may be measured by high income, by a large-sized operation, or by possession of wealth.

Enos (1958) studied the characteristics of laggards and innovators in the petroleum industry. He concluded, "A prosperous refiner is the innovator; an impoverished one is the laggard."[24] Mulford (1959) found that the Iowa communities who were innovative in adopting an organizational idea were much larger in size than the noninnovators. The new idea that Mulford studied was the establishment of local industrial development corporations.

Ross (1958) reviewed a number of studies dealing with the diffusion of educational ideas among public schools. He concluded the one variable most closely related to innovative-

24. This statement is supported by Mansfield (1961b) who studied some 5,000 steel, petroleum, and coal firms. He found that size of firm was directly related to innovativeness. The four largest firms accounted for 40 per cent of the innovations in steel, 50 per cent in petroleum, and 20 per cent in the coal industry. Sutherland (1959) found that laggard cotton spinning firms were small in size.

ness is wealth. Coleman and others (in press) found that doctor-innovators of gammanyn had patients of higher incomes who were better able to afford the high cost of a new drug.

Rogers (1961b) found that a much higher gross farm income was characteristic of innovators and early adopters. This relationship between farm income and innovativeness has also been reported in over 18 different studies.[25]

Wealth and innovativeness appear to go hand-in-hand. Do innovators innovate because they are rich or are they rich because they innovate? The answer to this cause-and-effect question cannot be answered on the basis of available data. However, there is adequate reason why wealth and innovativeness vary together. Greatest profits go to the first to adopt, therefore, the innovator gains a financial advantage through his innovations. Some new ideas are costly to adopt and require large initial outlays of capital. Only the wealthy units in a social system may be able to adopt these innovations. The innovators become richer and the laggards become poorer through this process. Because the innovator is the first to adopt, he must take risks that can be avoided by later adopters. Certain of the innovator's new ideas are likely to fail. He must be large enough to absorb the loss from these occasional failures. It should be pointed out that while wealth and innovativeness are high related, economic factors do not offer a complete explanation of innovative behavior (or even approach doing so). For example, while agricultural innovators tend to be wealthy, there are many rich farmers who are not innovators.

25. Some of these studies include Jones (1960), Marsh and Coleman (1955b), Copp (1956), Hoffer and Stangland (1958), Fliegel (1957), Rahim (1961), van den Ban (1957b), Straus (1960a), Sizer and Porter (1960), Lionberger and Coughenour (1957), Hobbs (1960), Lindstrom (1958), Rogers and Pitzer (1960), Rogers and Burdge (1961 and 1962), Blackmore and others (1955), Kreitlow and Duncan (1956), Sheppard (1960a), and Jones (1960).

4. SPECIALIZATION. *Earlier Adopters Have More Specialized Operations Than Later Adopters.* Innovators, especially, tend to be specialized, and place "all their eggs in one basket." For instance, farmer innovators concentrate on one farm enterprise such as hogs, sheep, or dairy (Rogers, 1961b). This specialization allows the innovator to keep up to date more easily in his specialty, and may lead him to seek more cosmopolite sources of information.

This generalization has relatively less empirical support than others in this section. Jones (1960), Rogers (1961b), and Rogers and Burdge (1962) found specialization related to innovativeness.

5. MENTAL ABILITY. *Earlier Adopters Have a Type of Mental Ability Different From That of Later Adopters.* Innovators must be able to adopt a new idea largely from mass media sources of information. They cannot simply copy the behavior of other members of their social system because these other members have not yet adopted the innovation. On the basis of this type of reasoning, one might expect innovators to possess a different type of mental ability than do laggards.

There are several research studies which lend at least fragmentary evidence in support of this generalization. Both Rogers (1961b) and van den Ban (in press) found low but positive relationships between innovativeness and "cloze" scores, which are a crude measure of intelligence.[26] Rogers and Beal (1959) found a high relationship between innovativeness and ability to deal with abstractions, a type of mental ability they measured by responses to stimulus pictures. There are also several studies (Rogers, 1957b; Sizer and Porter, 1960; and

26. Evidence that cloze scores are basically a measure of intelligence as well as readability (which the cloze procedure was designed to measure) may be found in Taylor (1956).

Photiadis, 1961) that indicate farm innovators have greater knowledge of technical agriculture than do laggards.

Several investigations indicate that earlier adopters are less dogmatic, less rigid, and more rational than later adopters. Rogers (1957b) found that more innovative farmers scored lower on a dogmatism scale and on a rigidity scale. Copp (1956) found in a study of Kansas cattlemen that innovators had greater mental flexibility than laggards. Dean and others (1958), Emery and Oeser (1958), Bemiller (1960), and Coughenour (1960b) found that more innovative farmers utilized more rational means to reach their goals. Burdge 1961), Goldstein and Eichhorn (1961), Rogers and Burdge (1962), and Copp (1956) concluded that laggards were relatively more work-oriented; that is, they viewed work as a goal in itself rather than as a means to other ends. Sutherland (1959) found that laggard cotton-spinning firms regarded the future only in terms of the short run, and claimed the best policy was to simply hang on to ideas presently on hand.

Mental ability[27] is a difficult dimension to measure, and it must be pointed out that the data supporting the present generalization are extremely weak.

Communication Behavior

Information sources vary on the basis of (1) stage in the adoption process, (2) the characteristics of the innovation, and (3) adopter category. The generalizations considered in the present section deal mainly with differences in the com-

27. Harp (1960) feels that the inclusion of personality variables in analyses of innovativeness will contribute little. He states that if other sociological variables are included in investigations of innovativeness, the effect of " . . . personality may disappear." At the present time, there are few studies that have related adequate measures of personality variables to innovativeness.

munication behavior on the basis of adopter category, and generally ignore the effect of adoption stages and characteristics of the innovation. A number of generalizations will be suggested, each of which is concerned with differences between adopter categories in some dimension of information sources.

1. IMPERSONAL SOURCES. *Impersonal Sources of Information Are More Important Than Personal Sources for Relatively Earlier Adopters of Innovations Than for Later Adopters.* This tendency is particularly marked at the evaluation stage and slightly less so at other stages, especially at the awareness stage (Figure 6-2). This generalization is supported by the findings of Bowers (1938), Ryan and Gross (1943), Wilkening (1952b, p. 19), Rogers and Beal (1958a), Beal and Rogers (1960, p. 16), Rahim (1961, p. 43), and van den Ban (in press). Personal influence is evidently not as necessary to motivate the earlier adopters to accept a new idea as it is for the later adopters. At the time the innovators and early adopters decide to use a new idea, few members of their social system have experience with it. As a result, the earlier adopters secure new ideas from impersonal sources. When earlier adopters report personal information sources, the sources are likely to be other earlier adopters or change agents.

2. COSMOPOLITE SOURCES. *Cosmopolite Sources of Information Are More Important Than Localite Sources for Relatively Earlier Adopters of Innovations Than for Later Adopters.* Cosmopolite information sources are those external to a social system. Most new ideas enter a social

Percentage of Communication Sources
Classified as Personal

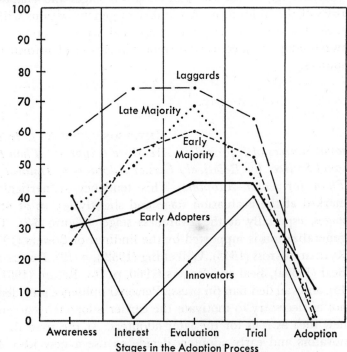

FIGURE 6-2. PERCENTAGE OF PERSONAL COMMUNICATION
SOURCES AT EACH STAGE IN THE ADOPTION PROCESS
BY ADOPTER CATEGORY FOR 2,4-D WEED SPRAY

In general, later adopters tend to depend more upon personal sources
of communication at each stage in the adoption process than do earlier
adopters. This tendency is particularly so at the evaluation stage and
slightly less so at the awareness, interest, and trial stages.

Source: Beal and Rogers (1960, p. 19). Used by permission.

system from outside. If one is an earlier adopter, he is likely
to secure his information about innovations from cosmopolite
sources. Support for the present generalization comes from

Campbell (1959), Rogers and Leuthold (1962), and Rogers and Burdge (1961 and 1962). Physician-innovators regarded out-of-town medical institutions as a more important information source than did laggards (Coleman and others, in press). Carter and Williams (1959) found that innovative industrial firms were more likely to seek new ideas from university researchers than were laggards. There is need to test the present generalization while controlling on stage in the adoption process.

3. CLOSER CONTACT. *Earlier Adopters Utilize Information Sources That Are in Closer Contact With the Origin of New Ideas Than Later Adopters.* The source of most innovations is scientists. Innovators have more direct contact with scientists (Rogers, 1958a; Rogers and Beal, 1960; Rogers, 1961b; Rogers and Burdge, 1961 and 1962; and Carter and Williams, 1959), and have more favorable attitudes toward scientists than do laggards (Beal and Rogers, 1959; and Rogers, 1961b).

Data from a sample of 200 Ohio farmers were analyzed by Rogers (1961b) to show that innovators had the greatest degree of contact with agricultural scientists (42 per cent had direct contact within the past year compared to 10 per cent for other adopter categories). The early adopters had greater contact with county extension agents than any other adopter category, including the innovators.

4. MORE SOURCES. *Earlier Adopters Utilize a Greater Number of Different Information Sources Than Do Later Adopters.* It has already been pointed out that earlier adopters tend actively to seek new ideas while later

adopters have a more passive or even negative attitude toward the new. Innovators and early adopters are willing to expand greater efforts to secure information about innovations (Hruschka, 1961). It is reasonable to expect that earlier adopters not only seek more impersonal, more cosmopolite, and more direct information sources, but that they seek a greater number of different information sources than later adopters.

This generalization is supported by the findings of Coughenour (1960b), Fliegel (1956), Marsh and Coleman (1955a), and Emery and Oeser (1958). Copp (1956, p. 12) found that earlier adopters used not only more information sources but also those that required greater effort to utilize.

Information sources can be classified on a number of different bases such as cosmopoliteness and personal-impersonal. The unit of analysis in the type of research reviewed in the present section is an individual seeking information about a new idea from some source. It is obvious that the dimensions of analysis in the present generalizations may be interrelated. For example, cosmopolite sources are likely to be less personal and also to be more direct to the origin of new ideas. A next research step is to perform a multivariate analysis of information sources in order to determine the degree to which use of information sources is a predictor of innovativeness.

Social Relationships

There are important differences in social relationships on the basis of adopter category.

1. COSMOPOLITENESS. *Earlier Adopters Are More Cosmopolite Than Later Adopters.* Cosmopolite-

ness is the degree to which an individual's orientation is external to a particular social system. It has already been shown that earlier adopters utilize more cosmopolite information sources than do later adopters. The innovators' reference groups are more likely to be outside rather than within their social system. They travel widely and are interested in affairs beyond the boundary of their social system. The cliques and formal organizations to which innovators belong are likely to also include other innovators as members.

Ryan and Gross (1943) found that hybrid corn innovators traveled more often to urban centers such as Des Moines than did the average farmer. In a later reanalysis of the same data, Gross and Taves (1952) found that trips to Des Moines were positively associated with adoption of 9 of the 10 farm innovations they studied.[28] Medical doctors who were innovators attended more out-of-town professional meetings than non-innovators (Menzel and Katz, 1955). Carter and Williams (1959) found that the most innovative industrial firms they studied were very cosmopolite. "There is extensive world-wide travel by executives, and a lively interest in progress at home and abroad. . . ." Ross (1958, p. 187) reported that teachers at more innovative schools were relatively more likely to get new educational ideas from outside their community. Foster (1956) found that Indian villagers who owned bicycles, an indication of cosmopoliteness, were more innovative. Goldsen and Ralis (1957, pp. 25–28) found that Thailand farm innovators were more likely to visit Bangkok. Cocking (1951) found that innovative schools were more cosmopolite.

Lionberger and Coughenour (1957) in Missouri, Rogers and Burdge (1961 and 1962) in Ohio, Emery and Oeser (1958) in Australia, and Jones (1960) in England found in-

28. It is interesting that Ryan and Gross (1943), Emery and Oeser (1958), and Benvenuti (1961) refer to cosmopoliteness as "urbanism." Perhaps this is because an orientation external to a farm community is often in an urban direction.

novative farmers were more cosmopolite. Rogers (1961a) found that innovators and early adopters were much more cosmopolite than late majority and laggards. The laggards, in fact, were semi-isolates who had relatively little interaction within or without their social system.

Tarde (1903, pp. 87–88) was a sociological forefather who recognized the cosmopoliteness of innovators. He stated, "To innovate, to discover, to awake for an instant . . . the individual must escape, for the time being, from his social surroundings. Such unusual audacity makes him super-social rather than social."

2. OPINION LEADERSHIP. *Earlier Adopters Have More Opinion Leadership Than Later Adopters.*[29] An individual who is more innovative than his peers is certainly in a position to influence their adoption decisions because of his prior experience with the innovation. This influence potential is not realized in many cases because of such mediating variables as the norms of the social system. Nevertheless, there is strong evidence for the present generalization from 17 research studies.[30]

The present generalization, while important in itself, does not provide enough information. It is important to know under what conditions an earlier adopter is an opinion leader and under what group situations he is not. Further detail on this point is reserved for Chapter VIII.

29. The present generalization looks at the relationship between innovativeness and opinion leadership from the opposite direction of a generalization in Chapter VIII which states that opinion leaders are more innovative than their followers.

30. Katz (1957), Lionberger (1953 and 1955), Marsh and Coleman (1954a), Young and Coleman (1959), Wilkening (1952b, 1958d, and 1962), Rogers (1955 and 1957c), van den Ban (in press), Chaparro (1956), Rogers and Burdge (1962), Barnabas (1958), Rahudkar (1960), Brandner (1960), and Rahim (1961, p. 58).

TABLE 6-4

A COMPOSITE PICTURE OF ADOPTER CATEGORIES

Adopter Category	Salient Values	Personal Characteristics	Communication Behavior	Social Relationships
Innovators	"Venturesome"; willing to accept risks	Youngest age; highest social status; largest and most specialized operations; wealthy	Closest contact with scientific information sources; interaction with other innovators; relatively greatest use of impersonal sources	Some opinion leadership; very cosmopolite
Early adopters	"Respect"; regarded by many others in the social system as a role-model	High social status; large and specialized operations	Greatest contact with local change agents	Greatest opinion leadership of any category in most social systems; very localite
Early majority	"Deliberate"; willing to consider innovations only after peers have adopted	Above average social status; average-sized operation	Considerable contact with change agents and early adopters	Some opinion leadership
Late majority	"Skeptical"; overwhelming pressure from peers needed before adoption occurs	Below average social status; small operation; little specialization; small income	Secure ideas from peers who are mainly late majority or early majority; less use of mass media	Little opinion leadership
Laggards	"Tradition"; oriented to the past	Little specialization; lowest social status; smallest operation; lowest income; oldest	Neighbors, friends, and relatives with similar values are main information source	Very little opinion leadership; semi-isolates

A Composite Portrait

In order to summarize the present section on characteristics of adopter categories,[31] Table 6-4 has been prepared.
This diagram shows the salient values for each adopter category and their three main characteristics that were presented:
personal characteristics, communication behavior, and social
relationships.

Most of the characteristics of the adopter categories decrease or increase consistently from innovators to laggards.
However, there are some variables which early adopters may
possess in highest degree, such as communication with local
change agents and opinion leadership. In most cases, only
minor differences may be noted between the early and late
majority. Gross (1942) stated, "The constant similarities of
the intermediate groups [early and late majority] indicate
that the two large midgroups, consisting of 68 per cent of the
adopters, may be conceived as one large homogenous aggregate rather than as two large intermediate groups."

Consistency of Innovativeness

While Table 6-4 helps one draw a composite portrait of
each adopter category, it should be remembered that *all* in-

31. A number of researchers have related single factors to innovativeness while statistically controlling on other factors. These analyses,
which were included in the present discussion, provide further insight
into the nature of innovativeness. For example, see Wilkening (1952a),
Copp (1956 and 1958), Fliegel (1956), Marsh and Coleman (1955b),
Rogers (1958a), Ross (1958), Coughenour (1960b), Emery and Oeser
(1958), Gross and Taves (1952), van den Ban (1957), Photiadis (1961),
Sizer and Porter (1960), Rogers and Havens (1961b), and Rogers and
Burdge (1962). These studies are reviewed in greater detail in Chapter X, and offer an example of the direction in which more sophisticated analyses need to proceed. It is not enough to know only
the zero-order relationship between a variable and innovativeness;
future research needs to show whether this relationship remains when
other variable are controlled.

dividuals in each adopter category may not possess the characteristics indicated. For example, Mansfield (1960, p. 19) found that innovative behavior among the industrial firms he studied was fairly consistent, but not perfectly so.

Taking two innovations that first appeared at about the same time, there is some tendency—the strength of which varies among industries—for the same firms to be relatively quick to begin using both. . . . But taking ones that appeared many years apart, this tendency is perceptibly weaker.

Parish (1954) found that the pattern of adoption of farm innovations among his sample of Australian farmers was generally consistent. Farmers who had adopted soil conservation innovations had also adopted livestock feeding ideas and also crop innovations. He concluded ". . . there is a tendency for farmers either to adopt innovations consistently, or consistently to fail to do so."[32]

There is no clear-cut evidence as to whether or not innovating behavior is completely consistent. Opinion Research Corporation (1960) found that families who adopted one consumer innovation, for example, home air-conditioning, were likely to adopt other consumer innovations.[33] There is less evidence, however, that a farm innovator is also an innovator in political ideology, consumer behavior, or other areas of life.[34]

In any event, it is doubtful whether an individual who is an innovator for one idea is a laggard for another idea.

32. Some support for the consistency of innovativeness among farmers is provided by factor analyses of innovativeness scales by Fliegel (1956) and Copp (1956). Additional support comes from intercorrelations of items in innovativeness scales by Rogers (1957a), Rogers and Rogers (1961), Sheppard (1960a), and Wilkening and others (1962, p. 56). Individuals may acquire an adoption or a rejection "set" and thus become habituated in their responses to new ideas.

33. There is support for this statement from several farm innovation studies and from the Coleman and others (in press) drug study.

34. Rogers and Havens (1961c) found a correlation of +.81 between adoption-of-farm-innovations scores and adoption-of-homemaking-innovations scores for a sample of 84 farm families in Ohio.

SELF-IMAGES OF ADOPTER CATEGORIES

An objective method of categorizing the individuals in a social system into adopter categories has been described. For some purposes, however, a more subjective rating of adopter category may be valuable. If an individual *perceives* himself as an innovator, then he may act as if he were an innovator.

For example, the farmers in an Ohio study (Rogers, 1961b) were asked: "About where would you rate yourself in respect to adopting new farm practices? (1) Among the first, (2) slightly before the average, (3) about average, (4) slightly later than average, or (5) among the last?" Self-images as to adopter category roughly corresponded to the five (objective) adopter categories determined on the basis of innovativeness scores. There is a general tendency for the self-images to be accurate.[35] Only about 24 per cent of the farmers had widely inaccurate self-images, and did not rate themselves in the same or an adjacent category to that determined by their innovativeness score. The self-images of innovators and early adopters are more accurate than those of laggards.[36]

There are several interesting and useful aspects of self-images as to adopter category that have not yet been fully explored. Do individuals with inaccurate self-images differ from those individuals with accurate self-images? For example, are "pseudo-innovators," individuals who are not innovators but who think they are, different from innovators in their social characteristics and communication behavior? It may be fruitful to determine the characteristics of self-perceived adopter

35. Robinson's "A" between adopter categories and self-images is .79, which is significant at the one per cent level. The general accuracy of self-images provides some evidence of the validity of adopter categorization on the basis of adoption-of-innovations scores.

36. Sheppard (in press) found that self-images on innovativeness were more accurate for some innovations than for others, and in some social systems than in others.

categories,[37] just as past investigations have sought to isolate the characteristics of objective adopter categories.

CHANGES IN ADOPTER CATEGORIES OVER TIME

The tone of this chapter may have implied that an innovator in a social system at one point in time will remain an innovator at a later time. Such is not necessarily the case. In fact, research studies show *there is considerable shifting of individuals in a social system from one category to another over time.* Adopter categorization is similar to a snapshot that pictures an individual at one time. He does not necessarily remain in the same position in the social structure at a later point in time.

Lackey (1958) found a considerable movement of farmers from one category to another. He utilized a panel study consisting of personal interviews with farmer respondents in 1947 and again in 1957. Seldom were more than 50 per cent of Lackey's respondents in the same adopter category in both 1947 and 1957.[38]

Rogers (1957c and 1959b) found about half of his sample of 104 Ohio farmers shifted from one category to another from 1957 to 1959. There were approximately as many respondents moving to an earlier adopting category as to a later adopting category (Figure 6-3). For most individuals, the shift was to an adjoining adopter category. Seldom did a farmer move more than two categories, either forward or backward.

37. One attempt to determine the characteristics of self-perceived innovators has been completed by Hildebrand and Partenheimer (1958), even though they did not realize it at the time (Rogers, 1959a).

38. Although part of this shifting may have been the result of inadequacies in Lackey's innovativeness scales, which contained relatively few items.

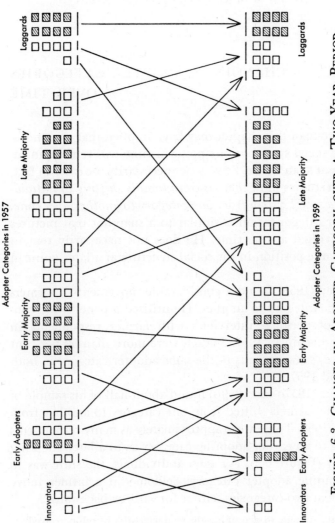

FIGURE 6-3. CHANGES IN ADOPTER CATEGORY OVER A TWO-YEAR PERIOD

The shaded squares represent farmers who did not shift from one category to another over the two-year period. *Source:* Rogers (1957c and 1959b).

It has been established that all individuals do not retain the same adopter category. But who drops out of the social system over a period of time? Rogers (1957c and 1959b) found in two different panel studies that those farmers leaving farming were much more likely to be laggards than innovators. They were older, less educated, and had smaller farms. Lackey (1958) found similar evidence in his New York panel study. He compared the characteristics of the "replacements" who entered farming with those farmers who left. The replacements had more education, a higher level of living, and larger farms. Their characteristics were very similar to those farmers who remained in farming over the ten-year period.

Although replacements may enter a social system in any of the five adopter categories, *laggards are most likely to drop out of the social system.* In fact, the shifting of individuals among adopter categories over time may be likened to a bell-shaped pile of potatoes. The potato pile rests precipitously near the edge of a table. As the potatoes rearrange their relative positions within the stack over time, an occasional potato is shoved over the edge of the table and out of the pile. New potatoes are constantly being added to the pile and distribute themselves throughout the stack. While the pile retains its bell shape over a time period, individuals within it may be changing positions.

SUMMARY

Adopter categories are the classifications of individuals within a social system on the basis of innovativeness. A variety of categorization systems and titles for adopter categories have been utilized in past research studies.

The writings of early sociologists, learning psychologists,

and students of the interaction effect provide theoretical reason for expecting adopter distributions to be normal. The interaction effect is the process through which individuals in a social system who have adopted an innovation influence those who have not yet adopted. Adopter distributions follow a bell-shaped curve over time and approach normality.

The continuum of innovativeness is partitioned into five adopter categories (innovators, early adopters, early majority, late majority, and laggards) on the basis of the two parameters of the normal distribution, the mean and the standard deviation. The resulting five categories are a somewhat arbitrary classification system, but when utilized by research workers, they should lead to a greater standardization of methodology. As a result, findings can be compared more meaningfully from one study to another.

The five adopter categories are ideal types, conceptualizations that are based on observations of reality and designed to institute comparisons. The dominant values of each category are: innovators, venturesome; early adopters, respect; early majority, deliberate; late majority, skeptical; and laggards, tradition. The relatively earlier adopters in a social system tend to be younger in age, have higher social status, a more favorable financial position, more specialized operations, and a different type of mental ability from later adopters. Earlier adopters utilize information sources that are more impersonal and cosmopolite than later adopters and that are in closer contact with the origin of new ideas. Earlier adopters utilize a greater number of different information sources than do later adopters. The social relationships of earlier adopters are more cosmopolite than for later adopters, and earlier adopters have more opinion leadership.

Research findings, although somewhat fragmentary at the present time, indicate there is a considerable shifting of individuals in a social system from one adopter category to another over time. Laggards are most likely to drop out of the social system.

CHAPTER VII

Innovators as Deviants: In Step with a Different Drummer[1]

> If a man does not keep pace with his companions, perhaps it is because he hears a different drummer.
>
> HENRY DAVID THOREAU, 1906

Perhaps the adopter category of greatest interest to sociologists is innovators. By definition, innovators are the first to adopt new ideas in their social system. However, the innovator is not always the most respected member of a system. He prefers venturesomeness to the respect of his peers. Innovation thus offers a fertile field in which to test theories of deviant behavior.

The innovator plays an important role in the process of change. The innovator may not be a respected "leader" of change, but there is no doubt that when the innovator adopts a new idea, he causes his peers to become aware of the innovation. If the innovation proves to be advantageous, the initial skepticism of the innovator's peers may change to a grudging admittance of its utility.

Thus, the innovator may not be identified as influential in his social system, but he may set the stage for change by

1. With A. Eugene Havens of The Ohio State University. An earlier version of this chapter was originally presented as a paper at the 1959 American Sociological Association. The authors wish to thank John Useem and Richard Adams of Michigan State University and John W. Bennett of Washington University for their insightful suggestions as to the study of innovators.

demonstrating new ideas to local opinion leaders. The new idea is injected into the social system from external sources by the innovator.

The purpose of this chapter is to describe the deviancy of innovators as perceived by other members of the social system, and as perceived by innovators themselves.

PAST VIEWS OF INNOVATORS

The deviancy of innovators has remained a controversy among social scientists. Linton (1952) stated, "Both the motives and the personalities of [innovators] appear to be varied, but it is safe to say that their personalities are rarely of the basic type. In fact, such persons are very frequently misfits in their societies, handicapped by atypical personalities."[2] Barnett (1941) found "The disgruntled, the maladjusted, the frustrated, or the incompetent are pre-eminently the acceptors of culture innovations and change." Innovators were characterized by Barnett (1953, p. 380) as the "truly marginal individuals." One attempt at reconciliating these views was by Adams (1951) who found that Barnett's view of innovators held true in cases where change is rapid and violent, but that the innovator has high prestige where change is gradual. Putney and Putney (1961) found that innovators had high prestige in a Mexican village with an atmosphere of radical change.

Pelto (1960) found similar evidence in his comparison of the status of innovators among the Skolt Lapps and the Pueblo Indians. The Lapps are an individualistic society in which innovation is rewarded, or, at least, not discouraged. Most innovations are of little consequence to persons outside

2. Professor Everett E. Hagen at MIT is investigating innovators' personalities in less developed countries by means of psychological tests.

of the innovator's own nuclear family. High status persons frequently are innovators among the Lapps. Among a more "conformity-oriented" society, such as the Pueblos, most innovations are of serious consequence for the whole community. Here the innovator has a lower status. In fact, the innovators have little to lose by innovation.

Although at first glance there would appear to be little consensus as to the deviancy of innovators, generalizations will be derived later in this chapter from theoretical writings and investigations of innovators. Unfortunately, previous research on innovators has suffered from two inadequacies: (1) standard means of selecting innovators were not utilized; and (2) generalizations were made on the basis of a small number of case studies. There is a need for research on larger samples of innovators.

INNOVATORS AND INVENTORS

Past research findings indicate that all individuals do not adopt a new idea at the same time. The innovativeness continuum may be divided into adopter categories (Chapter VI). The first 2.5 per cent of the adopters in a social system are innovators. The percentage is quite arbitrary. It is chosen because most adopter distributions over time have been found to closely approach normality and 2.5 per cent of the individuals are contained to the left of two standard deviations from the mean time of adoption (Rogers, 1958b). Individuals may be placed on the innovativeness continuum on the basis of either a *single* new idea or on the basis of their composite time of adoption of several innovations, as measured by an adoption-of-innovations scale.

Innovators are not necessarily the same persons as inventors. *Inventors* are the individuals who create new ideas.

They unite cultural elements into new combinations. Innovators adopt new ideas but they do not necessarily invent them. This does not say that innovators cannot be inventors or vice versa. The two terms are not mutually exclusive nor are they mutually inclusive.[3] We found that several Ohio farm innovators possessed home welders and developed their own new farm machinery. In certain fields, there may be little scientific research available, and here the innovators are likely to also be inventors.

In summary, innovators and inventors are distinct roles which may overlap, but are not necessarily the same.[4]

DEVIATION

Deviation is defined as departure from a social system norm.[5] A norm is the most frequently occurring pattern of overt behavior for the members of a particular social system.[6] Deviation is a matter of degree. It is important to note that deviant behavior in one social system may not be deviant behavior in another system. One must specify the social system from whose norms an individual is deviating.

3. The present distinction between innovators and inventors has also been made by a number of other writers. For examples, see Ruttan (1959) and Strassman (1959, pp. 9–10).

4. In fact, Enos (1960) found an average time period of 11 years between invention and innovation (first use) of 11 new ideas in the petroleum refining industry. This time period suggests a distinction between the two roles.

5. This definition of deviation is based upon Cohen (1959, p. 462), Zadrozmy (1959, p. 89), Benedict (1934), Lemert (1951, p. 30; 1959, p. 447), and Merton (1957, p. 176).

6. There have been attempts to define norms in two ways (1) as role expectations, and (2) as modal patterns of behavior. The present authors prefer the latter type of definition although both are probably reflected in most norm measures.

Laggards are deviants as well as innovators.[7] In a sense, laggards are overconformers. They overconform to traditional ideas by maintaining allegiance to them after they have been rejected by most members of a social system.

Merton (1959) and Dubin (1959) discussed overconformity as a type of deviant behavior. Merton stated, ". . . overconformity is the direct counterpart of under-conformity. It is a form of social deviation that involves 'too much' just as under-conformity involves 'too little' when judged by group standards" (1959). As Merton pointed out, the fact that overconformity exists has been noted before (Parsons, 1951, p. 323; LaPiere, 1954, p. 122). However, the distinction between types of conformity and deviance has not been made clear.

Laggards overconform to traditional ideas to such a degree that they are perceived as deviant.[8] The late-majority and early-majority categories are relatively low in deviancy since they display the average or modal patterns of behavior. However, they are distinct because the late majority overconform slightly while the early majority underconform slightly to the modal pattern. Early adopters underconform to a greater degree than early majority and thus are more deviant. Innovators underconform to norms to such a degree that they are perceived as highly deviant. Thus, a high degree of deviancy occurs under conditions of both overconformity and under-conformity.

7. Menzel (1960a) maintained that every innovator is not necessarily a deviant from norms as it is possible the norms in some social systems might strongly favor innovativeness. However, as innovators and deviation are defined in this book, all innovators are deviants as they are departing from social system norms.

8. Homans (1961, pp. 336–358) reviewed small group studies on conformity, status, and innovation to show that both upper- and lower-status individuals deviate from norms, but in different ways and for different reasons. "The upper-status man has little to gain by conformity, the lower-status one little to lose by its opposite, and so for different reasons the behavior of both is biased in the same way."

A simple paradigm may be used to summarize the relationships between conformity, deviancy, and adopter categories.

Adopter Category	Type of Deviation	Type of Conformity
Innovators	High Deviation	Underconformity
Early Adopters	Some Deviation	Some Underconformity
Early Majority	Low Deviation	Conformity
Late Majority	Low Deviation	Conformity
Laggards	High Deviation	Overconformity

ARE INNOVATORS DEVIANTS?
A RESEARCH STUDY

Data are taken from an investigation of agricultural innovators (Rogers, 1961b) in order to provide better understanding of the deviant behavior of innovators. Two different samples were utilized. Personal interviews were completed with a state-wide random sample of 104 Ohio farmers in 1957. This sample contained innovators as well as other adopter categories. Because there were so few innovators (only three) in this study, the sample of innovators was enlarged by asking 44 county extension agents in Ohio to nominate innovators in their counties. Of the 150 farmers nominated by county agents, 96 actually were innovators in terms of their adoption of new farm ideas; the other 54 farmers were discarded from the present analysis.

Innovators were separated from noninnovators among the farmers nominated by county agents by means of an adoption-of-farm-innovations scale. That is, an innovator must have adopted new farm ideas, on the average, before a certain time relative to when the average farmer adopted these innovations.[9] The present analysis is based primarily on data from a state-wide sample[10] of 99 innovators and 101 non-innovators in Ohio.

Determining Deviancy

Two methods are utilized in the present investigation to investigate the deviancy of innovators: (1) Deviancy in the eyes of *other group members*. Do other community members view innovators as deviants? (2) *Self-images*. Do innovators perceive themselves as deviants from norms?

1. OTHER GROUP MEMBERS. The 99 Ohio innovators were asked, "How do your neighbor-farmers feel about many of the new farm ideas that you use on your farm?"[11] More than half the responses were in terms of lack of respect from neighbors.[12] Typical replies illustrate this attitude:

9. It should be pointed out that all of the 99 members of this sample are innovators, but that there are other innovators among the farm audience in the 44 counties who are not included in the sample.

10. The statistical norms for innovators on this 25-item innovativeness scale were developed from the study of 104 commercial farmers. The 25 farm innovations were selected by a panel of agricultural experts to represent dairying, grain production, and other farm enterprises. The ideas included in the innovativeness scale were generally those that would yield a farmer profit if utilized correctly.

11. This question really asks the innovator how he perceives his neighbors' perceptions of himself. An improved research design would entail asking the innovators' neighbors directly how they feel toward innovators.

12. Wilkening (1949, p. 208) found a similar tendency for farmer innovators to be ridiculed. "To deviate from the norms of the neighborhood and kin groups . . . brings ridicule or other forms of punishment. The innovator in farming methods represents such a deviation."

The way I operate my farm is *not* the way to win popularity contests among one's neighbors.
Sometimes they shake their heads.
Fifty per cent *think* I am crazy; the other 50 per cent are *sure* I am.

Most of the other comments followed the general theme "my neighbors are skeptical at first, but they are convinced when the new ideas turn out successfully." One comment illustrates this attitude of the innovator's neighbors:

Some talk contempt, but they watch with interest and many of them follow.

This evidence, as well as the findings of Wilkening (1949), suggest that *innovators are perceived as deviants by other members of their social system.* Two important qualifications must be pointed out about this general statement.

1. The degree to which innovators are perceived as deviant is partly a function of the social system's norms on innovativeness. Adams (1951), Putney and Putney (1961), Pelto (1960), van den Ban (in press), Menzel (1960a), and Rogers and Burdge (1962) found that innovators are perceived as more deviant by the members of a social system when the system's norms are more traditional than when they are modern.[13]

2. Not only do the norms in a social system affect the way in which innovators are perceived; the respondents' adopter category also determines, in part, how favorably he views innovators. Table 7-1 contains data from two investigations of the relationship between adopter category and favorable-

13. Data supporting this point also come from Littumen's (1959) analysis of Finnish radio listener groups. The norms of a number of these discussion groups were judged as to innovativeness, and the passiveness of innovators in each group was determined. Littumen found innovators sought a passive role and withdrew from group discussion when the norms were traditional, but that innovators were active participants in groups with innovative norms. This study, like others, probably suffered from difficulties in measuring norms on innovativeness.

TABLE 7-1

FAVORABLENESS OF ATTITUDE TOWARD INNOVATORS BY ADOPTER CATEGORY

Adopter Category of Respondent	Per Cent Viewing Innovators Favorably	
	Iowa Farmers, 1957*	Ohio Farmers, 1961†
Innovators	100	100
Early adopters	100	80
Early majority	75	69
Late majority	36	54
Laggards	0	27
All Respondents	57	61

* Data come from 23 interviews with a random sample of farmers in one Iowa rural community; see Rogers and Beal (1958b). Used by permission.

† Data come from 83 vegetable growers in one Ohio county (Rogers and Burdge, 1962). Used by permission.

ness of attitude toward innovators. One's position in a social structure (of adopter categories) appears to determine one's view of the structure. Relatively earlier adopters tend to regard innovators more favorably than do later adopters. One reason for this relationship may be the degree of familiarity with innovators. For example, early adopters are more similar to innovators in their social characteristics (Chapter VI) and interact more with them.

2. SELF-IMAGES. *Innovators perceive themselves as deviant from the norms of their social system.*[14] The respondents in the Ohio study were asked whether they considered themselves "among the first," "slightly before the average to adopt," and so on, as is shown in Table 7-2. This

14. There is also some evidence for the support of this generalization from Beal and Rogers (1960).

TABLE 7-2

SELF-IMAGES AS TO DEVIANCY FOR INNOVATORS AND LAGGARDS*

Self-Image as to Deviancy	Adopter Category (as determined by an Innovativeness Scale)		
	Innovators	All Farmers	Laggards
"Among the first"	53	16	12
"Slightly before the average"	36	15	6
"About average"	10	49	35
"Slightly later than average"	1	14	23
"Among the last"	0	6	24
Total per cent	100	100	100
Total number	98	104	17

* Both innovators and laggards see themselves as more deviant from community norms than the average respondent. Innovators perceive themselves as deviating from community norms on innovativeness even more than laggards.

Source: Rogers (1961b).

question actually sought to determine the degree to which each adopter category perceived itself as deviating from community norms on innovativeness.

Table 7-2 shows that 89 per cent of the innovators (as determined by an innovativeness scale) actually perceived themselves as deviating from community norms on innovativeness. Fifty-three per cent said they were among the first to adopt in their community while 36 per cent said they were above average in adopting innovations. Forty-seven per cent of the laggards (as determined by an innovativeness scale) perceived themselves to be later than the average to adopt. Both innovators and laggards perceived themselves as more deviant from community norms on innovativeness than did the average respondent.

Reference Groups of Innovators

Cohen (1959, pp. 469–470) suggested three alternatives available to the deviant: (1) continue to conform despite frustration, (2) break with the norm-holding group and acknowledge other reference groups, or (3) proceed alone without the reinforcement that comes from group support. Past research suggests that the second alternative may be most often utilized by deviants; there is a need for allies in overcoming one's conformity to group norms (Asch, 1952, pp. 2–11). Deviants are characterized by a weak attachment to the norm-holding group and by ties to other groups or subcultures (Kelley and Volkhart, 1952; Festinger and others, 1950). One expected consequence of deviation is a shift or change in reference groups.

Some insights into the group relationships of innovators are available from the present study. The farm innovator's group relationships are likely to be spread over a much wider geographical area than are the noninnovators; the innovators' reference groups are different from the average farmer's. A cosmopoliteness scale was developed to measure differences in the geographical location of reference groups.[15] A cosmopolite is one who is oriented externally rather than inside of a particular social system, the respondent's community of residence in the present case. The data indicate that innovators are much more cosmopolite than other farmers.[16] An innovator *is* different from the average farmer; as such, he does not fit smoothly into the social relationships of the local community.

15. Typical items in this scale were the degree to which farm work and equipment were exchanged with neighbors, amount of visiting with neighbors, and importance of neighbors' opinions on the respondents' farming decisions.

16. Innovators' scores on the cosmopoliteness scale were significantly different from noninnovators' scores. Further evidence that innovativeness is related to cosmopoliteness comes from more than a half-dozen other studies reviewed in Chapter VI.

Responses of the 99 farm innovators indicated a wide perspective in terms of travel to learn about new farm ideas. The respondents were asked, "Within the past year, have you traveled outside your county to observe some new farm practices in operation?" Seventy-seven per cent of the innovators said they had done so (which was much greater than for noninnovators). In fact, almost half of the respondents had traveled not only outside their county but also outside their state. A few had even traveled outside the United States to observe new farm innovations. Some of the most cosmopolite replies are as follows:

Beef and dairy enterprises in South America, wheat practices in Canada, and new beef ideas in Colorado and Nebraska.

I visited with swine research men at the Iowa and Minnesota [Agricultural Experiment] Stations.

I was interested in dairy and beef nutrition in Michigan and potato growing automation in Pennsylvania.

In a study of Ohio irrigators, its was found that they were members of friendship cliques with other irrigators (Rogers and Pitzer, 1960). These irrigator-friends were often located over several counties, and 16 per cent of the irrigators reported irrigation friends outside of the state. Thus, the irrigators had a cosmopolite type of group support in their adoption decisions even though many of their close-by neighbors ridiculed the adoption of irrigation.

Innovators are often regarded by their neighbors with disrespect. The research findings suggest that innovators are impervious to this group pressure from their neighbors. But the present evidence also indicates that innovators receive group support for their ideas from another source. While their neighbors are relatively unimportant to them as a reference group,[17] the present findings suggest that innovators belong to a cosmopolite clique whose norms favor innovativeness. These reference groups provide consensual validation for the

17. In fact, a farm innovator may not sociologically be a member of his community to which he is assigned on the basis of his place of residence. The community is not a reference group to him.

innovator and give him psychological support with which to combat criticism from his local social system.

DISCUSSION

Nonagricultural Innovators

Although the present chapter has concentrated on studies of agricultural innovators, the generalizations obtained need to be tested with adequate samples of other types of innovators. Some evidence about the deviancy of nonagricultural innovators is already available. For example,[18] Menzel (1960a) found that doctor-innovators were emancipated from the local norms of their medical community. Enos (1960) found that almost all inventions in the petroleum industry in the past forty years ". . . were made by men close to the oil industry, but not attached to the major firms." Ben-David (1960) found that ". . . the pioneers in bacteriology and psychoanalysis illustrate the characteristics of scientific innovators who begin investigating problems defined at the time by scientific consensus as beyond the scope of science. Typically, the innovators were practitioners who were involved in research and academic teaching as a side-line. . . ." Miller (1957, p. 23) found similarly that the early adopters of inoculation for smallpox were marginal men on the edge of the medical profession.

Nonrecommended Innovations

Most of the research studies completed to date have studied the innovators of potentially successful innovations that are

18. Some of these examples actually concern the deviancy of inventors rather than innovators.

recommended by experts and scientists.[19] Will similar findings result when the innovation is judged as unsuccessful and is not recommended by scientists?

A partial answer is provided by Francis' (1960) study of the adoption of grass incubators. This innovation was manufactured and distributed by commercial concerns; it was not recommended to farmers by agricultural experts because of its cost and its dubious nutritional effects. Francis secured data from a nationwide sample of 88 farmers who had adopted the grass incubator. Only 34 per cent of the incubator owners were also innovators of recommended farm ideas. This finding provides some evidence that certain innovators (of recommended ideas) may also adopt nonrecommended ideas in a rash of venturesomeness, but that they generally discern more carefully between economic and noneconomic innovations.

The innovators who adopted the grass incubator, Francis found, tended to form a cosmopolite reference group composed of other grass incubator owners. The respondents in the grass incubator study exhibited elements of deviancy in their evaluations by peers and in their self-conceptions. It is even possible that innovators of nonrecommended ideas are regarded as deviant by the innovators of recommended ideas.

SUMMARY

Deviation is defined as departure from a social system norm. Deviation is a matter of degree and is relative to a particular social system. Innovators, as the first individuals in a social system to adopt new ideas, are necessarily deviant

19. It should be pointed out that nonrecommended innovations are those falling in the "rational rejection" typology of the paradigm presented in Chapter V.

in their time of adoption. Laggards are deviants as well as innovators, but laggards overconform to traditional ideas (even after the majority of the members of a social system have adopted a new idea), while innovators are underconformers in this regard.

Agricultural innovators were perceived as deviant by other members of their local social system. The degree to which innovators are perceived as deviant depends, in part, upon (1) the social system norms on innovativeness, and (2) the respondent's adopter category. Innovators perceive themselves as deviant from the norms of their local social system. However, agricultural innovators identify with other reference groups outside their community who consensually validate their behavior.

Thus, innovators *are* in step with a different drummer.

CHAPTER VIII

Opinion Leaders and the Flow of Ideas

The influential has arrived! And so has a dramatic new concept of mass media buying! Can you buy word-of-mouth advertising?

Post influence moves sideways—on every income level.

These P. I.'s (*Post* influentials) are the ad man's best friends. Reach them, and they start broadcasting your message like a tomtom beater with St. Vitus' dance.

AN ADVERTISEMENT FOR *The Saturday Evening Post* IN *Mediascope*, 1: 48–49, 1957

Just as it is obvious that all individuals do not adopt an innovation at the same time, so it is obvious also that all persons do not exert an equal amount of influence on the adoption decisions of others. Those individuals who have a greater share of influence are called "opinion leaders" because they take the lead in influencing the opinions of others. Opinion leaders are defined as those individuals from whom others seek advice and information.

The purpose of the present chapter is to describe the two-step flow of communication, to demonstrate the importance of personal influence, to examine methods of measuring opinion leadership, and to summarize what is known about the behavior of opinion leaders.

OPINION LEADERS

Throughout the present chapter, the term "opinion leaders" will be used to refer to individuals who are influential in approving or disapproving new ideas. The following list provides an indication of the variety of terms, other than opinion leaders, many writers have used.

Key communicators (Lionberger, 1960, p. 55)
Leaders (Marsh and Coleman, 1954a)
Informal leaders (Wilkening, 1952b)
Information leaders (Sheppard, 1960a, p. 43)
Adoption leaders (Rogers and Safilios, 1960, pp. 415–418)
Fashion leaders (Katz and Lazarsfeld, 1955, pp. 247–270)
Consumption leaders (Opinion Research Corporation, 1959)
Local influentials (Lionberger, 1953)
Influentials (Merton, 1957, pp. 387–420; and Stewart, 1947)
Influencers (Emery and Oeser, 1958, p. 48)
Tastemakers (Opinion Research Corporation, 1959)
Style setters (Coleman and others, in press)
Sparkplugs (Ross, 1958, p. 71)
Gatekeepers (Lewin, 1952, p. 459)

All of these terms refer to the same basic dimension, opinion leadership. Before these other terms were developed, Lazarsfeld and others (1944, p. 152) utilized the term "opinion leader." Of course, there are as many types of opinion leaders as there are *types* of opinions. For example, opinion leaders in fashions, in politics, and in the adoption of innovations have been studied.[1] There is nevertheless a need to standardize the terminology and the criterion for selection of opinion leaders.

Active and Passive Roles for Adopters and Rejectors

Some adopters are *active* in influencing other individuals to adopt. Others, after their own adoption decision, play a

1. In fact, the term "adoption leaders" is sometimes reserved for the particular type of opinion leaders who influences the adoption of new ideas. In the present chapters, however, this dimension will be referred to as "opinion leadership," a more general term.

passive role in spreading an innovation. Rejectors of an innovation may also be active or passive in communicating their opinion about an innovation to their peers.[2] An example of an active rejector was the farmer, described in Chapter IV, who blamed the death of his cattle upon his use of a new crop fertilizer.

Thus, a two-way classification of individuals in regard to an innovation is possible. Degree of influence is one dimension of analysis, and adoption-rejection is the other. The four cells in the two-by-two table are (1) active adopters,[3] who adopt the innovation and influence others to do so; (2) active rejectors, who reject the innovation and influence others to do so; (3) passive adopters, who adopt the innovation, but do not attempt to influence others to do so; and (4) passive rejectors, who reject the innovation, but do not attempt to influence others to do so. This paradigm is obviously an oversimplification of the rather complex interaction between the adopters of an innovation and those who have not adopted. Change agents seeking to diffuse an innovation may attempt to neutralize the active rejectors. These rejectors view the idea unfavorably and "let everyone know about it." At the same time, change agents may seek to locate the uncommitted opinion leaders and concentrate their promotional efforts upon them. Then the innovation may spread via

2. It should be pointed out that active rejectors may also be opinion leaders. They oppose adoption of the innovation and seek to influence others not to adopt. The respondents in most of the research studies reviewed in the present chapter are probably active adopters rather than active rejectors, although both are opinion leaders. Klapper (1960, p. 35) has pointed out that practically no research attention has been paid to the possible influence of opinion leaders in discouraging change. Several analyses are now under way on the diffusion of fluoridation among U.S. communities. These studies include an investigation of the role of active rejectors who lead the opposition to fluoridation.

3. It is possible that some individuals may actively promote an innovation among their peers even before they have adopted themselves.

word-of-mouth channels from the active adopters to the remainder of the change agent's audience.

An Example of Opinion Leadership Among Physicians

Figure 8-1 illustrates one method by which opinion leaders may be selected; their followers were asked from whom they secured information or advice about an innovation. The data shown in Figure 8-1 come from nine medical doctors in one community (Coleman and others, 1959). Doctor 05 is obviously the key opinion leader in the sociogram. Notice that most of the doctors have discussion relationships with several other doctors shown. This indicates the presence of a clique or network among these doctors. Doctor 05, the opinion leader, adopted a new drug relatively sooner than his eight followers. These physicians' adoption of the innovation probably followed soon after Doctor 05 adopted. On the other hand, if the opinion leader had viewed the new drug unfavorably or had rejected its use, the influence of his opinion would have likely retarded adoption of the innovation among his medical colleagues.

THE TWO-STEP FLOW OF INNOVATION

Sociologists once viewed America as a "mass society" in which mass media communicated in a one-way fashion with individuals who communicated little with each other. The mass media were seen as an all-powerful influence on behavior. A classic study of the 1940 Presidential election by Lazarsfeld and others (1944, p. 151) suggested that this image of modern America needed revision. These authors intended to study the role of mass media in clinching vote de-

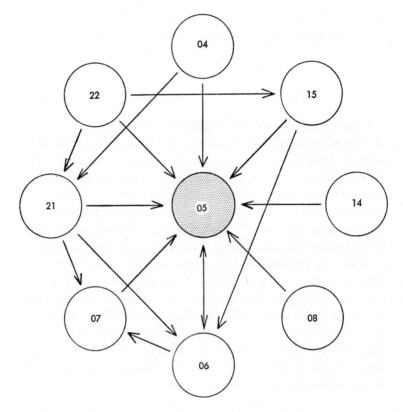

FIGURE 8-1. SOCIOGRAM OF DISCUSSION RELATIONSHIPS
AMONG MEDICAL DOCTORS

This sociogram shows the relationships among nine medical doctors in one community. They were asked to name the doctors with whom they most frequently discussed their cases. Doctor 05 is the key opinion leader in this clique. He is reported as a discussion partner by all eight of his colleagues. Doctor 06 has somewhat less opinion leadership; he is named by three others. This suggests that opinion leadership should be regarded as a matter of degree rather than a dichotomy of leaders and followers.

Source: Data are taken from Coleman and others (1959).

cisions, but actually completed an *ex post facto* analysis of personal influence. They found ". . . that ideas often flow from radio and print to opinion leaders and from these to the less active sections of the population." This so-called two-step flow hypothesis has been used in several studies and, with modification, is probably the most popular framework, explicitly or implicitly, utilized in diffusion research. A reformulation of the two-step flow hypothesis suggests that innovations spread from sources of new ideas via relevant channels to opinion leaders and from them by way of personal communication channels to their followers. It is likely that the first "step," from sources to opinion leaders, is mainly a transfer of information while the second step, from opinion leaders to their followers, may also involve the spread of influence.

The two-step flow hypothesis was not really well documented in the 1940 Presidential election study because the study design did not anticipate the importance of personal influence in voting decisions. The two-step flow of communication is a handy communication model for those studying the diffusion of innovations. A relay function, by which an individual receives new ideas from any relevant source and passes them along to others, is found throughout the diffusion process. Thus, whatever individual one takes as his point of reference in the diffusion process, there is likely to be a receiving and a sending of ideas.

Two major criticisms of the two-step hypothesis need to be mentioned at this point.

1. One criticism of the two-step flow hypothesis is its lack of integration with the idea of stages in the adoption process. Neither the originators nor most of the later students of the two-step flow idea seem to have taken into account the relative importance of the communication sources at different stages in the adoption process. Perhaps most individuals utilize mass media at the awareness stage. At the evaluation stage, personal communications are important for most

adopters. So perhaps the two-step flow hypothesis is simply a restatement of a generalization reported in Chapter IV. Most individuals become aware of innovations from mass media and then proceed to discuss these innovations with peers as they evaluate the idea.[4]

2. Essential to the idea of a two-step flow is a distinction between opinion leaders and their followers. Yet the criterion of opinion leadership varies considerably among the analyses of the two-step flow. In the original Presidential election study, any advice-giver was considered an opinion leader if he influenced only one other person (Katz, 1957). Some later studies have regarded opinion leaders as all individuals named by five or more peers as sources of advice. There is need to standardize the specific criterion of opinion leadership so that the findings of various studies may be more precisely compared.

In summary, transfer of information from person to person may take place as a two-step flow, but the process postulated from mass media to opinion leaders to audience is certainly an oversimplification. It is important to recognize that:

1. Recent research evidence suggests a multistep flow where opinion leaders may influence other opinion leaders and they, in turn, influence their followers. Perhaps models similar to those utilized in organic chemistry to show complex hydrocarbons are needed to depict the chains of influence relationships actually found in the diffusion process.

2. The process is more complex than the two steps first suggested, but there *are* two steps involved in information transmission at any *one point* in the diffusion process. Thus, if one wishes to do so, he may take a dyadic relationship as his unit of analysis in the diffusion process.

4. This argument does not necessarily imply there are no opinion leaders, only that there is no two-step flow hypothesis as it was originally formulated.

THE INTERACTION EFFECT

The proportion of an audience that are active adopters increases as the innovation diffuses through a social system. When an innovation is accepted by 10 per cent, there are relatively few active adopters, but there are many more when saturation reaches 90 per cent. The interaction effect is the process through which individuals in a social system who have adopted an innovation influence those who have not yet adopted.[5] This interaction or "snowball" effect[6] was first described by Ryan and Gross (1943):

There is no doubt but that the behavior of one individual in an interacting population affects the behavior of his fellows. Thus, the demonstrated success of hybrid seed on a few farms offers a changed situation to those who have not been so experimental. The very fact of acceptance by one or more farmers offers new stimulus to the remaining ones.

One investigation of interaction about an idea generated by active adopters was completed by Coleman and others (1957) in a study of a new medical drug (Figure 8-2). The adopter distribution for the opinion leaders was a "chain-reaction" or snowball model which grew as a function of the number of doctors who had already adopted. The adopter distribution for the "isolated" followers (or passive adopters), who received no sociometric choices as opinion leaders, followed a more constant rate of increase. A constant proportion of those who had not yet adopted appeared to do so each month; for example, if 15 per cent adopted during the

5. It should be pointed out that the interaction effect is simply a specific type of diffusion. In fact, the interaction effect and diffusion (defined as the process by which an innovation spreads) are essentially synonymous.

6. Coleman and others (1957) defined the "snowball process" as the process by which the number of individuals adopting an innovation in each time period increases in proportion to those individuals already converted.

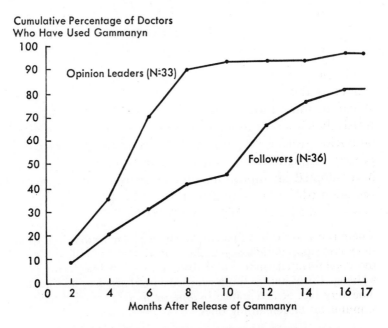

FIGURE 8-2. THE INTERACTION EFFECT CAUSES MORE
RAPID ADOPTION OF A NEW DRUG BY OPINION
LEADERS THAN BY FOLLOWERS

These data from the medical drug study show that opinion leaders are more innovative than followers. When earlier adopters talk to later adopters about a new idea, the rate of adoption proceeds more quickly than when this communication does not occur. The opinion leaders received three or more sociometric choices as social friends, while the followers shown above received no choices. The reader should be cautioned that very small samples of respondents are shown in this figure.

Source: Coleman and others (1957). Used by permission.

first month, then 15 per cent of those remaining should adopt the second month, and so on. The researchers interpreted the shape of the two adopter distributions to signify that interpersonal communication affects the rate of adoption of an idea.[7] In other words, when earlier adopters talk to later adopters about a new idea, the rate of adoption proceeds more quickly than when this communication does not occur.[8]

The interaction effect is generally similar to the process by which an infectious disease such as scarlet fever, diphtheria, or measles spreads through a social system. Bailey (1957, pp. 15–22) analyzes the infection process in terms of "infectives" (similar to active adopters of a new idea), "susceptibles" (those who are yet not infected), "removals" by death or isolation (similar to passive adopters), and the "incubation period" (similar to the adoption period). One of the interests of epidemiologists is predicting the point in a social system at which a disease becomes an epidemic. There is close theoretical similarity of the infection process to the diffusion process. Perhaps some of the complex mathematical equations obtained for different types of epidemics by Bailey (1957) might be fitted to the diffusion of innovations.[9]

IMPORTANCE OF PERSONAL INFLUENCE

Personal influence has been found to be an essential ingredient in all types of decision-making. *Personal influence* is defined as communication involving a direct face-to-face

7. If these data in Figure 8-2 are looked at in another way, they simply tell us that opinion leaders are more innovative than their followers.

8. It was shown in Chapter V that the amount of interaction about hybrid seed corn was more important in explaining its year-to-year rate of adoption than was profitability (Havens and Rogers, 1961b).

9. Rapoport (1956) and Karlsson (1958) attempted to develop mathematical diffusion models, but these models have not been tested empirically.

exchange between the communicator and the receiver, which results in changed behavior or attitudes on the part of the receiver.[10]

Opinion leaders are really ". . . men who exert personal influence upon a certain number of other people in certain situations" (Merton, 1957, p. 410). The definition of personal influence implies a relationship between people. Influence is not an abstract attribute of an individual; it is a *process* involving two or more people.[11]

Since its original "discovery" in the 1940 Presidential election study, several investigations have provided evidence of the crucial significance of personal influence in decision-making:

Katz and Lazarsfeld concluded that their consumer study found that personal influence figured both more frequently and more effectively in decisions than any of the mass media (1955, pp. 169–186). The extent of opinion leadership, as measured by the number of sociometric relationships, was more highly related to time of adoption of a new drug by medical doctors than any other factor studied (Coleman and others, 1957). Rahudkar (1958) found that neighbor-to-neighbor communication was of greater importance in the diffusion of farm innovations than any other communication channel in his study of India's villagers. Many of the respond-

10. This definition is based upon that of Rogers and Beal (1958a) and Merton (1957, p. 415) who stated, "Interpersonal influence refers to the direct interaction of persons in so far as this affects the *future* behavior or attitude of participants (such that this differs from what it would have been in the absence of interaction)." It should be pointed out that personal influence is more properly referred to as "interpersonal influence."

11. More research attention probably has been paid to those doing the influencing than to those being influenced. Recent laboratory experiments indicate that some individuals are considerably more persuadable than others (Klapper, 1960, p. 95). In any event, it is often empirically difficult to separate the roles of influencer and influencee. An individual may act first as a source of influence in a conversation, then as an influencee, and finally as an influencer again.

ents were illiterates or poorly educated and hence were unable to use mass media communications. Beal and Rogers (1957a) found word-of-mouth communication was more important than any other type of information source in convincing Iowa homemakers to purchase new fabrics of Orlon, Dacron, and nylon.

These findings and others have convinced most students of diffusion that it is impossible to ignore social relations in studying the spread of innovations. In fact, after an innovation is adopted by 10 to 20 per cent of an audience, it may be impossible to halt its further spread.

When Is Personal Influence from Peers Most Important?

Although personal influence is important throughout the diffusion process, it is of relatively greater significance in certain situations and for certain individuals than for others. The purpose of this section is to enumerate generalizations about the relative importance of personal influence that emanates from *peers*. These peers may be a medical doctor's colleagues, a farmer's neighbors, or a business executive's friends. It is expected that opinion leadership is largely exerted through personal influence from peers.[12]

1. EVALUATION STAGE. *Personal Influence from Peers Is Most Important at the Evaluation Stage in the Adoption Process and Less Important at Other Stages.* It has already been pointed out in a previous chapter that personal sources of communication (of all kinds) are most im-

12. In terms of the present definitions of personal influence and of opinion leadership, it is consistent to regard all personal influence from peers as coming from opinion leaders. Any peer that exerts influence is an opinion leader to some degree.

portant at the evaluation stage in the adoption process. Hence, peers are expected to wield their greatest degree of influence at the evaluation stage in the adoption process. This is where personal influences of all types (from change agents and from peers) have their greatest impact in the adoption process.

In Figure 8-3, the importance of peer influences has been separated from that of other types of personal influences. It is plain that influences flowing from peers have their greatest effect at the evaluation stage for both of the innovations.[13] Figure 8-3 also suggests that peer influences are of greater importance in the case of certain innovations than of others. For example, peer influences were more important than change agent influences at each stage in the adoption process for "miracle" fabrics. However, personal influence from commercial change agents was reported more often than peer influences in the case of antibiotic swine supplements (Beal and Rogers, 1960, p. 8).

2. LATER ADOPTERS. *Personal Influence from Peers Is More Important for Relatively Later Adopters Than for Earlier Adopters.* This dimension of analysis cannot be shown in Figure 8-3. It is probably equal in significance to differences in the importance of peer influences on the basis of adoption stage. Peer influences are much more important for laggards than for innovators and early adopters at each adoption stage. It was pointed out in Chapter IV that relatively earlier adopters are less likely to depend on personal influence of all types than are later adopters. The earlier adopters, even when influenced by personal sources, are

13. Support for this statement also comes from Rahim (1961). It should be cautioned that the importance of peers at the evaluation stage may result from their being one of the last communication sources used, and hence they are most easily recalled by respondents in research interviews (Sheppard, in press).

Per Cent of Information Sources
that are Personal Influence from Peers

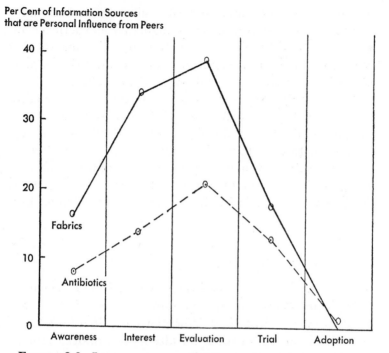

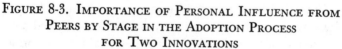

FIGURE 8-3. IMPORTANCE OF PERSONAL INFLUENCE FROM
PEERS BY STAGE IN THE ADOPTION PROCESS
FOR TWO INNOVATIONS

This figure shows that personal influence from peers is most important at the evaluation stage in the adoption process. It is at this
stage that opinion leaders have their greatest influence in the adoption process. Peer influences are also much more important for laggards
than for innovators and early adopters, although this dimension of
analysis is not shown. Data come from 148 farm operators and their
wives in one Iowa rural community. The innovations traced above are
"miracle" clothing fabrics and antibiotics for swine feeding.

Source: A reanalysis of Beal and Rogers (1957a and 1960, p. 8).

more likely to report that this personal influence comes from
change agents than from peers (Rogers and Beal, 1958a; and
Rahim, 1961, p. 43). This finding might be expected because

at the time the innovators and early adopters are deciding to use a new idea, fewer of their colleagues have experience and opinions about the innovation. But, by the time the late majority and laggards adopt, they are surrounded by legions of peers who have already adopted the new idea.[14]

One investigation is selected to illustrate the generalization under discussion, Bowers' (1938) analysis of a national sample of 312 ham radio operators. The innovators, who adopted before 1916, reported that 23 per cent of the influences leading to their adoption of ham radios came from peers. Those who adopted after 1925 reported that 51 per cent of the influences leading to their adoption came from peers.

(3.) UNCERTAIN SITUATIONS. *Personal Influence from Peers Is More Important in Uncertain Situations Than Clear-Cut Situations.* When an individual feels he has adequate information about the alternatives in decision-making, he is less likely to depend upon the opinions of his peers. However, when uncertainty prevails, he feels a need for reinforcement of his opinion through personal interaction with his peers.

Support for this generalization is provided by several research studies, although there is probably less direct evidence for this third statement than for the two previous generalizations.

Menzel and Katz (1955) reported that physicians depended more upon their colleagues when using new drugs

14. The accuracy or fidelity of the ideas after several tellings may be quite low. Copp and others (1958) pointed out that " . . . learning of a practice from relatives and other farmers is somewhat analogous to lifting oneself by one's boot straps, for ego's peers are not likely to be much better informed than ego." Interaction about an idea three- or four-hands removed from its source may amount to pooling of ignorance.

under ambiguous situations than when using drug innovations under more clear-cut circumstances. Coleman and others (1957), in another investigation of new drugs, found that ". . . A doctor will be influenced more by what his colleagues say or do in uncertain situations, whenever and wherever they may occur, then in clear-cut situations." Wilkening and others (1960) found Australian farmers depended more on personal influence from peers for innovations associated with greater economic risk. Van den Ban (1961b) found that 62 per cent of the pairs of friends he interviewed in the Netherlands had the same brand of milking machine. The probability by chance of both friends having the same model is only 15 per cent. The choice of a brand by a farmer is a very ambiguous decision because it is difficult to say that one model is better than another.

In summary, personal influences from peers are relatively more important (1) at the evaluation stage in the adoption process rather than other stages, (2) for later adopters rather than earlier adopters, and (3) in unclear situations rather than in clear-cut situations.

FUNCTIONS OF PERSONAL INFLUENCE

It has been established that individuals in decision-making situations usually rely heavily upon personal influence from others. This is particularly true when they are deciding whether to accept or reject an innovation. What are the functions performed by personal influence at each stage in the adoption process?

1. Awareness of an innovation may be created by personal influence from others. However, for most individuals, awareness is caused by impersonal communications such as mass

media. Personal influence is apt to be more important in making the relatively later adopters aware of an innovation than in creating awareness for innovators and early adopters.

2. Once formed, opinions about an innovation are reinforced by interaction with others. In the face of a high degree of uncertainty, most individuals wish to validate their opinions with those of others. Thus, personal influence not only helps to determine original opinions about an innovation at the awareness stage, but also consensually validates this opinion once it is formed.

3. Norms on innovativeness are generally communicated to group members via personal influence networks. These norms probably are most important at the evaluation stage where the individual is deciding whether or not to try the new idea.

4. A performance comparison of the innovation with existing ideas may be communicated from peers. This function of personal influence is most important at the trial stage of the adoption process. In fact, for those innovations that are not divisible for trial, personal influence from peers may in some ways replace a small-scale trial.

Thus, personal influence plays a somewhat different function at each stage of the adoption process.

Selectivity

Another way to view the functions performed by personal influence is in terms of three rather basic social-psychological processes (1) selective exposure, (2) selective perception, and (3) selective retention.[15] The three social-psychological processes are:

15. This discussion owes an intellectual ancestory to Lazarsfeld and others (1944), Rogers and Beal (1958a), Klapper (1960), Havens and Rogers (1961a), and, most of all, to van den Ban (1961b).

1. *Selective exposure* or the tendency for individuals to expose themselves to communications that agree with their existing opinions. Thus, it has been found that Democrats seldom watch Republican-sponsored television programs. Likewise, the members of an audience that a venereal-disease control campaign was designed to help most exposed themselves to campaign literature the least.

2. *Selective perception* or the tendency for individuals to interpret a new idea in terms of their past experience and existing opinions. For example, a new fertilizer may be perceived as a means to higher crop yields by an innovative farmer, but the same fertilizer may be perceived as a dangerous chemical powder by another farmer with different attitudes, values, and knowledge. The important point, of course, is that decisions are made by the individual on the basis of his perceptions, whether they are accurate or not.

3. *Selective retention* or the tendency for individuals to remember ideas that agree with their existing opinions. Thus, a physician may read hundreds of medical journal articles about new drugs but most of these leave little impression in the doctor's memory. News about a drug that promises to solve one of the physician's difficult cases, however, likely will be remembered, and perhaps adoption of the pharmaceutical innovation will eventually result.

These processes tend to inhibit the effectiveness of mass media campaigns designed to change opinions. Why is personal influence more likely to overcome these three barriers to communication effectiveness than are mass media messages?

1. Exposure to personal influence is often less selective than exposure to mass media. When one meets a friend, he does not know in advance what new ideas will be discussed.[16]

16. Deutschmann's (1961) analysis of the 1960 Nixon-Kennedy television debates indicates that personal conversations about the debates the following day reached many individuals who avoided watching the debate broadcasts.

2. When an individual misinterprets what you are saying, by perceiving only those parts of your message that agree with his existing opinions, you usually will grasp his misunderstanding and try to correct him. The communicator of a mass message is seldom in such a position to correct misunderstandings.

3. Personal discussions allow one to remind an individual about a new idea on several occasions even though he may not be initially interested in the innovation. Thus, selective retention may more readily be overcome by personal influence than by mass media.

DISTRIBUTION OF INFLUENCE

Opinion leadership is a fairly widespread trait, even though it is especially concentrated in a few individuals. Influence is a matter of degree and should properly be viewed as a continuous variable, rather than as a dichotomy of "leaders" and "followers." Some individuals are looked to for advice by many of their peers; others are asked for their opinions about an innovation by only a few.

One illustration of the distribution of influence is Rogers' (1955) study of 148 Iowa farmers living in one community. They were asked to whom they went for information and advice about farm innovations.[17] All but 43 of the 148 farmers

17. This type of question is undoubtedly at best an indirect means of assessing influence relationships. However, when the more direct question, "Who influences you to adopt farm innovations?" was asked in pretest interviews, the socially acceptable response of "no one" was received in most cases. When an individual asks a peer for information, he probably receives information and is at the same time influenced. The distinction between influence and information, while conceptually clear, is not always a sharp one in the empirical research studies reviewed in the present chapter.

had some degree of sociometric influence,[18] that is, they were named by at least one of their neighbors as an opinion leader. Fifty-one of the farmers received one sociometric choice, 28 received two, 13 received three, 7 received four, 4 received five, 1 received six, and 1 received seven choices. Thus, opinion leadership is a fairly widespread trait, even though it is especially concentrated in a very few individuals. The distribution of influence in the Iowa study generally is similar to that found in a number of other investigations of farmers.[19] These studies also provide evidence that opinion leadership is a matter of degree.

The Iowa data suggest one of the difficulties with the sociometric method of measuring opinion leadership. In addition to Rogers' (1955) 105 farmers with some sociometric influence, 97 individuals who resided outside of the community

18. It should be cautioned that the exact degree of concentration of opinion leadership depends partly upon such methodological points as the wording of the sociometric question and the number of sociometric choices allowed each respondent, and upon the social system's norms. For example, van den Ban (in press) asked three opinion leadership questions (with each worded differently) of a sample of Netherlands farmers. When the opinion leadership question was asked in one way, 64 per cent of the community residents received no sociometric choices, but when the opinion leadership question was asked in two other ways, 55 per cent and 32 per cent of the respondents, respectively, received no sociometric choices. There are certainly variations in the concentration of opinion leadership from one social system to another, just as the concentration of wealth varies from community to community. Perhaps there is a need to develop a standard measure of the concentration of opinion leadership in a social system. Such a measure might be somewhat similar in construction to the Gini ratio, an index of the concentration of incomes in a social system. This measure of opinion leadership concentration could then become the dependent variable in a research study in which social systems would be the units of analysis.

19. Among these studies are those of Lionberger (1953), Chaparro (1956), Wilkening (1958d, p. 376), Emery and Oeser (1958, p. 46), Wilkening and others (1960), van den Ban (in press), and Rogers and Burdge (1961 and 1962). Similar evidence that opinion leadership occurs as a continuous variable and as a positively skewed distribution is provided by a reanalysis of the Katz and Lazarsfeld (1955, p. 376) data.

boundaries were named as leaders. At the same time, there were obviously farmers living outside the area of study who chose opinion leaders within the community. However, these sociometric choices from outside the social system were not determined in the Iowa study because only the 148 farmers living within the community were interviewed. In short, the weakness of the Iowa study of farmer opinion leadership (and of the majority of other research studies) is that they ignore cosmopolite influence relationships.[20] It is possible, and likely, that an individual regarded as influential by his peers is not so regarded by individuals outside his social system. Likewise, an individual whose influence extends outside of his social system tends to be short-changed by the usual sociometric accounting of opinion leadership.

MEASURING OPINION LEADERSHIP

There are three main methods of measuring opinion leadership:

1. The *sociometric* technique consists of asking group members to whom they go for advice and information about an idea. A great number of respondents must be interrogated to locate a small number of opinion leaders. This method is probably more applicable to a research design where all members of a social system are interviewed, rather than where a relatively small sample within a larger universe is contacted. The sociometric method has been utilized more often in past research than any other method. Typical studies utilizing the sociometric method are Lionberger

20. Merton's (1957) data suggest there are two different types of opinion leaders, cosmopolites and localites, although he did not trace cosmopolite influence relationships from outside of the social system he studied.

(1953), Wilkening (1952b and 1958d), Marsh and Coleman (1954), Rogers (1955), Menzel and Katz (1955), Sheppard (1960a), Rogers and Burdge (1961), Rahim (1961), Coleman and others (1957), Wilkening and others (1960 and 1961), Chaparro (1956), van den Ban (in press), and Rogers and Burdge (1962).[21]

2. *Key informants* in a social system may be asked to designate the opinion leaders. The informants are selected subjectively as persons likely to know who the opinion leaders are. A similar use of key informants or "raters" has been made in social stratification studies to determine the prestige ratings of local people. Key informants are usually cost-saving and time-saving when compared to sociometric methods; however, both techniques suffer equally from lack of applicability to sample designs where only a portion of an audience is interviewed. Chaparro (1955) utilized the key informant method in a Costa Rica study, and van den Ban (in press) used the method in three Netherlands farm communities.[22]

3. The *self-designating* technique consists of asking a respondent a series of questions to determine the degree to which he perceives himself to be an opinion leader.[23] This method is dependent upon the accuracy with which respondents can identify and report their self-images. One advantage

21. Studies using the sociometric method to locate opinion leaders other than for innovations are Merton (1957), Stewart (1947), and many others.

22. Van den Ban (in press) asked six or seven farmers in each of the three communities to rate all the farmers in their community as to degree of opinion leadership on a ten-point scale. There was a generally high degree of agreement among the judges' ratings, although they were made independently. Correlations of the pooled judges' ratings with a sociometric measure of opinion leadership were .46, .64, and .66 in the three communities, respectively.

23. Katz and Lazarsfeld (1955, pp. 149–161, 353–362), Sokol (1959), Abelson and Rugg (1958), and Lazarsfeld and others (1944) utilized the self-designating technique, but not to locate opinion leaders for innovations.

of the self-designating technique is that it measures the individual's perceptions of his opinion leadership, which is actually what affects his behavior. As the W. I. Thomas theorem states, if men define situations as real, they are real in their consequences.

One study utilizing the self-designating method will be reviewed in some detail at this point.

A Self-Designating Opinion Leadership Scale

A serious weakness in previous uses[24] of the self-designating technique is the small number of items included in the opinion leadership scale. For example, only two questions were included in the original political opinion leadership scale: (1) "Have you recently tried to convince anyone of your political ideas?" and (2) "Has anyone recently asked you for your advice on a political question?" The distribution of scores on this simple opinion leadership scale were dichotomized into "leaders" and "followers."

A modification of the two items used in previous studies plus an additional four questions were utilized in a study of the diffusion of new farm ideas among Ohio farmers (Rogers, 1957c). Personal interviews were completed with a statewide random area sample of 104 farm operators. The self-designating opinion leadership scale consisted of six items:

1. During the past six months have you told anyone about some new farming practice?

2. Compared with your circle of friends (a) are you more or (b) are you less likely to be asked for advice about new farming practices?

3. Thinking back to your last discussion about some new farm practices, (a) were you asked for your opinion of the new practice or (b) did you ask someone else?

24. Such as Lazarsfeld and others (1944).

4. When you and your friends discuss new ideas about farm practices, what part do you play? (a) mainly listen or (b) try to convince them of your ideas?

5. Which of these happens more often, (a) do you tell your neighbors about some new farm practice, or (b) do they tell you about a new practice?

6. Do you have the feeling that you are generally regarded by your friends and neighbors as a good source of advice about new farm practices?

These six items yielded a higher reliability than the two-item scale used in previous studies.[25] The greater reliability of the six-item scale is consistent with the general principle that higher reliability can be obtained by lengthening a scale. There is some evidence[26] that the scale measures a single dimension and does not overlap with other self-perceptions.

The sociometric technique of selecting opinion leaders was utilized as one validity check on the self-designating opinion leadership scale. Each of the respondent's neighbors was asked from whom he would seek advice and information about farm innovations. Respondents who received one or more sociometric choices had significantly higher scores on the self-designating opinion leadership scale.[27]

25. For example, the Katz and Lazarsfeld (1955, pp. 376–377) scale yielded a test-retest reliability of .149 and a split-half reliability of .486 for public affairs opinion leaders. The present six-item opinion leadership scale yielded a split-half reliability of .703. A test-retest reliability of .238 and a split-half reliability of .563 were computed for the Katz and Lazarsfeld fashion opinion leaders.

26. The opinion leadership scale was subjected to a Guttman scale analysis to determine the degree to which the scale measured a single dimension. A coefficient of reproducibility of 91.4 per cent provides some evidence of the unidimensionality of the six-item scale. Items number 1, 3, and 4 ask respondents about their past behavior while items 2, 5, and 6 are more directly concerned with self-perceptions; nevertheless, the items appear to measure a single dimension.

27. Correlation between the number of sociometric choices and opinion leadership scores is .225. One reason for this relatively low relationship may be found in the crude nature of the sociometric data.

The available evidence indicates that the six-item self-designating opinion leadership scale is reliable, valid, and unidimensional. It may be administered in less than five minutes of a research interview. The nature of the items suggests they may be adapted to studies of almost any type of opinion leadership.

WHAT IS KNOWN ABOUT OPINION LEADERS

The undertaking of the present section is to synthesize the research evidence from several investigations of opinion leaders. In this section, and much of the remainder of the chapter, "opinion leaders" and "followers" will be referred to as if the degree of opinion leadership were a dichotomy.[28] This oversimplification is for the sake of clarity. Opinion

---

Often only one or two of a respondent's neighbors were asked who they regarded as an opinion leader in their neighborhood. This was done because the sample was composed of small area clusters.

In a study of 76 vegetable growers in one Ohio county, Rogers and Burdge (1962) utilized both sociometric choices and the self-designating measure of opinion leadership. The two methods were correlated .408 which is significant at the 1 per cent level. In a recent study of 145 dairy farmers in Central Ohio, the three methods of measuring opinion leaders were utilized (Havens, 1962). The self-designating opinion leadership scores were correlated .300 with the number of sociometric choices and .640 with composite opinion leadership ratings by four key informants. The number of sociometric choices correlated .876 with the composite key informants' ratings. All three correlations were significant at the one per cent level.

Stewart (1947) provides some evidence of the similarity of results obtained when both the sociometric and self-designating techniques are utilized. Katz and Lazarsfeld (1955, pp. 149—161, 353—362) also found their two-item opinion leadership scale was validated by sociometric data. Abelson and Rugg (1958) demonstrated that a self-designating measure of political opinion leadership was positively related to degree of political activity for a national sample of 1,059 U.S. businessmen.

28. The "followers" should more accurately be termed "nonleaders."

leadership is actually a matter of degree. The following generalizations about opinion leaders will each be discussed in detail.

Opinion leaders conform more closely to social system norms than the average member. There is little overlapping among the different types of opinion leaders. For example, an individual who is an opinion leader for innovations is not likely to be also influential in political affairs. Opinion leaders differ from their followers in information sources, cosmopoliteness, social participation, social status, and innovativeness.

Conformity to Norms

Opinion leaders have often been found to be just like their followers, only more so. *Opinion leaders conform more closely to social system norms than the average member.* Homans (1950, p. 427) stated, "The leader must live up to the norms of the group—all the norms—better than any follower."

One evidence of this generalization comes from a 1950 study of 13 Kentucky neighborhoods by Marsh and Coleman (1954a).[29] Their conclusions suggest that leaders do not deviate very far from the system's norms (Figure 8-4). In modern neighborhoods, the leaders were much more innovative than their followers. The leaders in traditional neighborhoods were relatively less innovative, as compared to their followers.

Another test of this generalization comes from an investigation of 83 truck growers residing in seven different communities by Rogers and Burdge (1962). The seven com-

29. The Marsh and Coleman study, and several closely related investigations, will come under more detailed scrutiny in a later section where the degree of opinion leadership by adopter category is discussed.

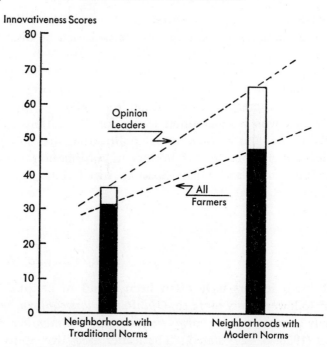

Innovativeness Scores

FIGURE 8-4. INNOVATIVENESS SCORES OF OPINION LEADERS
AND FOLLOWERS IN NEIGHBORHOODS WITH TRADITIONAL
AND MODERN NORMS

These data suggest that opinion leaders do not deviate very far from
the norms of the social system. The innovativeness scores of leaders
in the traditional neighborhoods were only slightly higher (five points)
than their followers, while leaders in the modern neighborhoods were
18 points ahead of their followers. Where the neighborhood norms
encourage innovativeness, opinion leaders place an even higher value
on innovativeness. But where the neighborhood norms discourage innovativeness, the leaders tend to reflect this value also.

Data come from 393 farmers in 13 neighborhoods in Washington
County, Kentucky, who were interviewed as to their adoption of 21
farm innovations. The neighborhoods were categorized into (1) modern
neighborhoods, and (2) traditional neighborhoods. Leaders were selected within each neighborhood by sociometric methods of asking
respondents to indicate which farmers they sought for information.

Source: An illustration of data from March and Coleman (1954a).
Used by permission.

munities offered a wide range in their norms.[30] A deviancy-from-norms score was computed for each opinion leader and follower by a ratio of the absolute difference between the respondent's innovativeness score and the community norm, to the range in all innovativeness scores in the community.[31] In other words, this measure of deviancy indicated how far the individual's behavior deviated from social system norms. The deviancy scores for opinion leaders averaged .101 and for their followers averaged .617. The opinion leaders conformed much more closely to community norms than did the followers.

Further evidence of the generalization that opinion leaders conform more closely to social system norms than the average member is provided by van den Ban's (in press) study of three Netherlands farm communities.[32] The norms in two of the communities were modern, and the correlation in these communities between opinion leadership and innovativeness was .48. However, in the third community, whose norms were traditional, the correlation between opinion leadership and innovativeness was .34.[33] In other words, when

30. Community norms were measured by averaging the innovativeness scores of the farmers residing in each community (as was discussed in Chapter III).

31. When expressed in equation form, the deviancy score $= \dfrac{|X_1 - X_n|}{\sigma}$ where $X_1 =$ each respondent's innovativeness score; $X_n =$ community norms on innovativeness for the community in which the respondent lives (the individual's innovativeness score was not included in computing the mean community innovativeness score to avoid possible redundancy); $\sigma =$ standard deviation of the innovativeness scores in the respondent's community.

32. Some caution should be exerted about the present generalization which, although it is reasonable on social-psychological grounds and is supported by the findings of Marsh and Coleman (1954a), Rogers and Burdge (1962), and van den Ban (in press), is not supported by the findings of Rahudkar (1960) or Lionberger (1960, p. 61) as will be shown later in this chapter.

33. The difference between these correlations is in the expected direction, but is not significant at the 5 per cent level.

the community norms were modern and favored innovativeness, the opinion leaders were more innovative than when the community norms were traditional.

Lack of Overlap

Merton (1957, pp. 413–415) pointed out that opinion leaders may differ as to the breadth of their spheres of influence. Some opinion leaders, termed "monomorphic" by Merton, exert their influence only in one rather narrowly defined area such as politics or fashion. Other opinion leaders are "polymorphic." They exert influence in a number of areas.

The majority of the research findings indicates *there is little overlapping among the different types of opinion leaders.* For example, Katz and Lazarsfeld (1955, p. 334) concluded:

The fact that a woman is a leader in one area has no bearing on the likelihood that she will be a leader in another. . . . By and large, . . . the hypothesis of a generalized leader receives little support in this study. There is no overlap in any of the pairs of activities. Each area, it seems, has a corps of leaders of its own.

Two studies dealing directly with opinion leaders of innovations support the generalization that most opinion leaders are monomorphic. Emery and Oeser (1958, p. 51) concluded, "Thus the three outstanding men [opinion leaders on farm innovations] are not leaders in local politics or other community affairs." Ryan (1942) found that farmers influential in farm innovations were different from church opinion leaders or from leaders on school issues.

Perhaps in less developed countries and in other social systems where the norms are traditional, opinion leaders are more likely to be polymorphic than monomorphic. There is probably a greater separation of roles in more developed societies than in traditional societies. Hence, a greater degree of overlap among the different types of opinion leaders in social sytems with more traditional norms is expected. In an investigation of a Pakistani village, Rahim (1961, p. 60) found that many of the farm opinion leaders were also the formal leaders of the village, although there was not complete overlap. However, Rahudkar (1961) found in a study of 339 farmers in Central India that the village headman was seldom influential in farmers' decisions to adopt new farm ideas. Further research is needed to determine more exactly the relationship of social system norms to the degree of overlap of different types of opinion leaders.

While opinion leaders of innovations do not overlap with other types of influentials, there is less evidence available to indicate whether opinion leaders for one innovation are also opinion leaders for other innovations. Wilkening and others (1962) found that Australian farmers sought different opinion leaders for information about different types of innovations. The leaders for dairy innovations were not the same, in many cases, as those for hog, pasture, or irrigation ideas. However, the same opinion leader was often sought for information about closely related ideas such as pastures and irrigation.

Opinion Leaders Differ from Followers

Opinion leaders differ from their followers in information sources, cosmopoliteness, social participation, social status, and innovativeness.[34]

34. It should be cautioned that the characteristics of opinion leaders depend in part upon (1) the type of sociometric question asked or other opinion leadership measurement technique used, and (2) the social system norms, as van den Ban (in press) has demonstrated.

INFORMATION SOURCES. *Opinion leaders use more impersonal, technically accurate, and cosmopolite sources of information than do their followers.* The mass media are generally more accurate sources of information about innovations than is personal communication. There is less chance of message distortion by mass media than when new ideas are transmitted from person to person.

Lionberger (1953) found that more influential farmers subscribed to a greater number of farm magazines and newspapers. Menzel and Katz (1955) reported that more influential medical doctors were most likely to receive information about drug innovations from professional journals. Rogers (1955) found farmer opinion leaders subscribed to more farm magazines and papers, and watched more TV farm shows than their followers.

Rahim (1961, p. 58) found farm opinion leaders in a Pakistani village made greater use of such printed media as magazines, newspapers, and Extension Service bulletins.

Not only do opinion leaders make greater use of the mass media,[35] but they also tend to seek other technically accurate information sources. For example, farm opinion leaders have more contact with county extension agents than do farmers with less influence.[36] Emery and Oeser's (1958) study of Australian farmers illustrates the relatively greater communication of opinion leaders with extension change agents. Most of the farmers without extension contact communicated with an opinion leader who had extension contact, although this is not necessarily true in other communities that have been studied.

35. This statement is also supported by findings from studies of other types of opinion leaders. Lazarsfeld and others (1944, p. 51), Katz and Lazarsfeld (1955, pp. 311–318), and Berelson and others (1954, p. 111) all reported that opinion leaders had relatively greater exposure to mass media than did their followers.

36. Evidence is provided by Emery and Oeser (1958, pp. 49–53), Rogers and Capener (1960), Rogers and Burdge (1962), and van den Ban (1961 and in press).

Probably the most direct means for farmers to secure technical information is to contact agricultural scientists at state colleges. Both Rogers (1955), and Rogers and Burdge (1961 and 1962) found that opinion leaders were more likely to have direct contact with agricultural scientists than were their followers (see Figure 8-5). The fact that farm opinion leaders have (1) greater extension contact and (2) more direct communication with agricultural scientists suggests that opinion leaders utilize more cosmopolite information sources than their followers. Messages emanating from outside the social system are often, but not necessarily, more technically accurate than are localite sources.[37]

The information sources utilized by opinion leaders and followers have been compared, but not while controlling on the stage in the adoption process. This type of analysis needs to be completed.

COSMOPOLITENESS. Not only are opinion leaders more cosmopolite in their communication behavior but also in other types of social relationships.[38] *Opinion leaders are more cosmopolite than their followers.*

Katz (1957) reported that among his sample of medical doctors, the opinion leaders were more likely to participate in out-of-town medical meetings. Lionberger (1953) found that his farm opinion leaders tended to belong to formal organizations located outside (rather than inside) the rural

37. Some indirect evidence that opinion leaders utilize more cosmopolite information sources was found by Rogers and Leuthold (1961). More direct support for the generalization is provided by Rogers and Burdge (1962) and by van den Ban (in press).

38. Katz and Lazarsfeld (1955, pp. 243–300) reported that their fashion leaders and public affairs leaders, but not their movie or marketing opinion leaders, were more cosmopolite in their reading of books and magazines than were the less influential. Stewart (1947) found little relationship between the degree of influence an individual possessed and his cosmopoliteness.

Missouri community in which they lived. Rogers (1955) found that the more influential Iowa farmers in his sample were more cosmopolite in their friendships, formal organization attendance, and reading behavior.

Van den Ban (in press) found that farm opinion leaders in the Netherlands had many more contacts with urban centers during the preceding year than did their followers. This relationship between the degree of opinion leadership and cosmopoliteness held for each of three communities he studied, but opinion leadership was more closely related to cosmopoliteness in the modern communities than in the community with more traditional norms. These findings again demonstrate the point that the characteristics of opinion leaders vary somewhat on the basis of the norms of the social system. Rahudkar (1960) concluded that the opinion leaders in the Indian villages he studied had more informal and formal contacts outside the village than did their followers.

Thus, opinion leaders form a communication link with sources outside of the social system and provide an avenue for the entrance of new ideas.

SOCIAL PARTICIPATION. In order for opinion leaders to pass along their personal messages about innovations, they must have direct contact with their followers. That is, opinion leaders must be accessible. Accessibility is the degree to which an individual is socially and physically available for social interaction. Face-to-face communication contacts could be expected to occur both at meetings of formal organizations and through informal discussion.

Lionberger (1953) and van den Ban (in press) found farm opinion leaders had greater participation in formal organizations than did farmers with less influence. Rogers (1955) concluded that opinion leaders had a greater degree of both formal and informal social participation. Rahim (1961, p. 58) reported that opinion leaders in a Pakistani village were members of more organizations than their followers. Van den Ban (in press) found opinion leaders had more formal participation than followers in each of three Netherlands communities he studied. *Opinion leaders have more social participation than their followers.*[39] Opinion leaders, however, are not necessarily the powerholders or the formal leaders in their communities.

SOCIAL STATUS. When individuals are asked to specify persons to whom they go for advice and information, it might be expected that they would name opinion leaders with a somewhat higher social status than their own.[40] On the other hand, it is unlikely that individuals would seek opinions from those who have a much higher social status.[41] These higher status individuals can no longer serve as a somewhat comparable "role model." Nevertheless, a generalization is plain from the available research findings: *opinion leaders have higher social status than their followers.*

39. This statement is also supported by Merton (1957), Stewart (1947), Berelson and others (1954, p. 113), and Katz and Lazarsfeld (1955, pp. 243–300).

40. Findings from investigations of opinion leaders (in areas other than innovativeness) have not yielded completely consistent findings on the relative social status of opinion leaders. For example, see Katz and Lazarsfeld (1955, p. 273), Stewart (1947), Lazarsfeld and others (1944, p. 50), and Berelson and others (1954, p. 113). These inconsistent findings may be the result of differences in the communities studied.

41. Tarde (1903, pp. 221–224) recognized that opinion leaders should ideally have higher social status than their followers, but not "too much" higher. "Invention can start from the lowest ranks of the people, but its extension depends upon the existence of some lofty social elevation, a kind of social *water-tower,* whence a continuous water-fall of imitation may descend. . . . The influence of the model's example is efficacious inversely to its *distance* as well as directly to its superiority. *Distance* is understood here in its sociological meaning."

Lionberger (1959) found that farm opinion leaders were generally distributed throughout the social class structure but were concentrated in the upper part. On the average each farmer tended to seek advice from opinion leaders who were slightly above him in social status, but not "out of sight" (Lionberger and Coughenour, 1957). In another study, Lionberger (1953) reported that opinion leaders were more likely to own their farm, to live on a relatively larger farm, to earn a higher gross farm income, and to have higher community prestige. Chaparro (1956) found that opinion leaders had higher status than followers in four Costa Rica communities. Fliegel (1957) found opinion leaders earned annual farm incomes that were about 40 per cent higher than the average farmer's. Emery and Oeser (1958, pp. 49–53), Rahim (1961, p. 58), van den Ban (in press), and Rogers and Burdge (1962) stated that farm influentials operated larger farms. Rogers (1955 and 1957c) concluded that opinion leaders had larger farms, higher farm incomes, and higher social status than followers.

INNOVATIVENESS. If opinion leaders are to be widely recognized as experts on innovations, it is likely that they adopt (or reject) new ideas before their followers. The available research evidence indicates that *opinion leaders are more innovative than their followers.*[42]

Katz (1957) found that doctors who were influential in convincing their colleagues to adopt a new medical drug were, themselves, relatively earlier adopters of the innovation.

Influential farmers have been found to be above average

42. One caution should be mentioned about this generalization. It may state a circular relationship; opinion leaders might be expected to be above average in innovativeness when the data are obtained from a sociometric opinion leadership question such as, "From whom do you seek information and advice about innovations?"

in innovativeness by Lionberger (1953 and 1955), Marsh and Coleman (1954a), Young and Coleman (1959), Wilkening (1952b, 1958d, and 1961), Rogers (1955 and 1957), van den Ban (in press), Chaparro (1956), Rogers and Burdge (1962), Barnabas (1958), Rahudkar (1960), Brandner (1960),[43] and Rahim (1961, p. 58).

An investigation of leader-group differences in innovativeness in seven Ohio truck-growing communities was completed by Rogers and Burdge (1962). The average innovativeness score for the sociometric leaders was 28 per cent higher than for the average truck growers in the sample. All but one of the 14 opinion leaders were more innovative than the average grower in their community.

The research findings do not indicate, however, that opinion leaders are necessarily innovators.[44] There seem to be some opinion leaders in almost every adopter category. However, it is clear that opinion leaders are generally more innovative than their followers.

An opinion leader who is able to communicate with his followers and have high rapport with them must not be very different from his followers.[45] For the average individual, the early adopter probably is an ideal role model. He is slightly earlier than the average member at adopting innovations but not "too early." For example, there is evidence from several investigations that laggards are seldom influenced by innovators. There is too wide a social gap between the two categories for an influence relationship to occur fre-

43. Brandner (1960) actually found self-designated opinion leadership related to adoption of hybrid sorghums in one section of Kansas but not in another (where the innovation was not recommended by change agents).

44. Hruschka (1961) termed individuals who combine the role of innovators and opinion leaders as *initiativpersons* or literally, initiative-persons.

45. This tendency for people with similar values and opinions to interact with one another has been called "value homophily" by Katz and Lazarsfeld (1955, p. 59). Actually, it is difficult to determine whether the common values precede rather than follow from interaction.

quently. Sociometric analyses generally indicate that *each adopter category is mainly influenced by individuals of the same or a more innovative category.* This generalization is supported by the findings of Lionberger (1953 and 1955), van den Ban (1961 and in press), Rogers and Burdge (1961 and 1962), and Rogers and Leuthold (1962). Figure 8-5 illustrates this generalization with sociometric data from interviews with 28 Ohio vegetable growers (Rogers and Burdge, 1961). Only 4 of the 25 information-seeking relationships shown are from the respondent to a less innovative farmer.[46]

It has now been stated that (1) opinion leaders are more innovative than their followers, and (2) each adopter category is mainly influenced by individuals of the same or a more innovative adopter category. These generalizations are, in fact, complicated by the effect of social system norms on innovativeness.

At first glance, it appears there is contradictory evidence on whether opinion leaders are innovators. For example: Menzel and Katz (1955) reported that in one study of new medical drugs, the opinion leaders tended to be innovators. In another study, however, there was little overlap between innovators and opinion leaders. Wilkening (1952b) in a North Carolina study found that only 3 of 15 farm innovators were opinion leaders. Lionberger (1953), in a Missouri study, found considerable overlap between opinion leaders and farm innovators, as did Rogers and Burdge (1962) in an Ohio study.

A partial solution to these inconsistent findings is available from the Marsh and Coleman (1954a) Kentucky results (Figure 8-4). Opinion leaders in modern neighborhoods were mostly innovators and early adopters, but in traditional neigh-

46. It is interesting that in the present data, at least, three of the four sociometric choices that do not follow the generalization are mutual choices.

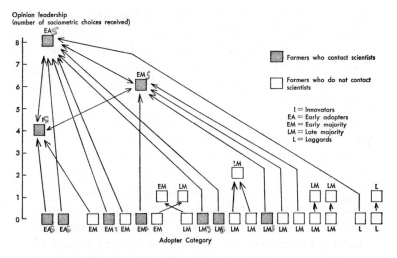

FIGURE 8-5. OPINION LEADERS ARE GENERALLY MORE
INNOVATIVE THAN THEIR FOLLOWERS

Each of the 28 truck growers shown in this sociogram were asked
from whom they secured advice and information about vegetable-
growing innovations. A general tendency can be observed for each
adopter category to be influenced by individuals in the same adopter
category or in a more innovative category. Only 4 of the 25 influence
relationships shown are exceptions to this statement.

The sociogram also suggests that a two-step flow of innovations may
occur. Innovations seem to flow from the agricultural scientists to the
opinion leaders and from them to their followers. The reader should
be cautioned, however, that this tendency cannot be generalized to all
farmers. These respondents were highly specialized, lived in only two
communities, and the scientists were geographically nearby.

Source: Rogers and Burdge (1961). Used by permission.

borhoods the opinion leaders were probably in the early majority category. Thus, *social system norms on innovativeness
seem to determine, at least in part, the innovativeness of
opinion leaders.*

Young (1959b), in a 1955 study of the Kentucky neighborhoods analyzed by Marsh and Coleman in 1950, found additional support for the original conclusions.[47] There was a wider difference in innovativeness between opinion leaders and their followers in modern neighborhoods than in traditional neighborhoods.

Some very weak support for the Marsh and Coleman generalization was obtained from the Ohio study of seven truck-growing communities (Rogers and Burdge, 1962). In the modern communities, the opinion leaders' innovativeness scores were 19 per cent higher than the average farmer's, while in the more traditional communities, the opinion leaders' innovativeness scores were 16 per cent higher. In the modern communities, the sociometric leaders tended to be innovators and early adopters. In the communities with more traditional norms, the leaders were more likely to be early majority.

Van den Ban's (in press) study of three Netherlands farm communities also supports the present generalization. He found that when the community norms favored innovativeness, the opinion leaders were more innovative than when the community norms were traditional.

Sheppard (1960b) has recently criticized the Marsh and Coleman (1954a) conclusions. He points out that the wider

47. Rahudkar (1960) found contradictory evidence to the original Marsh and Coleman (1954a) data on leader-group differences. In a more modern area in India, Rahudkar found that opinion leader's innovativeness scores were closer to those of all farmers (a difference of only 13.5) than in a traditional area, where the leader-group differences in innovativeness scores were 27.0. Lionberger (1960, p. 61) similarly found a greater difference in innovativeness between opinion leaders and followers in a traditional Missouri community (a difference of 31 in innovativeness scores) than in a modern community, where the leader-group difference in innovativeness scores was 24. Only three areas were involved in the India study and two communities in the Missouri study, while 13 neighborhoods were utilized in the Kentucky study. Nevertheless, the point remains that the India and Missouri data are exactly contrary to those of Marsh and Coleman.

difference in innovativeness between opinion leaders and followers in modern neighborhoods than in traditional neighborhoods may *not* be due to differences in the social systems' norms on innovativeness. Sheppard claims the difference is due merely to the greater variation in innovativeness scores within modern social systems. On the basis of his research, Sheppard suggests that opinion leaders may have innovativeness scores that are about 20 per cent higher than their followers, whether the social system's norms are modern *or* traditional. A reanalysis of the Marsh and Coleman (1954a) data by the present author, however, indicated little support for either the 20 per cent figure or for the idea of a proportional difference between leaders and followers.[48]

At least one conclusion may be drawn from these various studies on the innovativeness of opinion leaders. Social system norms should be taken into account when one is making generalizations about whether or not opinion leaders are innovators. Further inquiry is needed to determine general statements about the magnitude of leader-group differences in innovativeness under varying social system norms.

BARRIERS TO THE FLOW OF IDEAS IN A SOCIAL SYSTEM

A tacit assumption throughout much of the present chapter is that opinion leaders influence the "nonleaders" in a

48. The leaders were 16 per cent higher in innovativeness scores (than all farmers) in the traditional Kentucky neighborhoods and 38 per cent higher in the modern neighborhoods. When the Kentucky innovativeness scores were converted to approximate percentiles by the present author using data from Marsh and Coleman (1954c and 1954a), the leaders in traditional neighborhoods were 32 per cent higher than all farmers in innovativeness scores, and in modern neighborhoods, 27 per cent higher.

social system. Are the nonleaders really "followers" of the opinion leaders? Is there really a flow of ideas in a social system by which opinion leaders influence the adoption decisions of the other members of the social system?

Social Status as a Barrier

The research evidence needed to supply a complete answer to these questions is not yet available. However, several studies provide insights into the flow of ideas. It is likely that differences in (1) social status, and (2) innovativeness *can* act as barriers to the flow of ideas as in a system. Lionberger (1959) and Chaparro (1956) both found that seldom do the highest status members of a social system influence, at least directly, those of lowest status.

In fact, a high status opinion leader may not always be an appropriate role model for someone of lower status. An example of this point comes from an investigation by van den Ban (in press) in a Netherlands agricultural community. He found that only 3 per cent of the opinion leaders had farms under 50 acres in size but 38 per cent of all farms in the community were smaller than 50 acres. The wisest farm management decision for the large farmers was to purchase mechanized farm equipment as a substitute for hired labor. However, the wisest economic choice for those on farms of under 50 acres was to ignore power equipment and begin intensive horticultural farming. Van den Ban found, as might be expected, that the small farmers were following the example of the opinion leaders on the large farms, even though the example was inappropriate for their situation.

Extreme differences in social status between a communicator and a receiver may impede communication and slow up the trickle-down of new ideas.

Innovativeness as a Barrier

Another barrier to the flow of ideas is difference between opinion leaders and nonleaders in innovativeness. Past research findings have already been reviewed to show that (1) each adopter category is mainly influenced by individuals of the same or a more innovative adopter category, and (2) the social system norms on innovativeness seem to determine, at least in part, the innovativeness of opinion leaders. If the more innovative members of a social system rarely communicate directly with laggards, change agents cannot count on a flow of ideas to reach the last to adopt in a social system.

The degree to which differences in innovativeness act as a barrier to the diffusion of new ideas varies on the basis of social system norms. This is demonstrated by van den Ban (in press) who computed a measure of association (gamma) between the innovativeness of each "seeker" of new ideas and the person he "sought" (an opinion leader) under conditions of traditional and modern community norms. He included data from nine communities in the Netherlands, Missouri, and Wisconsin. The measure of association between the innovativeness of seekers and those sought varied from +.03 in the most traditional community to +.51 in the most progressive community. The trend was consistent in the nine communities from most traditional to most modern. In other words, the followers who interacted with opinion leaders in modern communities were more likely to be in the same adopter category as the opinion leaders they sought. In the traditional communities, however, the followers sought opinion leaders across the entire range of adopter categories. In a more innovative social system, one interacts with others like oneself. The van den Ban findings (while they should be regarded as somewhat tentative until supported by additional studies) suggest the following generalization: *Differences in innovativeness between individuals are a more important barrier to the flow of ideas in a social system where the norms are modern than where they are traditional.* Analyses similar to that of van den Ban could be accomplished with his methods to determine the importance of social status differences, geographical distance, and other variables as barriers to the flow of ideas under conditions of different social system norms.

Followers and Nonfollowers

One measure of the importance of barriers to diffusion in a social system is the percentage of the members who are followers, that is, who communicate directly with the opinion leaders. Actually, few analyses have been completed of the nonfollowers, those individuals who are not linked through sociometric networks to the opinion leaders. The single research study comparing followers with nonfollowers was Sheppard's (1960a, p. 4) investigation of grassland farmers in England. He found that the followers who communicated directly with opinion leaders were no different on most social characteristics from the nonfollowers.

NEEDED RESEARCH

In spite of the volume of research already completed on opinion leaders, there are several important aspects of opinion leadership about which little is known. Although a great deal is already known about the social characteristics of opinion leaders, no investigation has yet been designed to determine *why* certain individuals, rather than others, are chosen as opinion leaders. It might also be important to know whether opinion leaders maintain their position in a social system over a period of time, or whether there is a high rate of turnover.

The correlates of opinion leadership, such as social status, cosmopoliteness, innovativeness, and social participation, are probably highly interrelated. Investigations should be directed to determine the amount of variation in opinion leadership explained by each of these variables when the effect of the others is controlled statistically.[49] Such analyses should prove fruitful in terms of theoretical significance and implications for action.

The present generalizations about opinion leaders suggest a question that is not full answered: Who influences the influential? One implication for a strategy of change is for change agents to concentrate their efforts upon opinion leaders. There is some evidence, for example, that extension agents may be concentrating their communication efforts upon farm opinion leaders.[50] However, influential medical doctors were less likely to depend upon drug salesmen as an information source about new drugs than were their less influential colleagues (Menzel and Katz, 1955). More certainly needs to be known about what influences the opinion leaders.

SUMMARY

Opinion leaders are those individuals from whom others seek advice and information. They play an important role in

49. The statistical tool to accomplish this purpose is multiple correlation. One attempt to explain the variation in the dependent variable, opinion leadership, was similar in method to the prediction of innovativeness (a topic reviewed in Chapter X). Rogers and Burdge (1962) explained 26 per cent of the variation in opinion leadership with three variables, deviancy from system norms, social status, and innovativeness.

50. However, Hruschka (1961) found that there was some tendency for German extension agents to select innovators as local missionaries for their educational program rather than farmers who possessed higher opinion leadership and were less innovative.

the diffusion and adoption of innovations. It is impossible to ignore opinion leaders in studying the spread of ideas. The two-step flow of communication hypothesis originally stated that ideas flowed through mass media channels to opinion leaders and from them to their followers. There is now evidence that the diffusion process is much more complex than the two steps originally suggested, but there are two steps involved in information-transmission at any one point in the diffusion process.

Personal influence is communication involving a direct face-to-face exchange between the communicator and the receiver which results in changed behavior or attitudes on the part of the receiver. Personal influence from peers is most important (1) at the evaluation stage in the adoption process and less important at other stages, (2) for relatively later adopters than for earlier adopters, and (3) in uncertain situations rather than in clear-cut situations. The three types of selectivity partially explain why personal influence functions more effectively than mass media in overcoming resistance to change. *Selective exposure* is the tendency for individuals to expose themselves to communications that agree with their existing opinions. *Selective perception* is the tendency of individuals to interpret a new idea in terms of their past experience and existing opinions. *Selective retention* is the tendency of individuals to remember ideas that agree with their existing opinions.

Opinion leadership is a fairly widespread trait, even though it is especially concentrated in a few individuals in most social systems. Three methods have been utilized to measure opinion leadership: (1) sociometry, (2) key informants, and (3) self-designating scales. Opinion leaders conform more closely to social system norms than the average member. There is little overlapping among the different types of opinion leaders. For example, an individual who is an opinion leader for innovations is not likely to also be influential in political affairs. Opinion leaders use more impersonal, technically accurate, and cosmopolite sources of information than their followers. Opinion leaders are more cosmopolite, have more social participation, higher social status, and are more innovative than their followers.

Each adopter category is mainly influenced by individuals of the same or a more innovative adopter category. Social system norms on innovativeness seem to determine, at least in part, the innovativeness of opinion leaders. Differences in innovativeness between individuals are a more important barrier to the flow of influence in a social system where the norms are modern than where they are traditional.

CHAPTER IX

The Role of the Change Agent and the Consequences of Innovation

Throughout the world, the "developing countries" are attempting in a relatively brief span of time to narrow the gap between themselves and those nations with a richer technology and a higher standard of living. To achieve this, they are launching and carrying forward nation-wide programs of change and are inviting from outside thousands of specialists to strengthen these programs. . . . It is sometimes assumed that understanding the *change-agent* role in any program for social change means the ability to apply techniques of change or to speak glibly of the strategy of change. This is a part of the role, to be sure, but only a narrow part. . . . Thus far, techniques and strategy have not usually been considered in their effects upon other programs . . . or in their effects upon other aspects of life than the one to which action is directed.

COUNCIL ON SOCIAL WORK EDUCATION, 1959, p. ix

The primary concerns of this chapter are the role of the change agent, his strategy of change, and his responsibility for the social consequences of the innovations he introduces.

A *change agent* is a professional person who attempts to influence adoption decisions in a direction that he feels is desirable. In most cases, a change agent seeks to secure the adoption of new ideas, but he may also attempt to slow the diffusion and prevent the adoption of certain innovations. A new idea may compete with or supersede an old idea sponsored by the change agent. A change agent may seek to prevent the adoption of a nonrecommended innovation, as county extension agents did in the case of the grass incubator. Francis' (1960) analysis of this innovation suggests that county agents in the United States may be more effective in preventing the adoption of nonrecommended ideas than in promoting the spread of recommended farm innovations. The dual role of the change agent, as both an opponent of nonrecommended innovations and a promoter of recommended ideas, is recognized in the present description of the change agent's functions.

Almost every area of public concern has at least one type of change agent. Examples of various types of change agents are: technical assistance workers in less developed countries; county extension agents; detail men who promote medical drugs with physicians; salesmen and dealers of new products; public health officials, nurses, and medical doctors; and school administrators and teachers.

The term "change agent" was first used in laboratory studies of small groups in 1947 (Lippitt and others, 1958, p. 10). The term has since been utilized by a number of research workers in their analyses of the diffusion of innovations.[1]

ROLE OF THE CHANGE AGENT

Most change agents are local-level bureaucrats whose purpose is to inject a cosmopolite influence to innovate into a client social system. The change agent functions as a communication link between two social systems. For example, a

1. Among those utilizing the term "change agent" are Loomis and Beegle (1957), Council on Social Work Education (1959), Rogers (1960), and Stabler (1958). Winston (1933) used the term "diffusion agent." Barnett (1953, pp. 291–295) preferred to use the term "professional advocate" or "advocate of change."

detail man provides linkage between his professional system, the drug company, and the client system of medical doctors that he contacts. Similarly, a technical assistance worker provides linkage between the United States and a less developed country in which he is introducing innovations.

Emery and Oeser (1958, p. 52) pointed out that while an Australian District Agricultural Officer (D.A.O.) may live in the same community with his clients, he is still an "outsider" to them. In order to be effective in diffusing new ideas, he must secure linkage with his client system.

. . . A D.A.O. is not accountable for his professional actions to anyone in the locality. He is accountable only to a somewhat remote organization, the Department of Agriculture. Even if all the sheep die, his salary will continue. In essence the definition of an "outsider" rests on the direction and location of a person's accountability. No matter how highly regarded he may be, the D.A.O. remains, sociologically speaking, an outsider.

Factors in the Success of Change Agents

Because a change agent's social position is located midway between the bureaucracy to which he is responsible and the client system in which he works, he is subjected to various role conflicts. The change agent is often expected to engage in certain behaviors by his professional system and, at the same time, he is expected by his client system to carry on quite different actions. Preiss (1954) studied the resulting role conflicts among Michigan county extension agents. His analysis suggests that the more successful county agents were those who disregarded the expectations of the extension service bureaucracy in favor of those of their local client system.

Studies by Wilkening (1958b) of Wisconsin county extension agents and by Bible and Nolan (1960) of Pennsylvania county agents indicate there is considerable disagreement between (1) the role expectations by the local client system of the county agent and (2) the agent's self-definition of his role. For example, the change agents perceived their role as one of basic education, but their clients expected them to provide services such as finding speakers for organizations.

Nye (1952) analyzed factors contributing to the success of county extension agents in Missouri. His measure of success was a composite rating by supervisors, colleagues, and clients. The success score included, among other dimensions, the results secured in introducing innovations. Nye was able to explain statistically 63 per cent of the variation in the rated success of the change agents. The amount of variation explained by each of the five variables was, in percentage of variation in rated success: personality, 28 per cent; training, 15 per cent; vocational interests, 11 per cent; attitudes, 9 per cent; learning ability, 0 per cent.

Perceptions of the change agent by his client system may affect his success in securing change. These perceptions vary on the basis of the social characteristics of his clients, and partly determine how much communication a client will have with a change agent. Research results show that change agents reach the upper social status portion of their clientele disproportionately more than the lower strata.

The illustration in Chapter I of the water-boiling campaign in a Peruvian village demonstrates this differential perception of a change agent on the basis of social class. Lower-status housewives saw the change agent, a public health nurse, as a "dirt inspector." Upper-status housewives had more favorable perceptions of the change agent and more communication with her.

Promotion Efforts by Change Agents
and Rate of Adoption

Several research studies suggest that *the extent of promotional efforts by change agents is directly related to the rate of adoption of an innovation.* The relative advantage of an innovation over the idea it supersedes may be emphasized by the promotional efforts of change agents. Actually, there are few adequate research studies that test the effectiveness of efforts by change agents to speed the rate of adoption of a new idea. There is a need to know much more about the variables which mediate or intervene in the relationship between the extent of a change agent's efforts and the results he secures, as measured in terms of the rate of adoption of new ideas.

Hoffer (1944) provides one of the earliest studies supporting the previous generalization about change agents' efforts and rate of adoption. Hoffer correlated certain promotional activities by county agents (such as the number of farm visits, newspaper articles published, and circular letters written) with the adoption of new ideas by farmers. Hoffer's main concern was to determine why some diffusion methods were more likely to result in the adoption of innovations than were other methods.

Ross (1952) found that the rate of adoption of driver training programs by high schools was much more rapid than the rate of adoption of other educational innovations. He attributed this rapid rate of adoption to the promotion efforts of car dealers, insurance companies, and the American Automobile Association.

Armstrong (1959), in an ingenious analysis of secondary data, determined the relationship between different types of promotional activities by change agents and resulting changes in the adoption of innovations by their clients.[2] Armstrong

2. Armstrong's methodology is patterned closely after that of Cutright and Rossi (1958) who attempted to predict the vote for Democratic party candidates from the extent of election campaign activities by precinct workers, after removing the effect of the social characteristics of the precinct members.

found that for the Kentucky counties he analyzed, the greater the promotional efforts by county extension agents, the greater the adoption of innovations by farmers in their counties.

Stone (1952, p. 16) analyzed the amount of effort spent by 18 Michigan county extension agents from 1943 to 1950 in promoting a new farm idea, the artificial breeding of dairy cattle. Figure 9-1 shows the number of dairy cows bred artificially in Michigan. From 1943 to 1946, the adoption of the innovation roughly paralleled the amount of the change

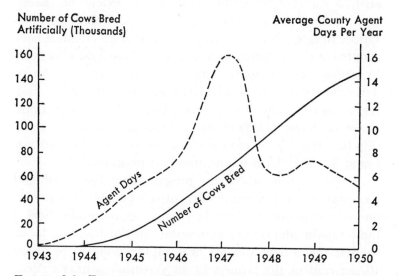

FIGURE 9-1. EXTENT OF CHANGE AGENTS' EFFORTS AND THE RATE OF ADOPTION OF ARTIFICIAL BREEDING OF DAIRY COWS

These data show that Michigan farmers continued to adopt artificial breeding of dairy cows at almost a constant rate even after county extension agents' promotional efforts slackened after 1947. Much of this increase in adoption after 1947 is the result of word-of-mouth diffusion from farmer to farmer about the new idea.

Source: Stone (1952, p. 16). Used by permission.

agents' efforts, as measured by the number of agent days per year spent on the idea. After 1947, the county agents' efforts decreased, but the farmers continued to adopt the new idea at almost a constant rate. A large portion of this increase in adoption after 1947 is probably due to word-of-mouth diffusion of the idea from farmer to farmer. Many of the earlier adopters of the innovation were probably opinion leaders who, after experience with artificial breeding, helped influence their neighbors to adopt.

The results of this study suggest that there is not necessarily a direct relationship between the extent of change agents' efforts and the resulting rate of adoption of an innovation. In fact, after a certain percentage of his clientele have adopted, a change agent may utilize his time most effectively by letting word-of-mouth diffusion of the innovation occur. The reader should be cautioned against generalizing the findings from the study of one farm idea to all other situations. However, Stone (1952) claims a somewhat similar relationship between rate of adoption and change agents' efforts was found for other farm innovations that he studied.

Another caution about the present generalization should be mentioned at this point. It is entirely possible that the extent of promotional efforts by change agents results *from* a rapid rate of adoption of an innovation! For instance, let us suppose that a new idea has been rapidly adopted by about 10 per cent of the farmers in an extension worker's client system. The change agent is then likely to interpret the rapid rate of adoption as an indication of his client's need for the new idea, and decide that he should concentrate his promotional efforts upon securing wider adoption of the idea. Thus, rapid adoption may cause greater promotional efforts by change agents, rather than the reverse. In any event, for some innovations that have been studied, the two variables, rate of adoption and change agents' efforts, seem to occur concurrently.

How Change Agents Adopt New Ideas

One attempt has been made to determine how change agents first become aware of an innovation, how they were convinced of its utility, and then recommended it to their clients. The case is similar to the adoption process described in Chapter IV except that "adoption" for a change agent may amount to recommending the new idea to his clients.

Rogers and Yost (1960) secured data from a sample of 44 Ohio county extension agents on their "adoption" of stilbestrol, a growth-producing sex hormone feed for beef cattle. Not all of the 44 county agents were "adopters" of the innovation at the time of the investigation. Different sources of information created (1) awareness of the new idea among the county agents than (2) convinced them to recommend the idea to farmers in their counties. The average change agent in the Ohio study required about two years to pass through the adoption process. The awareness and adopter distributions generally tended to approximate an S-shaped curve (Figure 9-2). The generalizations stated in Chapter IV regarding the adoption process appear to apply to the way in which change agents, as well as others, adopt new ideas.

COMMERCIAL CHANGE AGENTS

There are many different types of change agents, as was emphasized earlier. The purpose of this section is to present generalizations about the role of commercial change agents.

The adoption of a new idea almost always entails the sale of a new product. Most companies have organized market research departments to conduct research on how their new

Number of County Extension Agents

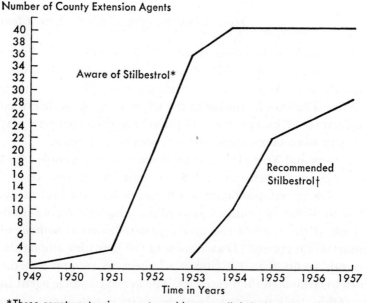

*Three county extension agents could not recall their date of awareness.

†Six county extension agents could not recall the date they recommended Stilbestrol, and ten county extension agents had not yet recommended Stilbestrol.

FIGURE 9-2. THE DATE COUNTY EXTENSION AGENTS BECAME AWARE OF AND RECOMMENDED STILBESTROL TO THEIR CLIENTS

These data show how 44 Ohio county extension agents became aware of stilbestrol, a growth-producing sex hormone feed for beef cattle. The awareness and the "adopter" distributions for these change agents generally tended to approximate an S-shaped curve.

Source: Rogers and Yost (1960, p. 26). Used by permission.

products diffuse and why they are purchased by customers. For some innovations and under some conditions, commercial change agents are of great significance in the diffusion of innovations. Ryan and Gross (1943), for example, found that hybrid seed salesmen were reported by almost half of the sample of Iowa farmers as their source of awareness information. Salesmen were relatively less important as an information source at the evaluation stage than in creating awareness of hybrid seed.[3]

At least two generalizations about the relative importance of commercial change agents in diffusing innovations may be observed in Figure 9-3.

1. *Commercial change agents are more important at the trial stage than at any other stage in the adoption process.*[4] This generalization holds true, in fact, for each of the five adopter categories shown in Figure 9-3. The generalization is supported by the findings of Ryan and Gross (1943) for hybrid corn, by Beal and Rogers (1957) for a new clothing fabric, and by Copp and others (1958) for three farm innovations. The individual purchases a small amount of the new product at the trial stage. It is at this point that he relies most heavily upon commercial change agents for information on how to use the new idea.

2. *Commercial change agents are more important for earlier adopters than for later adopters at the trial stage.* This generalization can be observed in Figure 9-3 and is also supported by Beal and Rogers (1957b) and by Ryan and Gross (1943).

3. The Ryan and Gross (1943) data also show that commercial change agents were relatively more effective in creating awareness for those who were the first to become aware than for those who became aware later. For example, 70 per cent of those who learned about hybrid seed in 1930 named salesmen as their source while only 5 per cent reported neighbors. Three years later, in contrast, these figures were 27 per cent and 61 per cent, respectively. A somewhat similar pattern was found for medical doctors (Katz, 1961).

4. One possible explanation for this generalization is that it may be more socially respectable to admit being influenced by a friend than by a salesman or by advertising at the evaluation stage.

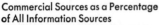

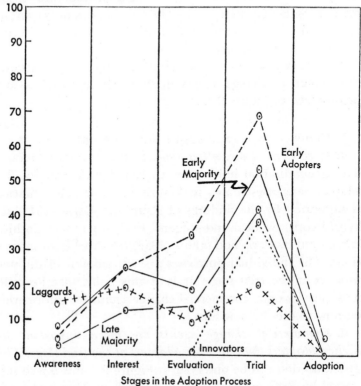

Commercial Sources as a Percentage
of All Information Sources

FIGURE 9-3. IMPORTANCE OF COMMERCIAL SOURCES OF
INFORMATION BY STAGE IN THE ADOPTION PROCESS AND
ADOPTER CATEGORY FOR 2,4-D WEED SPRAY

These data show that commercial sources of information are more important at the trial stage than at any other stage in the adoption process. Commercial change agents are generally more important for earlier adopters than for later adopters at the trial stage. The reader should be cautioned that while these relationships can be observed for this innovation, there is little research evidence to support these generalizations other than from studies of agricultural innovations.

Source: Beal and Rogers (1960, p. 16). Used by permission.

There is evidence from a number of studies that most individuals place less credibility in commercial change agents than in other types of change agents. Rogers (1957c) found that farmers placed much greater credibility in neighbors than in salesmen. Ninety-seven per cent of Rogers' respondents stated they would more likely be convinced of a new farm idea if they talked with a neighbor about it than a farm salesman. Some typical responses illustrate reasons for the lack of credibility in commercial change agents.

The salesman's job is to sell—he's partial. Salesmen, heck, they try to blow everything [new products] up.

A salesman would try to sell you anything, but a neighbor would know if the new idea worked on his farm.

The commercial change agent's motives, as perceived by his clients, may be one reason for the relatively low credibility they place in his recommendations. They feel that he may seek to promote the overadoption of new ideas to secure higher sales. However, in some communities that the author studied, local farm store dealers were widely respected by farmers and their recommendations were often followed. The reason that these dealers had such high credibility was often the result of the strong primary group relationships they developed with their clients. The farmers regard the dealers as friends, rather than as change agents promoting a new product.

Similar reasons may be suggested for the higher credibility farmers place in farmer-dealers (farmers who are selected by companies to sell their products such as fertilizer, seed, and machinery on a part-time basis) than in salesmen or dealers.[5] A neighboring farmer-dealer is often regarded by his clients as a peer, rather than in his role of seller. Personal influence with his clients is hence more likely to result in their adoption of a new product.

5. Some evidence for this statement is available from an investigation of the diffusion of new fertilizer ideas by Rogers and Leuthold (1962).

Studies of the diffusion of new medical drugs among physicians shed some light on the role of one type of commercial change agent, the detail men who promote new drugs for pharmaceutical firms. Menzel (1959) found no differences in the importance of detail men as an information source on the basis of adopter category.[6] In other words, laggards were as likely as innovators to report commercial change agents as an information source about new drugs.

Opinion leader doctors were less likely than their followers to mention drug salesmen as an information source (Menzel and Katz, 1955). In practice, the detail men were not utilizing the two-step flow of communication. By reaching the opinion leaders, the change agents might have indirectly reached their followers, but such was not the case. The detail men reached the opinion leaders less than their followers.

Hawkins (1959b), after reviewing a number of market research studies by drug companies, concluded that commercial change agents are of considerable importance as a source of information to physicians about new drugs. Hawkins pointed out that most respondents are likely to "underreport" the importance of commercial sources of information. Ferber and Wales (1958) asked 210 physicians to maintain diaries in which they recorded their sources of information about new ideas. It appeared from the diaries that detail men were a more important source of information than the doctors admitted in personal research interviews.

It is reasonable to assume that many respondents underreport the significance of commercial sources of new ideas. It is not fully acceptable to admit one has been influenced by commercial change agents. Further evidence of this point is provided by van den Ban (1961b). When a sample of about 200 Wisconsin farmers were asked their most important

6. To be more precise, Menzel (1959) found no relationship between importance of detail men as an information source and innovativeness of physicians. One reason for this lack of relationship may lie in the blanket exposure of doctors to detail men. The average physician visited with several detail men per week (Coleman and others, in press).

source of farm information in 1952, only about 3 per cent mentioned commercial change agents. The same respondents were reinterviewed in 1957 and asked their information sources for the specific farm ideas they had adopted from 1952 to 1957. Over 30 per cent named commercial change agents! When a more specific question was asked, many more respondents reported commercial change agents as an information source.

CROSS-CULTURAL DIFFUSION OF INNOVATIONS

One particular type of change agent is the technical assistance worker who seeks to transfer new ideas from one culture to another. The problems of interpersonal communication encountered by any change agent are heightened in the case of the technical assistance worker because he seldom shares a common culture with his client. This point is emphasized by Peter and Schlesinger (1959) who stated, "The carrier of new ideas and procedures from one culture to another needs to learn special skills in the germination, nourishment, and development of these transplantations."

The importance of technical assistance change agents is indicated by the growing list of technical assistance agencies and by the number of their employees. Observers estimate that about 40,000 foreign nationals come each year to study, receive training, or teach in the United States.[7] At least 20,000 Americans go abroad each year for similar purposes. The U.S. Agency for International Development, AID (and its predecessor agencies such as Point Four and ICA), have trained over 52,000 participants from over 60 countries. The

7. These foreigners, when they return to their home countries, are operating as cross-cultural change agents to the extent that they have absorbed a portion of U.S. culture during their stay.

number trained annually is increasing by more than 6,500 each year. The more recently initiated Peace Corps will add several thousand more each year to the number of change agents who work in cultures different from their own.

A communication problem for all change agents, but especially for those in less developed areas, is that of securing "linkage" or communication relationships with their clientele. Most isolated Indian villages, for example, regard strangers with distrust. One reason for the general success of the village-level worker program in India (and a similar program in Pakistan) is its method of training. A local person from a village is given a minimum education and then returned to his village. Socially, he is not a stranger and, supposedly, he can understand the local villager's values.[8]

Rahudkar (1959) investigated the factors contributing to the success of village-level workers in India. He found, surprisingly, that the change agents with only a high school education were more successful in introducing innovations to villagers than were those with a college education. Rahudkar explained this finding on the basis that high-school-educated change agents were able to maintain linkage with their clients more effectively than were the college-educated.[9]

The problem of securing linkage with his client system is particularly bothersome to the change agent in less developed areas who seeks "reentry" to his social system after leaving to gain further training. Examples are the African student who travels to the United States for a college degree or the Indian

8. However, the communication gap previously existent between government officials and local people may now exist between government officials and the village-level worker.

9. The opposite kind of problem seems to be occurring for many county extension agents in the United States. At one time, the county agent was about the only college-educated expert available to farmers in his county. However, the "educational gap" between a county agent and his clients has decreased in recent years as more farmers have college degrees. As a result, the more innovative farmers do not regard the county agent as the same degree of expert that he once was.

government official who returns after a year of technical training abroad. The reentry problem is so important that the Agency for International Development (AID) provides many foreign trainees with a week-long seminar in diffusion techniques just before they return to their home countries. Over 2,000 AID-sponsored trainees are given these understandings each year. The results have convinced U.S. leaders that technical training of foreign personnel is not enough. They must also be shown how to secure the adoption of the new ideas.

A number of research studies[10] have recently been completed on the diffusion of innovations in less developed countries. Straus (1953) investigated the role of change agents in introducing innovations in a less developed area. He found that Ceylon had a relatively well staffed extension service, but that their goal of higher crop yields was seldom realized. The extension service was organized from the top downward, rather than the bottom upward. Extension agents carried on "drives" to promote the raising of castor seeds or cotton or chillies, whether these innovations were appropriate to the locale or not. It is difficult for Ceylonese to order their relationships with those of lower status on any other basis than one of superiority. Even when administrators issued directives to extension agents to treat villagers as equals, the agents could not bring themselves to do so.

Social Status and Communication with Change Agents

Almost every analysis of any change agent's clientele shows that *change agents have more communication with higher-*

10. Among these investigations are those of Paul (1955) in South America; Welikala (1959) and Straus (1953) in Ceylon; Bose (1961 and 1962), Foster (1956), and Rahudkar (1961) in India; Polson and Pal (1955) in the Philippines; Goldsen and Ralis (1957) in Thailand; Chaparro (1955) in Costa Rica; and Rahim (1961) in Pakistan.

status than with lower-status members of a social system.[11] Evidence supporting this generalization comes from investigations of county agents and soil conservationists in the United States, of technical assistance workers, and of local-level change agents in less developed countries.[12]

One illustration is taken from Foster's (1956) analysis of the activities of a village-level worker (VLW) in one Indian community. Using mainly participant observer methods, Foster gathered data on who the VLW reached among the villagers. The VLW concentrated on upper-class households and tended to neglect the lower classes. In fact, the lower their status, the more the VLW neglected them. He contacted all of the upper-class villagers both personally and in group meetings. Only about 25 per cent of the lower class were contacted.

The VLW achieved the most adoptions of ideas per hour of effort spent on the upper classes. Fewer adoptions resulted per hour of effort spent on each succeeding lower class. Practically speaking, the VLW probably allocated his efforts in optimum proportions. He did not totally neglect the lower classes where the need for knowledge was greatest, and he adequately covered the upper classes where adoption was easiest to effect.

Another reason why change agents work more closely with clients of higher social status is that the status differences that often exist between the change agent and his cli-

11. An even more general statement might be that change agents communicate more with clients who have social characteristics most similar to their own.
12. Among the research studies that found change agents work more closely with higher-status members of a social system are Foster (1956), Welikala (1959), Mendras (1958), Neinhaus (1953), Rogers and Burdge (1962), van den Ban (1953, 1957b, 1961a, and in press), von Blankenburg (1960), Osborne (1961), Rogers and Havens (1961a), Wickers (1958), Rogers and Capener (1960), Coleman (1951), Parish (1956), Scantland and others (1952), Slocum and others (1958), Niederfrank and others (1948), and Emery and Oeser (1958).

entele. It is likely that wide status differences between any two individuals act to impede effective communication. As a result, change agents tend to interact most effectively and most often with clients who have a similar status to their own.[13] The VLW was probably in the middle or upper status in the Indian village; he communicated most with people of his own status.

The way in which a change agent handles his status relationships with his clients obviously has much to do with his relative effectiveness in introducing new ideas. Erasmus (1961, p. 84) pointed out that native change agents in some less developed countries avoid the stigma of working with their hands to demonstrate new ideas. Manual labor is symbolic of a lower social status. As a result, change agents are more likely to tell farmers what to do rather than to show them. "In Colombia, I have seen highland agricultural extension agents go into the field in a black double-breasted suit with tie, scarf, and black Homburg. They were far more eager to demonstrate their social distance from the farmer than to demonstrate improved agricultural practices" (Erasmus, 1961, p. 84).

SOCIAL CONSEQUENCES

The change agent plays an important role in securing the adoption of innovations. What is his responsibility for the social consequences of these new ideas after their adoption?

13. The tendency for change agents to work more closely with their higher-status clients does not necessarily imply that change agents do not have a potential for securing changes in the behavior of their lower-status clients. McKain and others (1958, p. 2) found that personal influence from change agents was relatively more effective in securing higher milk consumption among lower-status persons than those of higher status.

Research studies generally indicate that many of the consequences of innovations cannot be accurately predicted before their adoption.[14] The ultimate results are often far-reaching and unintended, in a similar way to the side effects from a new medicine.

This point was emphasized by the Council on Social Work Education (1959, p. 1).

The professional person can no longer shrug his shoulders and claim merely to be a practitioner in a narrow specialty; more and more, he is forced to take responsibility for the kinds of changes brought about by the programs in which he is directly involved. Some of these changes can be anticipated and planned for; many others, perhaps the majority, are not usually foreseen.

The change agent has a responsibility for the consequences of the innovations he introduces. Almost every program of planned change results in a myriad of social consequences in the client system. Opler (1954, p. 5) pointed out that virtually ". . . no technical assistance can in fact be provided that does not touch some economic, political or social nerve end." Nearly every program to hasten economic development, for example, produces a host of reactions that run throughout the social structure of the client system.

The anthropological diffusion tradition, more than any other, has concentrated upon the social consequences of innovation. In fact, a classic type of research topic for anthropologists in past years has been the analysis of changes in a primitive society after contact with a modern society. Certain of the other research traditions on diffusion that were described in Chapter II gave some attention to the results of technological change. For example, some industrial engineers and industrial sociologists have investigated the consequences of automation.

In the past, rural sociologists have usually assumed that the

14. The present section can properly be regarded (as can the entirety of the present book) as part of the sociology of science, which is the study of the antecedents to scientific discoveries and their consequences.

consequences of farm innovations were universally desirable. Seldom have these consequences been subjected to scientific analysis. However, the current emphasis on agricultural adjustment to technological change has made it imperative to concentrate more rural sociological research efforts on the consequences, rather than the antecedents, of innovation.

The case example that follows describes the social consequences that resulted from the introduction of the wagon into an Indian village in southern Arizona.

In the Wake of the Wheel: A Case Illustration of Social Consequences[15]

The Papago Indians of southern Arizona knew nothing of the wheel until its introduction by white men. Because of their relative isolation in the desert, they did not adopt wagons until after 1900. Papago acceptance of wheeled vehicles came about as the result of a deliberate program by the U.S. Bureau of Indian Affairs. The far-reaching consequences of the wagon upon the simple routine of life in the desert villages was partly unanticipated.

The present case materials center on the first wagon to be introduced in one remote Papago village. Three brothers of the village headman saw wagons in use when they were employed off of the reservation in railroad construction. When they returned to their village, they persuaded the headman to order a wagon from the Indian agent.

When the wagon arrived about a year later, it immediately began to cause changes in the Papago culture. The wagon was used intensively from the beginning and soon replaced the pack horses which had been the Papago's primary means of transportation. The wagon was used to carry water from

15. This case illustration is adapted from Bliss (1952, pp. 23–33). Used by permission.

springs to the village households. Previously, pottery jars were used for fetching water, but these were easily broken by the wagon. The Papagoes soon turned to metal barrels which were unbreakable, and pottery making rapidly declined as a craft among the women.

Changes in other aspects of Papago culture soon resulted from the wagon. A road was constructed for the wagon. Lengthy trading journeys into Mexico by pack horse were replaced by short wagon trips into nearby towns. Crops and firewood were marketed through use of the wagon. The gathering of firewood soon developed as an occupation for men instead of piecemeal gathering by women and children. The shift from subsistence to a market economy and the need for manufactured harness and metal barrels linked the Papagoes with the general American society in new ways.

In the Papago case little conscious control of the innovation was exercised by the change agent. One wonders if the new idea would have been so completely accepted if the innovator had not been the village leader. Some consequences like the need for roads and the disuse of pack horse transportation might have been expected by anyone who planned ahead. Other effects were not so obvious. The wagon resulted in shifts in the division of labor, increased dependence on the American economy, and influenced the relations of Papagoes with surrounding peoples.

Direct and Indirect Consequences

There have been several research studies on the consequences of technological change; four somewhat typical investigations are:

1. Ogburn and Gilfillian (1933, p. 153) listed 150 effects of the radio in U.S. culture. These consequences spread out

in primary, secondary, and tertiary levels. The most direct effects, in turn, caused more ultimate consequences.

2. Bertrand and others (1956) found the consequences of farm mechanization in the South included larger farms, less tenancy, greater commercialization, and an increased demand for more skilled farm labor.

3. Karpat (1960) investigated the social effects of a farm mechanization program in Turkey ten years after its inception. He found such direct and indirect consequences as urbanization resulting from a decrease in farm labor needs, altered food habits, new occupations such as village mechanics, and a wider income gap between rich farmers with tractors and poor farmers without tractors.

4. Pollack (1957) discussed the consequences of industrial automation in the U.S. Included in the direct effects of automation are technological unemployment, the need for more highly skilled workers, more abundant leisure, and a trend to larger-sized businesses.

These four research studies indicate that many authors divide the social consequences of innovation into two types: (1) the *direct* or manifest consequences are adjustments in the social system that are intended and recognized by the participants, and (2) the *indirect* or latent consequences are adjustments in the social system that are neither intended nor recognized by the participants at their time of adoption.

An illustration of the direct and indirect consequences of a new idea is the anthropological study of the adoption of wet rice farming by a native tribe (Linton and Kardiner, 1952, pp. 222–231). The tribe had been a nomadic group that cultivated rice by dry-land methods. After each harvest they would move to a different location. Many social changes resulted in the tribe's culture after the adoption of wet-land farming. A pattern of land ownership developed, social status differences appeared, the nuclear family developed, and tribal government changed. The consequences of the technological change were far-reaching and unanticipated. A second gen-

eration of consequences from wet rice growing spread from
the more direct results.

WINDFALL PROFITS

In addition to the consequences of innovation for an entire
social system, special advantages may occur for certain individuals rather than others within the system. Laggards are
the last to adopt innovations. By the time they adopt a new
idea, they are often forced to do so by economic pressures. On
the other hand, innovators, by being the first in the field,
frequently secure a special kind of economic gain called
windfall profits.

Windfall profits are economic returns over costs that are
earned by the first adopters of a new idea in a social system
because their unit costs are usually lowered and their additions to total production have little effect on the price of the
product.[16] However, when all members of a social system
adopt a new idea, total production or efficiency increases and
the price of the product or service often goes down. This
offsets the advantage of lowered unit costs.

The innovator must take risks in order to earn windfall
profits. All new ideas do not turn out successfully, and oc-
casionally the innovator "gets his fingers burned." It is possible, of course, that adoption of a noneconomic innovation
could result in "windfall losses" for the first individuals who
adopt.

Windfall profits are a relative type of economic gain that

16. Windfall profits, in a more general sense, could be measured
in social as well as economic terms. An example is the prestige that the
innovator of consumer products may obtain by being the first to use
a new idea.

one individual in a social system receives and others do not. Hence, windfall profits are a reward for innovativeness and a penalty for laggardness. In one sense, new ideas may tend to make the rich richer and the poor poorer.

Many individuals realize the importance of windfall profits. Some innovators are probably motivated to be the first to adopt new ideas by a desire to earn these profits. As one innovator farmer remarked to the author in a research interview: "I think that almost every farmer realizes that all the new things that come out . . . on the majority of them you've got to take advantage of them as quickly as possible to get the full benefit out of them. After they've been on the market for several years, you don't get that advantage."

In order to illustrate the nature of windfall profits, data from the Iowa hybrid seed corn study by Gross (1942) were reanalyzed. The innovators of this farm idea, who adopted in the late 1920's, earned almost $2,500 more than the laggards, who adopted hybrid seed in 1940–1941. The innovators earned these windfall profits because (1) of a higher market price for corn before most farmers adopted hybrid seed and corn production was increased, (2) of their larger corn acreages (for example, the innovator who adopted in 1927 averaged 124 acres of corn while the typical laggard who adopted in 1941 raised only 70 acres of corn), and (3) of the greater number of years they received the higher yields from hybrid seed.[17]

The reader should be cautioned that hybrid seed is probably not a typical farm innovation in terms of its windfall profits. The innovation was characterized by large relative advantage (high profitability) and a relatively slow rate of adoption. Both of these factors result in relatively larger

17. Gross (1942) presented these data on the basis of average years of *trial*. It was necessary to adjust these data with a factor measuring the length of the trial-adoption period in order to plot them on the basis of year of *adoption*.

windfall profits. The windfall profits also may have been affected somewhat by the Depression which occurred in the early 1930's.

Nevertheless, the general distribution of windfall profits on the basis of innovativeness may hold true for other new ideas. There is certainly need for a similar type of economic analysis of other innovations in agriculture and in other fields.[18]

A STRATEGY OF CHANGE

It is impossible to state a series of universal recommendations for all change agents in all situations. Such recommendations are often useless outside of a very specific situation because they are rarely general in their application. The present section is an attempt tentatively to state a more general strategy of change,[19] which, although *illustrated* with specific examples, should apply to a broad range of change agent-client relationships.

1. A PROGRAM OF CHANGE SHOULD BE TAILORED TO FIT CULTURAL VALUES AND PAST EXPERIENCES.
One example of this statement comes from a Latin American

18. In fact, agricultural economists in the United States have paid relatively much less research attention to the economics of farm innovations than their sister social science, rural sociology, has paid to the social relationships involved in the diffusion of innovations. Some of the investigations of new farm ideas by agricultural economists are Hess and Miller (1954), Hildebrand and Partenheimer (1958), and Toussaint and Stone (1960).

19. The present strategies of change were obtained mainly from Goldshmidt (1952, pp. 149–151), Rogers (1960, pp. 456–458), and Mead (1955, pp. 288–303).

country. United Nations powdered milk was distributed for the first time in a remote village, and that same week a smallpox epidemic broke out. Local people blamed the disease on the powdered milk. Needless to say, later efforts by change agents to secure the acceptance of powdered milk were unsuccessful.

An irrigation engineer from a Far East country, who had received AID training in the United States, returned home convinced of the value of building wells in order to irrigate rice. Over 100 wells had been constructed in isolated villages before the engineer realized they were not being used. Local people regarded the irrigation water from wells as "artificial" and felt it was not as natural as rainfall. Since they feared it would harm their crops, they refused to adopt the new idea. All 100 wells have now passed into complete disuse.

Other illustrations of the importance of planning a program of change in terms of cultural values were provided in the present book. The hot-cold complex in the Peruvian village, compatibility in the case of hybrid sorghums in Kansas, and U.S. consumers' rejection of a headache pill to be taken without water all help illustrate the importance of cultural values and past experiences.

Most change agents possess values which differ somewhat from those of their client system. This is particularly true for cross-cultural change agents. Unless he is aware of his clients' values, the change agent is likely to destroy his linkage with his clients by his actions in introducing new ideas (Rohrer, 1955).

It has repeatedly been emphasized throughout this book that the norms of a social system, particularly the norms on innovativeness, have a considerable effect upon the diffusion of new ideas. This point suggests that perhaps a change agent should seek to alter his client system's norms on innovativeness, rather than promote single innovations. This strategy is sociologically sound, but in practice may be difficult to accomplish (van den Ban, 1961a).

2. A Change Agent's Clients Must Perceive a Need For an Innovation Before It Can Be Successfully Introduced.

The potential need for an idea must exist in a client system, although a change agent can help develop such a need.

In fact, Dobyns (1951) summarized his analysis of the unsuccessful introduction of irrigation farming on the Papago Indian reservation with the following statement, "An induced technological change will succeed to a degree proportionate to the extent to which the [client system] feels a need for it, are brought into its planning and execution, and feel it to be their own."

Not only should a change agent's clients perceive a need for a new idea before it can be successfully introduced, but a change agent should select innovations for introduction on the basis of existing needs among his clients.[20] Mead (1955, p. 258) stated, "Experience has taught us that change can best be introduced not through centralized planning, but after a study of local needs."

3. Change Agents Should Be More Concerned With Improving Their Clients' Competence in Evaluating New Ideas And Less With Simply Promoting Innovations Per Se.

Young (1959a) suggested that a long-range program to change values may be a more appropriate strategy of attack for some change agents than just a "single-innovation" approach to change.[21]

20. A successful change agent should ideally keep one eye on the stock of available innovations in his field and the other eye fixed on the needs of his clients. The need for careful program planning of the change agent's efforts, using some of the generalizations available about the adoption process and adopter categories, is obvious.

21. Some change agencies seek to secure the adoption of new ideas through offering a cash payment. Subsidies for the adoption of certain farm innovations can be found in England, Sweden, the United States, and several other countries. The Netherlands no longer makes cash

Many writers imply that a desirable philosophy for change agents is a simple "the more, the better" (Young, 1959a). Obviously, *all* innovations should not be recommended to *all* members of a social system. This point is emphasized by Young (1959a).

If we may compare with factory production for a moment, a producer of textile machinery would not be prepared to claim that a given piece of machinery will produce greater profits for all kinds of factories of all sizes and capacities. Neither, then, will a given farm practice. "Scientific" farming thus far has emphasized particular techniques without regard to the enterprise as a whole. Perhaps now the agricultural economist or business management person should evaluate a given [farm] practice in terms of whether and when an enterprise of a certain capacity should adopt it.

Perhaps change agents should seek to provide their clients with a more favorable basic attitude toward new ideas and spend fewer efforts in campaigns to secure the adoption of single innovations.[22] In fact, there is some research evidence that campaigns are seldom very successful in changing behavior, at least in the short range (Havens and Rogers, 1961a).

4. CHANGE AGENTS SHOULD CONCENTRATE THEIR EFFORTS UPON OPINION LEADERS IN THE EARLY STAGES OF THE DIFFUSION OF AN INNOVATION. The existence

---

payments to farmers to encourage the adoption of farm ideas. It found that farmers adopted only to get the cash, and were oftentimes not really convinced of the utility of the innovations. At the first opportunity, the innovations were likely to be discontinued.

22. This statement implies a long-range rather than a short-range approach to change. It might mean, for example, that a change agent in a traditional social system would encourage innovativeness through youth organizations. There are few research studies on the effectiveness of youth organizations, such as 4-H Clubs, in introducing innovations. Strams and Estep (1959) and Olson (1959b) found that adult farmers who had been in 4-H Clubs as youth were more innovative.

of opinion leaders in a social system offers change agents a "handle" whereby they can prime the pump from which new ideas flow through an audience via the "trickle-down" process. A study in Ceylon (Welikala, 1959, p. 141), for example, indicated that the rate of adoption of new ideas closely followed that of the village leaders. Hrushka (1961) found that German county agents tended to select demonstration farmers that were too high in innovativeness and too low in opinion leadership for greatest effectiveness in diffusing new ideas.

5. THE SOCIAL CONSEQUENCES OF INNOVATIONS SHOULD BE ANTICIPATED AND PREVENTED IF UNDESIRABLE. The studies of consequences of innovations presented earlier in this chapter illustrate this strategy. Unfortunately, however, many of the consequences of an innovation cannot be anticipated.

As part of the U.S. technical assistance program in one Middle East country, new crop varieties, fertilizers, and farm machinery were introduced. Food production increased considerably as a result of the program of change, but the resulting social consequences of the program were mainly unanticipated. Before the program was initiated there was a majority of low-income farmers in the country and a small number of elite farmers. The innovations, particularly farm machinery, were of special advantage to the larger farmers. While the peasants' incomes were raised slightly, the elite landowners' incomes were multiplied many times. The income gap between the peasants and elite farmers was considerably widened, and the U.S. program was subject to much criticism in the Middle East country.

SUMMARY

A change agent is a professional person who attempts to influence adoption decisions in a direction that he feels is desirable. The change agent serves as a communication link between a professional system and his client system. The extent of promotional efforts by change agents is directly related to the rate of adoption of an innovation. However, the relationship between the extent of change agents' efforts and rate of adoption may not be linear. Once a certain percentage of the client system have adopted, the innovation may spread by word-of-mouth diffusion with little further effort from the change agent.

Commercial change agents, such as salesmen and dealers, are more improtant (1) at the trial stage than at any other stage in the adoption process, and (2) for earlier adopters than for later adopters at the trial stage. Several research studies indicate commercial change agents are seldom perceived as credible by their clients. The clients may feel the commercial change agent seeks to promote the overadoption of new ideas.

Change agents have more communication with higher-status than with lower-status members of a social system. The social consequences of innovation are of two types (1) direct or manifest consequences that are intended and recognized, and (2) indirect or latent consequences that are neither intended nor recognized by the participants at their time of adoption. Windfall profits are economic returns over costs that are earned by the first adopters of a new idea in a social system because their unit costs are usually lowered and their additions to total production have little effect on the price of the product.

A general strategy of change was suggested which included

the following: (1) a program of change should be tailored to fit the cultural values and past experiences; (2) a change agent's clients must perceive a need for an innovation before it can be successfully introduced; (3) change agents should be more concerned with improving their clients' competence in evaluating new ideas, and less with simply promoting innovations per se; (4) change agents should concentrate their efforts upon opinion leaders in the early stages of diffusion of an innovation; and (5) the social consequences of innovations should be anticipated and prevented if undesirable.

CHAPTER X

Predicting Innovativeness [1]

A leading drug company asked sociologists to chart the probable pattern of adoption of a new beef-cattle hormone feed they were about to release. The company's advertisers made no special appeal to the self-starters who seek new products from scientists, directed their first farm magazine campaign at the middle-of-the-roaders, and after a year's delay, aimed a local farm paper campaign at the bulk of the prospects. Five years after release, use of the hormone by beef farmers has come within 2 per cent of predicted sales.

[Adapted from *Business Week*, March 21, 1959]

One of the goals of sociological theory is to provide grounds for predicting human behavior.[2] The empirical prediction of human behavior is not meaningful unless it is theoretically based and logically consistent. The present chapter is an attempt to demonstrate two means of predicting innovativeness. When research on this topic reaches the point where we may predict "when" and "who"

1. With A. Eugene Havens, The Ohio State University. Some of the material in the present chapter previously appeared in Rogers and Havens (1962a). Used by permission.
2. As Merton (1957, p. 98), pointed out. Not all sociologists agree with this point of view. For example, Simpson (1959, p. 58) stated: "Much popular thinking about science and scientific method is surfeited with clichés. None appears more persistently than the statement that the aim of science is to predict. Like all clichés this one hides a problem, it does not settle one."

will adopt new ideas in a social system, valuable theoretical and practical consequences should result.

The nature of this topic necessarily means that this chapter will be somewhat more theoretical and methodological than the preceding chapters.

PAST PREDICTION STUDIES

Social scientists have completed studies in attempts to predict:

1. Academic success in high school and college
2. Success in Air Force pilot training
3. Chronicity of welfare cases
4. Juvenile delinquency
5. Parole and probation success
6. Marriage success

In these analyses the basic approach has been to derive probability statements indicating the likelihood of certain individuals behaving in a particular manner. Stochastic (or probability) models of human behavior have predominated in past prediction studies. The methods utilized in these past prediction studies should prove useful in attempting to predict innovativeness. Most prediction analyses have employed multiple correlation as the statistical tool for analysis.[3]

3. Several diffusion studies by rural sociologists have attempted to predict the adoption of single innovations with a battery of personal characteristics. Examples are Gross and Taves (1952) and Marsh and Coleman (1955b). Lackey (1958) and Lackey and Larson (1961) used innovativeness scores for farmers at one point in time to predict innovativeness five years later. These studies are not directly in the particular mainstream of diffusion research on predicting innovativeness that is the central concern of the present chapter.

PREDICTION WITH MULTIPLE CORRELATION

Multiple correlation is a statistical method whereby a series of "independent" variables are related to one "dependent" variable,[4] which in the present case is innovativeness. Innovativeness is the degree to which an individual is relatively earlier to adopt new ideas than the other members of his social system. The goal of the multiple correlation approach to prediction is to explain a maximum of the variation in the dependent variable. It is possible to determine the relative contribution of each independent variable in explaining the dependent variable.

Several rural sociologists have used multiple correlation to predict innovativeness in past studies with varying degrees of success. From 17 to 56 per cent of the variation in innovativeness has been predicted in these analyses. The results are summarized in Table 10-1. Five types of variables are most prevalent in past prediction studies. They are individual attitudes, nature of the business operation, social structure, group relationships of the respondent, and communication behavior. It should be cautioned that different definitions and dissimilar measures have been utilized in these studies, so an exact comparison is difficult. However, all of the studies utilized the same basic approach.[5] It is important

4. A dependent variable is the main factor investigated in a research study. The independent variables are those related to the dependent variable in the research study. Thus, whether a particular variable is regarded as dependent or as independent is arbitrary, and depends upon the design of the study.

5. One exception is Kivlin (1960), who computed an index which measured the relative rate of adoption for each of 43 different innovations. Twenty judges were asked to rate the characteristics of each innovation, such as compatibility, complexity, and relative advantage. Kivlin succeeded in explaining about 51 per cent of the variance in rate of adoption with these characteristics. It should be emphasized that Kivlin was predicting *rate of adoption* of various innovations, and not *who* will adopt an innovation. Other attempts to predict the rate of adoption are reviewed in detail in Chapter V.

TABLE 10-1

SUMMARY OF PAST ATTEMPTS TO PREDICT
INNOVATIVENESS BY MULTIPLE CORRELATION
METHODS

Investigator	Main Independent Variables Utilized	Per Cent of Variance in Innovativeness Explained
1. Copp (1956)	Gross farm income Professionalism Mental flexibility	50.00
2. Fliegel (1956)	Familism Information contact Level of living Attitude toward innovations	32.00
3. Copp (1958)	Gross farm income Membership in farm organizations Discerning ability Level of living	52.00
4. Rogers (1958a)	Attitude toward change Social status Communication competence	17.00
5. Armstrong (1959)*	Economic position of farmers Degree of urbanization Farm specialization	42.10
6. Hobbs (1960)	Attitude toward commercial change agents Cosmopoliteness Brand awareness Knowledge about innovations Management vs. traditional work orientation Gross farm income Farm size	29.70
7. Sizer and Porter (1960)	Knowledge about innovations Social status Education Social participation	25.88

8. Straus (1960)	Net worth	33.64
	Education	
	Wife role supportiveness	
9. Rogers and Havens (1961b)	Gross farm income	56.27
	Age	
	Belief in agricultural magic	
	Venturesomeness	
	Social status	
10. Cohen (1962)	Mobility (cosmopoliteness)	54.76
	Individual values	
	Family income	

* It should be pointed out that Armstrong used Kentucky *counties* as his units of analysis rather than *farmers*. He constructed a farm innovations adoption score for each of the 115 Kentucky counties. The use of counties as units of analysis provides relatively higher correlations because much farmer-to-farmer variation is eliminated from the analysis.

to note that all but one of these studies were completed with farmer respondents. There is little evidence to date that these relationships will hold in other types of social systems.[6]

An Example: Predicting Innovativeness among Truck Farmers

One prediction study is described in detail so the reader may more fully understand the procedures involved. Data

6. One nonfarmer study of prediction was completed by Carter and Williams (1959) of English industrial firms. About 78.54 per cent of the variation in innovativeness was explained when the dependent variable (a crude rating of the innovativeness of each firm) was correlated with one independent variable that was constructed by "pooling" a number of separate variables known to be related to innovativeness. Hence, the Carter and Williams study cannot be compared with the studies listed in Table 10-1, as its methodology is quite different.

The case is similar for the Pierce (1947, p. 10) analysis of factors related to the innovativeness of public schools. Sixty-four per cent of the variation in a composite measure of innovativeness was explained by 19 community characteristics.

come from personal interviews with a random sample of 76 truck vegetable farmers in one Ohio county. It should be noted that the adoption-of-innovations scale was more sensitive than previous scales utilized since it took into account not only adoption versus nonadoption of each innovation, but also the relative time each of the 17 truck-growing innovations were adopted.

Four criteria should be employed in selecting variables to be correlated with the dependent variable in a multiple correlation prediction analysis.

1. Each independent variable should be highly related to the dependent variable.

2. Each independent variable should have a relatively low interrelationship with each other independent variable.

3. The total number of variables should be minimized because of the amount of computational effort required and to increase practicality.

4. There should be a theoretical and practical relevance for the relationship of each independent variable with the dependent variable.

Using these four criteria, five independent variables were selected in a multiple correlation analysis to predict innovativeness. These independent variables are community norms on innovativeness, size of farm operation, self-designated opinion leadership, directness of communication behavior with scientists, and social status.

The theoretical and practical relevance of these five variables to the prediction of innovativeness may be described in the following manner.

1. Social status is an indication of one's position in the social structure. It may either inhibit or enhance an individual's access to sources of information and his willingness to deviate from group norms.

2. Norms are the most frequently occurring patterns of overt behavior for the members of a particular social system.

The community norm on innovativeness[7] is a matter of group expectation to which the individual feels obligated to conform.

3. Communication behavior is an indication of the degree to which an individual is willing to seek information and advice and is expected to be more innovative than in the case of the individual who does not.

4. Size of farm operation is an indication of scale and of the amount of potential resources available for investment in innovations.

5. Opinion leadership is measured by a self-designated technique. Individuals who possess a greater degree of opinion leadership are expected to be more innovative.

These five independent variables were related to innovativeness in a multiple correlation approach.[8] The results indicated that 64.1 per cent of the variation in innovativeness, the dependent variable, was explained by the combined effect of the five independent variables. This is the highest amount of variance explained in the innovativeness dimension yet reported. The amount of variation in innovativeness explained by each of the five independent variables is: community norms on innovativeness, 20 per cent; size of operation, 14.4 per cent; opinion leadership, 14.4 per cent; communication behavior, 8.9 per cent; and social status, 6.4 per cent.

When compared to previous studies (Table 10-1), the relatively larger amount of variation (a total of 64.1 per cent) explained by the present multiple correlation approach to prediction is mainly because of the inclusion of a previously unused variable, community norms on innovativeness. This

7. The community norm on innovativeness was obtained by averaging the adoption-of-truck-crops-innovation scores of the farmers interviewed in each community. This method of measuring norms was discussed, along with other norm measures, in Chapter III.

8. The present study is, in effect, ex post facto. The variables were not chosen on any a priori basis, although in future research it is suggested that this should be done.

finding suggests the importance of relating individual innovativeness to social system norms, as well as to social characteristics, in future research.[9]

A prediction equation may be obtained from the present data in which the value of each independent variable is inserted, and which will yield a value which is a prediction of an individual's innovativeness. The five variables have been shown to explain a considerable portion of variance in innovativeness; future studies in analyzing similar behavior may use these variables in a multiple correlation approach to predict the adoption of a new innovation or innovations. It may be possible to utilize the five variables presented in the current study to make predictions for a population of individuals in which the outcomes are not known—a so-called validation sample. There is an understandable desire in most cases to predict innovativeness among future samples.

A CONFIGURATIONAL APPROACH
TO PREDICTION

A second approach to prediction of some desired outcome is the configurational approach. This method consists of dividing a sample of respondents into relatively homogeneous subsamples on the basis of each of several independent variables.[10] Each subsample is regarded as a separate

9. Straus (1960a) found a significant addition to the explained variation in innovativeness by including a measure of "wife role supportiveness" in his analysis which already included farmers' education and net worth. Straus emphasized the importance of including "group" variables such as norms, as well as individual factors, in analyses of innovativeness.

10. The present discussion of the configurational approach to prediction is largely based upon Stuckert (1958), but the present application of the configurational method differs from that utilized by Stuckert.

unit for analysis since it has a unique configuration of independent variables. After successive breakdowns on the basis of the independent variables, which are usually dichotomized or trichotomized, the probability of a desired outcome is calculated.

The configurational approach to the prediction of innovativeness is illustrated with data from the same Ohio investigation as in the previous case of prediction with a multiple correlation approach. Four independent variables, community norms on innovativeness, size of farm operation, opinion leadership, and directness of communication behavior with scientists, were utilized in Figure 10-1 to predict innovativeness. These variables were chosen merely to demonstrate the configurational approach and were the four variables which explained the greatest amount of variation in innovativeness in the multiple correlation problem. The configurational approach is designed to predict from data with relatively imprecise measures.

An inspection of Figure 10-1 indicates the configurational approach may have potential in predicting innovativeness. The relative degree of success in predicting innovativeness is shown in Table 10-2.[11]

Even with the tentative data shown in Figure 10-1, however, it is possible to spot certain deviant configurations such as the three farmers who are Hi-Hi-Hi-Lo.[12] One farmer with this configuration lives in a community with an innovative norm, is "Hi" in farm size and possesses "Hi" opinion leadership, has a "Lo" degree of communication behavior, but is an innovator. Perhaps he learns about innovations from his innovative peers in his community. This il-

11. Robinson's "A," a measure of agreement, is .320 for the data in Table 10-2, which is an indication of the relative success of the configurational approach in the present case.

12. In fact, Emery and Oeser (1958, p. 94) originally suggested this type of "tree" diagram in Figure 10-1 as a method of better understanding the data, rather than for use as a method for predicting innovativeness.

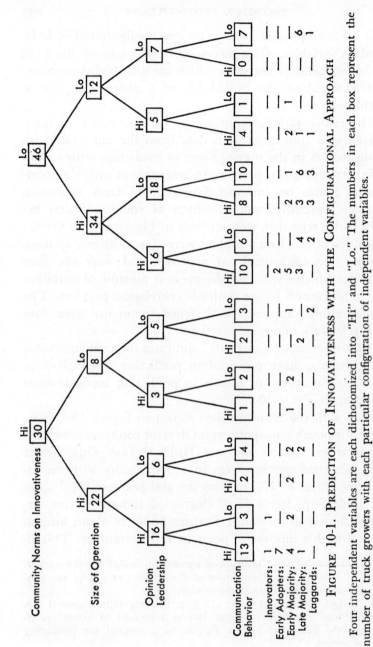

FIGURE 10-1. PREDICTION OF INNOVATIVENESS WITH THE CONFIGURATIONAL APPROACH

Four independent variables are each dichotomized into "Hi" and "Lo." The numbers in each box represent the number of truck growers with each particular configuration of independent variables.

Source: Rogers and Havens (1962a).

TABLE 10-2

RELATIVE EFFECTIVENESS OF THE CONFIGURATIONAL APPROACH IN PREDICTING INNOVATIVENESS

| | ADOPTER CATEGORY | | | | | |
Configuration	Innovators	Early Adopters	Early Majority	Late Majority	Laggards	Total
Four Hi's	1	7	4	1	—	13
Three Hi's, One Lo	1	2	10	3	2	18
Two Hi's, Two Lo's	—	—	8	12	6	26
One Hi, Three Lo's	—	—	3	6	3	12
Four Lo's	—	—	—	6	1	7
Total	2	9	25	28	12	76

lustration demonstrates one advantage of the configurational approach over the multiple correlation method. The configurational method points out exceptions or deviations from the general relationships among the variables. The configurational approach forces the researcher to become better "acquainted" with his data. The investigator is able to follow a particular individual through the various independent variables, and determine exactly which factors account most for his position on the innovativeness dimension.

FUTURE APPROACHES TO PREDICTION

The present chapter attempted to demonstrate two methods, multiple correlation and the configurational approach, for predicting innovativeness. At this time, several suggestions may be made for more fruitful future research on predicting innovativeness.

Future efforts need to select independent variables for the prediction of innovativeness with more attention to theoretical considerations. Most past research on prediction of innovativeness has simply studied the characteristics of individuals associated with innovativeness. The raw empiricism of this past research era has served a useful purpose, but it is now time to set forth a model to explain theoretically how adoption of an innovation takes place in a social system.[13] Then, the ability of this model to predict innovativeness may be assessed either with a multiple correlation or with a configurational approach. A major step forward would be an a priori selection of variables to be utilized in a prediction attempt. In the present chapter the variables utilized were selected on an a posteriori basis. Consequently, no claims are made toward advancing a *theory* of innovativeness on the basis of the present findings. The purpose was merely to demonstrate methods available for prediction.

Attempts to explain yet higher portions of the variation in innovativeness may lie in the direction of improving measures of innovativeness and of such dependent variables as cosmopoliteness, opinion leadership, and communication behavior. Additional dependent variables may be included in future studies. An example of the usefulness of this suggestion is contained in the present chapter, where inclusion of social system norms on innovativeness added 20 per cent to the amount of variation in innovativeness explained.

Utilizing an approach essentially similar to that of Kivlin (1960), it should be possible to predict the rate of adoption of an innovation from its characteristics such as relative advantage, divisibility, compatibility, communicability, and complexity. This approach to prediction might be particu-

13. Examples of past efforts to set forth such a model are Emery and Oeser (1958), Coughenour (1960b), Hobbs (1960), Straus (1960b), Fox and others (1961), and Rahudkar (1961).

larly useful when combined with the configurational method since it is likely that each configurational subsample may perceive the characteristics of an innovation differently. In other words, future research might include independent variables which measure how individuals *perceive* the characteristics of an innovation, as well as variables measuring the individual's social characteristics, attitudes, and group relationships. It may be that individuals who have a large operation, high opinion leadership, and high communication behavior, but perceive an innovation as unprofitable, for example, would be relatively slow to adopt the particular innovation in question.

Computer Simulation and Game Theories

Complex mathematical and statistical approaches may offer fruitful methods which can turn a searchlight on the dark waters of predicting innovativeness. Within very recent years, the method of computer simulation has been utilized to predict the adoption or rejection of innovations. The Simulmatics Corporation (1961a), a research organization composed of social scientists, is seeking to predict the acceptance by communities of fluoridation of municipal water supplies for the U.S. Public Health Service.[14]

Computer simulation is a technique for solving complex problems through the use of high-speed electronic computers which digest and interrelate immense quantities of data according to a program of instructions given the machine. Two conditions are necessary for successful simulation: (1) a body of knowledge about the behavior to be simulated, and (2) availability of data about the units in a social system that are to be simulated. Computer simulation

14. A similar study is underway by National Analysts (1961).

has been utilized for several years in the physical sciences, but only recently in the social sciences.

Probably one of the more impressive uses of computer simulation in the social sciences was the prediction of voting behavior in a national Presidential election by Pool and Abelson (1961).[15] Simulations of the diffusion of farm innovations and other new ideas have been made by Hagerstrand (1952, 1953, and 1960) with some degree of success. Hagerstrand is a Swedish geographer, and his approach to simulating diffusion has been largely on the basis of ecological or spatial factors.

Hagerstrand (1960), Walker and others (1960), and Dillon and Heady (1961) utilized Monte Carlo game theory techniques to simulate the diffusion and adoption of farm innovations.[16] Game theories generally state certain rules of decision-making that are followed by individuals when faced with a choice among alternatives. These game theories may be utilized to study adoption decisions, just as they have been used as models to analyze consumer or election decisions or war strategies. One recent adoption investigation by Klietsch (1961) made use of game theories to predict the acceptance or rejection of bulk milk tanks by farmers on the basis of four types of decision-makers (traditionalists, rationalists, evaluators, and affectors) whose strategies of choice were derived from the von Neumann and Morgenstern (1953) game theories.

Computer simulation can be useful in predicting the *consequences* of the adoption of ideas, even before the innovation is released in a social system. An example is the simulation of the national economy of a less developed country by Gillespie (1961). His simulation of the effects of currency

15. Another example of simulation is that by Orcutt and others (1961), who simulated the U.S. labor force.

16. Monte Carlo techniques have also been used to simulate the spread of infectious diseases. In one study epidemiologists mimicked the spread of measles in a boarding school (Bailey, 1957, pp. 153–155).

devaluation in a developing country indicated that the undesired results more than negated the desired effects.

Another use of simulation is to predict the acceptance of new ideas of a nontechnological nature. For instance, the Simulmatics Corporation (1961b) has proposed an investigation of the acceptance of new farm programs by the U.S. farm population.

Usefulness

Obviously, an underlying assumption of the present discussion is that predicting innovativeness is a worthwhile effort for social scientists. The prediction of innovativeness has utility for research organizations and for commercial companies who wish to know which individuals in their audience will be the first to adopt an innovation they are about to release. There is also great practical utility in prediction for change agents who wish to understand more clearly the independent factors related to innovativeness, and the interrelationships among these independent variables.

CHAPTER XI

Toward a Theory of the Diffusion
and Adoption of Innovations [1]

A science without a theory is blind because it lacks that element which alone is able to organize facts and give direction to research. Even from a practical point of view the mere gathering of facts has very limited value. It cannot give an answer to the question that is most important for practical purposes—namely, what must one do to obtain a desired effect in given concrete cases? To answer this question it is necessary to have a theory, but a theory which is empirical and not speculative. This means that theory and facts must be closely related to each other.

KURT LEWIN, 1936

A search of the diffusion literature reveals (1) a general lack of agreement upon sociological concepts involved in adoption behavior, and (2) absence of a synthesis of these concepts into a general theory that might be tested by empirical research. The many studies that have been completed provide an excellent base for an attempt to formulate a general theory of the diffusion and adoption of innovations.

Ordinarily, one would expect theoretical considerations to appear in the early chapters of a book. They could then serve as a framework for the entire volume. However, in the present case it is our belief that any theoretical statement must be so highly tentative that it is more appropriately

1. With A. Eugene Havens, The Ohio State University. A portion of this chapter was originally presented as a paper at the 1961 Rural Sociological Society.

placed at the end rather than at the beginning of the present work. The purpose of this chapter is to state a direction in which analysis should proceed toward a general theory of the diffusion and adoption of new ideas.

THEORETICAL APPROACH

Perhaps one of the most effective means of conceptualizing adoption and diffusion behavior is first to view this behavior in its most basic and elementary form, and then to develop some of the complex variables affecting this behavior. At one level of conceptualization, adoption of a new idea by an individual is a type of action. According to Parsons and Shils (1952, p. 56), an act consists of three basic elements: (1) an actor (2) orienting to (3) a situation. This conceptualization of human behavior implies:

1. Behavior is oriented toward attaining *ends* or goals.
2. It takes place in *situations*.
3. It is *normatively regulated*.
4. It involves an expenditure of *effort* or "motivation."

The ultimate goal or end which individuals seek to attain is interpersonal security (Sullivan, 1953). *Security* is that subjective state of well-being which minimizes tension. "Ends" are not used in the present case to mean verbalizations or rationalizations for behavior. For example, if a farmer says that he adopted an innovation because he felt it would increase his farm income, higher income is not an end but a verbalization of the end. At a more general level of abstraction, the farmer's goal is security.[2]

2. The concept of security may be at such a high level of abstraction that difficulties will be encountered in measuring it. There has been no attempt reported in the literature to relate a measure of interpersonal security to innovativeness.

Behavior takes place in situations. Individuals do not exist as a mass of disconnected units. They are members of social systems, and these memberships in social systems have important effects upon their behavior. The situational fields[3] in which behavior occurs do not necessarily follow community or organizational boundaries. One may be psychologically identified with a group and take the group's perspective as his own without being on the membership list. Of course, physical proximity, along with social status and other psychological identifications, are factors influencing frequency of interaction.

Behavior is normatively regulated. Interaction with others in a situational field provides the individual with a sense of identity. The "others" in a situational field are significant to the individual and influence his behavior. These "significant others," or reference groups, aid an individual in developing his self-identity. The manner in which an individual identifies himself influences his behavior; an example is the physician who feels, "As a progressive, scientific doctor, I adopt new medical ideas."

Some individuals identify with change agents and scientists to a greater degree than others. Other individuals interact with earlier adopters, develop a similar self-identification, and eventually become more like the persons with whom they interact.

Behavior involves an expenditure of effort or motivation. In the case of adoption and diffusion, the individual must exert energy to seek information about the new idea, to try it out, and to adopt it. In order for adoption to occur, the individual must perceive that the potential rewards of adoption outweigh the expected efforts required for adoption.

3. The term "situational field" (Cottrell, 1942) is somewhat preferable to "situation," as the former does not imply time boundaries, while the latter does. "Situation" tends to connote a given time and place. *Situational field* is defined as that part of the environment which is perceived by an actor as significant for him.

Perception

The concept of perception is a key dimension in understanding the diffusion of ideas. Although a new idea may be regarded as advantageous by experts in some field, a particular actor may not perceive the innovation in a similar manner. *Perception* is the way in which an individual responds to any sense or impression which he detects (Lindesmith and Strauss, 1956, p. 85).

Perception is a function of the situational fields within which the individual operates. Knowledge of these situational fields, the manner in which the individual identifies himself, his sense of security, and the normative regularities may enable the theoretical specification of some of the conditions for adoption behavior.

As Cottrell (1924) stated, "Items of behavior such as attitudes, traits, etc., studied apart from the context provided by the actor's definition of the situation, yield meaningless results." Thus, it is essential that the present model for adoption behavior account for the actor's perceptions of the situation.

DIFFUSION OF AN INNOVATION

The diffusion of an innovation takes place within a social system. A social system may embrace many different situational fields. The segments of a social system employed as a frame of reference cause individuals to display varying degrees of innovativeness. The situational fields themselves, when employed as a frame of reference, display greater homogeniety in characteristics of individuals and a smaller range in the innovativeness of actors. The five categories, innovators, early adopters, early majority, late majority, and laggards, may each be regarded as a situational field.

It is possible to view the individuals within a particular adopter category as employing certain dominant values which determine the means used to achieve the ultimate end of security. These dominant values are most appropriately viewed as ideal types which may be objectively found in actual situations, but which may not be possessed by *each* actor within a particular adopter category.

The dominant value of innovators is venturesomeness. Innovators appear to gain interpersonal security by being more venturesome than other members of a social system. Therefore, innovators are frequently viewed as deviants from the system's norms. In fact, innovators often operate within situational fields external to the social system. In terms of the situational field within which innovators operate, they may not perceive their decisions as venturesome. Innovators frequently bypass change agents and use more cosmopolite sources of new ideas. The innovator may have knowledge of an innovation before a change agent.

The dominant value of those individuals in the early adopter category is respect from their peers. Early adopters may perceive that respect enhances their security. They rate higher in opinion leadership within a social system than other adopter categories, although this depends, in part, upon the norms of the system. Opinion leaders may operate in the same situational field with change agents. Of course, not all opinion leaders are early adopters. To some extent, each adopter category may have its own opinion leaders. Opinion leaders "consensually validate" other individuals' perceptions of a new idea, and enhance or retard the adoption of innovations.

The dominant value of the early majority is deliberation. By deliberating on adoption decisions, they attempt to enhance their own security. The early majority do not adopt a new idea until other respected individuals within their social system have accepted an innovation and it has proved successful.

If every individual completely limited his identification to other individuals within a situational field, diffusion would be a slow process. However, some individuals are marginal to two or more situational fields. These marginal individuals bridge the gap between adopter categories.

The late majority category possess a dominant value of skepticism. These individuals doubt the value of innovations until they are convinced by a legion of their peers. Late majority individuals feel more secure in following tradition than in accepting new ideas (until the ideas become somewhat traditional for the social system).

The dominant value of laggards is tradition. When viewed in terms of the total social system, laggards are deviants. However, their deviancy does not derive from too rapid adoption of innovations, but from their unwillingness to accept new ideas even after they have become widely used in the social system. Laggards derive their security by resisting innovations.

ADOPTION OF AN INNOVATION

The paradigm[4] of the adoption of an innovation by an individual (Figure 11-1) contains three major divisions: (1) antecedents, (2) process, and (3) results. Antecedents are those factors present in the situation prior to the introduction of an innovation. Antecedents are of two major types: (1) the actor's identity, and (2) his perceptions of the situation. The actor's identity, which affects the adoption of in-

4. The paradigm suggested here owes certain of its ideas to the models of Emery and Oeser (1958), Coughenour (1960b), Hobbs (1960), Straus (1960b), Rahudkar (1961), and Fox and others (1961).

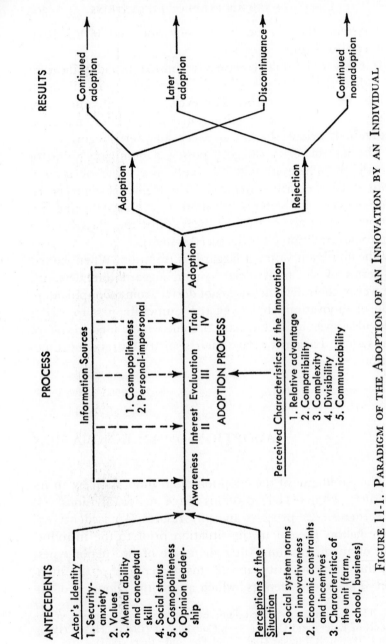

FIGURE 11-1. PARADIGM OF THE ADOPTION OF AN INNOVATION BY AN INDIVIDUAL WITHIN A SOCIAL SYSTEM

ANTECEDENTS

Actor's Identity
1. Security-anxiety
2. Values
3. Mental ability and conceptual skill
4. Social status
5. Cosmopoliteness
6. Opinion leadership

Perceptions of the Situation
1. Social system norms on innovativeness
2. Economic constraints and incentives
3. Characteristics of the unit (farm, school, business)

PROCESS

Information Sources
1. Cosmopoliteness
2. Personal-impersonal

Awareness Interest Evaluation Trial Adoption
I   II   III   IV   V
ADOPTION PROCESS

Perceived Characteristics of the Innovation
1. Relative advantage
2. Compatibility
3. Complexity
4. Divisibility
5. Communicability

RESULTS

Adoption
Rejection

Continued adoption
Later adoption
Discontinuance
Continued nonadoption

novations, is comprised of his sense of security, his dominant values, his mental ability and conceptual skill, his social status, and his cosmopoliteness.

The actor's perception of the situation affects his adoption behavior. The social system's norms on innovativeness serve as incentives or restraints on his behavior. Individuals in a social system with a modern norm will act differently from the way they would where the norms are traditional. The economic constraints and incentives, and the characteristics of the unit (such as the farm, business, or school) also affect adoption behavior.

Information sources are important stimuli to the individual in the adoption process. The individual becomes aware of the innovation mainly by impersonal and cosmopolite sources such as the mass media. At the evaluation stage the individual forms his perception of the characteristics of the innovation. Localite and personal information sources are more important at the evaluation stage.

The conclusion of the adoption process is either adoption or rejection of the idea. An innovation may be adopted at the conclusion of the adoption process and may be (1) used continuously, or (2) rejected at a later date, a discontinuance. The innovation may be rejected at the end of the adoption process, but adopted at a later date. It is also possible the innovation will be continuously rejected.

It is the authors' opinion that the theoretical position outlined in this section is researchable and may enhance the prediction of innovative behavior. It is not presented as *the* theory of adoption or as the only theory that may be advanced. Instead, it is a summary of current research and theory that has been reported in the fields of social psychology, cultural anthropology, sociological theory, and the traditions of diffusion research. It is hoped that this discussion may stimulate others to give greater attention to the basic theoretical framework upon which future diffusion research might be designed.

GENERALIZATIONS AND HYPOTHESES

This chapter attempted to state an approach to a theory of the diffusion and adoption of innovations. The action theory of Parsons and Shils provided a general frame of reference which was applied to consideration of how ideas spread. This framework suggests (1) generalizations that have been tested in previous research and summarized here, or (2) hypotheses capable of being tested by empirical means. The generalizations will be listed after a brief discussion of conceptual variable analysis.

Conceptual Variable Analysis

Theory consists of the postulated relationships among concepts. The empirical testing of these relationships is the task of research. Conceptual variable analysis is a method of relating theory to research and research to theory.[5]

The essential steps in conceptual variable analyses may be described as follows.

1. The first step is to express all concepts as variables. A *concept* is defined as a dimension stated in its most basic or "primitive" terms. A conceptual variable is thus a concept expressed in variable form. One example of a conceptual variable utilized throughout the present book is innovativeness, defined as the degree to which an individual is relatively earlier to adopt new ideas than the other members of his social system. A concept ideally should be as general or ab-

5. Many of the ideas contained in this section owe their development to Merton (1957) and to Professor Robert L. Hamlin of Washington University. Certain of these notions first appeared in Rogers (1958a). Used by permission.

stract as possible so that it may be utilized to describe behavior in many different types of social systems. For example, the innovativeness concept has been studied in industry, education, farming, and primitive tribes.

2. The postulated relationship between two conceptual variables is called a *general hypothesis*. An example of a general hypothesis tested in several research studies cited in Chapter VI is: innovativeness varies directly with cosmopoliteness. In this example, innovativeness and cosmopoliteness are conceptual variables, and the general hypothesis postulates a positive relationship between them. The sociological reasoning[6] is that individuals who have communication with sources external to their social system are more innovative. If one has reference groups outside a social system, greater deviation from that system's expectations for one's behavior is likely, and the adoption of new ideas may result.

3. A general hypothesis is tested by means of testing an *empirical hypothesis* (or hypotheses), defined as the postulated relationship between two operational measures of conceptual variables. An *operation* is the empirical referent of a concept and may be a scale, index, or other measure. The degree to which an operation is a valid measure of a concept is called an *epistemic relationship*. Unfortunately, this linkage between concept and operation cannot be tested except by intuitive means.

A conceptual variable analysis of the relationship between innovativeness and cosmopoliteness is illustrated with an example from the Ryan and Gross (1943) hybrid corn study in Iowa.

4. An empirical hypothesis is often accepted or rejected on

6. The development of general hypotheses may also be a result of derivations from other general hypotheses. For example, if concept *A* varies directly with concept *B,* and concept *B* varies directly with concept *C,* then it is postulated that concept *A* varies directly with concept *C.*

General Hypothesis: Innovativeness   varies   cosmopoliteness
                   (Concept)   directly   (Concept)
                     | with |

(Theoretical   (Epistemic   (Epistemic
  level)   relationship)   relationship)
---   ---   ---   ---   ---   ---   ---   ---   ---
(Empirical | |
  level)

Empirical Hypothesis: The time   varies   the number
                 of adoption   directly   of trips to
                 of hybrid   with   Des Moines
                 corn
                 (Operation)   (Operation)

the basis of statistical tests of significance, but other criteria
might be used. In the hybrid corn study, Ryan and Gross
(1943) reported a positive significant relationship between
time of adoption of hybrid seed and the number of trips outside of the Iowa communities in which the respondents resided.

5. A general hypothesis is supported or rejected on the
basis of the tests of corresponding empirical hypotheses.
Truth claims may be added to a general hypothesis by
similar findings from other analyses of the two conceptual
variables in a variety of different social systems. As additional support is added to a general hypothesis, greater confidence may be placed in the relationship between the two
concepts, and this relationship may be considered a generalization and eventually perhaps a principle.

6. The relationships between each of the two concepts and
other concepts may be analyzed, and, as findings of this na-

ture gradually accumulate, a body of general sociological theory is developed. In this fashion evidence is accumulated in an integrated and consistent manner. The eventual goal is the development of a body of more general sociological theory composed of the matrix of interrelationships among a number of relevant concepts.

Some critics of conceptual variable analysis might argue that most scientists intuitively use the essential features of this approach to theory without going through the mechanics of specifying concepts, operations, and epistemic relationships. This is undoubtedly true, but in the case of diffusion research, there is probably need more adequately to formalize the wealth of findings available in terms of more general concepts than have been used in most past studies. Conceptual variable analysis not only offers potential usefulness in future diffusion research but also provides one method for synthesizing past research findings.

Generalizations

Throughout the book, a number of generalizations have been presented to synthesize the major findings. A total listing of these generalizations provides a skeleton summary of the major conclusions of what is now known about the diffusion of innovations.

1. Innovativeness of individuals is related to a modern rather than a traditional orientation.
2. An individual's innovativeness varies directly with the norms of his social system on innovativeness.
3. Relatively later adopters are more likely to discontinue innovations than are earlier adopters.
4. Impersonal information sources are most important at

the awareness stage, and personal sources are most important at the evaluation stage in the adoption process.

5. Cosmopolite information sources are most important at the awareness stage, and localite information sources are most important at the evaluation stage.

6. There is little evidence that lack of knowledge about innovations actually delays their adoption.

7. Awareness occurs at a more rapid rate than does adoption.

8. The first individuals to adopt innovations require a shorter adoption period than do relatively later adopters.

9. The awareness-to-trial period is longer than the trial-to-adoption period.

10. The awareness-to-trial period is shorter for relatively earlier adopters than for later adopters.

11. The trial-to-adoption period is longer for relatively earlier adopters than for later adopters.

12. Earlier adopters try innovations on a smaller scale than later adopters.

13. A crisis emphasizes the relative advantage of an innovation and affects its rate of adoption.

14. The relative advantage of a new idea, as perceived by members of a social system, affects its rate of adoption.

15. The compatibility of a new idea, as perceived by members of a social system, affects its rate of adoption.

16. The complexity of an innovation, as perceived by members of a social system, affects its rate of adoption.

17. The divisibility of an innovation, as perceived by members of a social system, affects its rate of adoption.

18. Relatively earlier adopters may perceive divisibility as more important than later adopters.

19. The communicability of an innovation, as perceived by members of a social system, affects its rate of adoption.

20. Adopter distributions follow a bell-shaped curve over time and approach normality.

21. Earlier adopters are younger in age than later adopters.

22. Earlier adopters have higher social status than later adopters.

23. Earlier adopters have a more favorable financial position than later adopters.

24. Earlier adopters have more specialized operations than later adopters.

25. Earlier adopters have a type of mental ability different from that of later adopters.

26. Impersonal sources of information are more important than personal sources for relatively earlier adopters of innovations than for later adopters.

27. Cosmopolite sources of information are more important than localite sources for relatively earlier adopters of innovations than for later adopters.

28. Earlier adopters utilize information sources that are in closer contact with the origin of new ideas than later adopters.

29. Earlier adopters utilize a greater number of different information sources than do later adopters.

30. Earlier adopters are more cosmopolite than later adopters.

31. Earlier adopters have more opinion leadership than later adopters.

32. There is considerable shifting of individuals in a social system from one category to another over time.

33. Laggards are most likely to drop out of the social system.

34. Innovators are perceived as deviants by other members of their social system.

35. Innovators perceive themselves as deviant from the norms of their social system.

36. Personal influence from peers is most important at the evaluation stage in the adoption process and less important at other stages.

37. Personal influence from peers is more important for relatively later adopters than for earlier adopters.

38. Personal influence from peers is more important in uncertain situations than in clear-cut situations.

39. Opinion leaders conform more closely to social system norms than the average member.

40. There is little overlapping among the different types of opinion leaders.

41. Opinion leaders use more impersonal, technically accurate, and cosmopolite sources of information than do their followers.

42. Opinion leaders are more cosmopolite than their followers.

43. Opinion leaders have more social participation than their followers.

44. Opinion leaders have higher social status than their followers.

45. Opinion leaders are more innovative than their followers.

46. Each adopter category is mainly influenced by individuals of the same or a more innovative adopter category.

47. Social system norms on innovativeness seem to determine, at least in part, the innovativeness of opinion leaders.

48. Differences in innovativeness between individuals are a more important barrier to the flow of ideas in a social system where the norms are modern than where they are traditional.

49. The extent of promotional efforts by change agents is directly related to the rate of adoption of an innovation.

50. Commercial change agents are more important at the trial stage than at any other stage in the adoption process.

51. Commercial change agents are more important for earlier adopters than for later adopters at the trial stage.

52. Change agents have more communication with higher-status than with lower-status members of a social system.

It is not difficult to criticize the wording of most of these generalizations in terms of (1) their lack of succinctness and (2) their lack of generality. As an example of the former criticism, consider the generalization that "opinion leaders have higher social status than their followers." In more succinct terms this generalization would be "opinion leadership varies directly with social status." In the case of several generalizations, succinctness was sacrificed for the added clarity of a more lengthy statement.

The lack of general sociological concepts in many of the generalizations indicates these statements are, at best, in the "middle range" and need to approach greater generality before they are considered at the level of general sociological theory. As an example, consider the generalization that "earlier adopters have more specialized operations than do later adopters." Perhaps after further research findings are available from a wider range of contexts, the more general statement may be made that "innovativeness varies directly with specialization."

Future Directions

Many specific suggestions for future research were mentioned in each of the preceding ten chapters. At this point, only one further methodological recommendation should be made, the need for "survey experiments" or "field experiments" to test some of the basic generalizations listed in this chapter. There is a limit to what findings from the usual type of correlational analysis of survey data can tell us. For example, little of a cause-and-effect nature about innovativeness can be definitely determined until a research design with a before-after measurement with an adequate control is utilized. There are remarkably few before-after designs with a control that have been used in natural or field conditions, and it is this type of study that offers great promise in testing the present generalizations under more adequately controlled conditions.

This book is actually the first of two volumes. The second volume can perhaps be written in ten or fifteen years after the leads for research suggested here have been followed up and expanded upon.

Bibliography

The references included in this bibliography are organized under two general headings (1) the research studies on diffusion cited in the present book, and (2) general references cited for their relevance to the diffusion of innovations but which are not diffusion research studies. The former heading of "research cited" includes annotations for some of the major diffusion investigations. The research tradition for each diffusion study is coded in the following fashion.*

    A — Anthropology
    ES — Early Sociology
    RS — Rural Sociology
    E — Education
    I — Industrial
    MS — Medical Sociology
    O — Other studies not included in the six
         major diffusion research traditions.

DIFFUSION RESEARCH CITED

HELEN C. ABELL (1951), *The Differential Adoption of Homemaking Practices in Four Rural Areas of New York State,* Ph.D. Thesis, Ithaca, N.Y., Cornell University.–RS

* The assignment of research studies to traditions was somewhat arbitrary in a few cases.

HELEN C. ABELL (1952), "The Use of Scale Analysis in a Study of the Differential Adoption of Homemaking Practices," *Rural Sociology*, 17: 161–167.–RS

HELEN C. ABELL and others (1957), *Communication of Agricultural Information in a South-Central New York County*, Ithaca, New York Agricultural Experiment Station Mimeo Bulletin 49.–RS

DAVID F. ABERLE and OMER C. STEWART (1957), *Navaho and Ute Peyotism: A Chronological and Distributional Study*, Boulder, University of Colorado Studies, Series in Anthropology 6.–A

RICHARD N. ADAMS (1941), "Personnel in Culture Change: A Test of a Hypothesis," *Social Forces*, 30: 185–189.–A

DAVID ADLER (1955), *An Analysis of Quality in the Associated Public School Systems Through a Study of the Patterns of Diffusion of Selected Educational Practices*, D.Ed. Thesis, N.Y., Teachers College, Columbia University.–E

MANUEL ALERS-MONTALVO (1957), "Cultural Change in a Costa Rican Village," *Human Organization*, 15: 2–7.–A

HARLEY EARL ALLEN (1956), *The Diffusion of Educational Practices in the School Systems of the Metropolitan School Study Council*, D.Ed. Thesis, N.Y., Teachers College, Columbia University.–E

ANGELO ANASTASIO (1960), *Port Haven: A Changing Northwestern Community*, Pullman, Washington Agricultural Experiment Station Bulletin 616.–A

MARVIN A. ANDERSON (1955a), *Informational Sources Important in the Acceptance and Use of Fertilizer in Iowa*, Knoxville, Tennessee Valley Authority Report P 55–1.–RS

MARVIN A. ANDERSON (1955b), *Statistical Supplement to Informational Sources Important in the Acceptance and Use of Fertilizer in Iowa*, Knoxville, Tennessee Valley Authority Report SSP 55–1.–RS

MARVIN A. ANDERSON and others (1956), *An Appraisal of Factors Affecting the Acceptance and Use of Fertilizer in Iowa, 1953*, Ames, Iowa Agricultural Experiment Station Special Report 16.–RS

F. J. ANSCOMBE (1961), "Estimating a Mixed-Exponential Response Law," *Journal of American Statistical Association*, 56: 493–502.–O

ANACLETO APODACA (1952), "Corn and Custom: Introduction of Hybrid Corn to Spanish American Farmers in New Mexico," in Edward H. Spicer (ed.), *Human Problems in Technological Change*, N.Y., Russell Sage Foundation.–A

ANTONIO M. ARCE (1959), *Rational Introduction of Technology on a Costa Rican Coffee Hacienda: Sociological Implications*, Ph.D. Thesis, East Lansing, Michigan State University.–A

JOSEPH B. ARMSTRONG (1959), *County Agent Activities and the*

Adoption of Soil-Building Practices, M.S. Thesis, Lexington, University of Kentucky.–RS

HERBERT A. AURBACH and HAROLD F. KAUFMAN (1956), *Knowledge and Use of Recommended Farm Practices,* State College, Mississippi Agricultural Experiment Station Information Sheet 540.–RS

KURT W. BACK (1958), "The Change-Prone Person in Puerto Rico," *Public Opinion Quarterly,* 22: 330–340.–O

ANDREW W. BAIRD and WILFRID C. BAILEY (1960), *Test Demonstration and Related Areas: Review of Literature,* State College, Mississippi Agricultural Experiment Station Mimeo Bulletin.–RS

JASPER N. BAKER (1954), *A Study of the Relative Effectiveness of Sources from Which Farmers Get Information Regarding Agricultural Station Results,* Ph.D. Thesis, Minneapolis, University of Minnesota.–RS

BERNARD BARBER and LYLE S. LOBEL (1952), "Fashion in Women's Clothes and the American Social System," *Social Forces,* 31: 124–131.–ES

A. P. BARNABAS (1958), "Characteristics of 'Lay Leaders' in Extension Work," *Journal of the M.S. University of Baroda,* 7: 1–21.–RS

A. P. BARNABAS (1960), *Social Change in a North Indian Village,* Ph.D. Thesis, Ithaca, N.Y., Cornell University.–RS

HOMER G. BARNETT (1941), "Personal Conflicts and Culture Change," *Social Forces,* 20: 160–171.–A

HOMER G. BARNETT (1953), *Innovation: The Basis of Cultural Change,* N.Y., McGraw-Hill.–A An anthropological and psychological analysis of the adoption of new ideas by individuals.

THOMAS M. BARRINGTON (1953), *The Introduction of Selected Educational Practices into Teachers Colleges and Their Laboratory Schools,* N.Y., Columbia University Teachers College, Bureau of Publications.–E

ALLAN BARTON (1961), Unpublished data, N.Y., Columbia University, Bureau of Applied Social Research.–O

GLEN T. BARTON and RALPH A. LOOMIS (1957), "Differential Rates of Change in Output Per Unit of Input," *Journal of Farm Economics,* 39: 1551–1561.–O

BATTEN, BARTON, DURSTINE, and OSBORN ADVERTISING AGENCY (1958), *Colortown: A Profile of Color Set Owners,* N.Y., National Broadcasting Company.–O

WARD W. BAUDER (1960), *Iowa Farm Operators' and Farm Landlords' Knowledge of, Participation in and Acceptance of the Old Age and Survivors Insurance Program,* Ames, Iowa Agricultural and Home Economics Experiment Station Research Bulletin 479.–RS

WARD BAUDER (1961), *Influences on Acceptance of Fertilizer Practices in Piatt County,* Champaign, Illinois Agricultural Experiment Station Bulletin 679.–RS

GEORGE M. BEAL (1958), "Information Sources in the Decision-Making Process," Paper presented at the Rural Sociological Society, Pullman, Wash.–RS

GEORGE M. BEAL and JOE M. BOHLEN (1957), *The Diffusion Process,* Ames, Iowa Agricultural Extension Service Special Report 18.–RS

GEORGE M. BEAL and EVERETT M. ROGERS (1957a), "Informational Sources in the Adoption Process of New Fabrics," *Journal of Home Economics,* 49: 630–634.–RS

GEORGE M. BEAL and EVERETT M. ROGERS (1957b), "Time of Adoption of New Fabrics," unpublished paper, Ames, Iowa State University.–RS

GEORGE M. BEAL and EVERETT M. ROGERS (1958), "The Communication Process in the Purchase of New Products: An Application of Reference Group Theory," paper presented at American Association of Public Opinion Research, Chicago, Ill.–RS

GEORGE M. BEAL and EVERETT M. ROGERS (1959), "The Scientist as a Referent in the Communication of New Technology," *Public Opinion Quarterly,* 22: 555–563.–RS

GEORGE M. BEAL and EVERETT M. ROGERS (1960), *The Adoption of Two Farm Practices in a Central Iowa Community,* Ames, Iowa Agricultural and Home Economics Experiment Station Special Report 26.–RS

GEORGE M. BEAL and others (1957), "Validity of the Concept of Stages in the Adoption Process," *Rural Sociology,* 22: 166–168.–RS

GEORGE M. BEAL and others (1958a), *The Fertilizer Dealer: Attitudes and Activity,* Ames, Iowa State University, Rural Sociology Mimeo Report.–RS

GEORGE M. BEAL and others (1958b), *The Role of the Retail Dealer in the Adoption of Commercial Fertilizer by the Ultimate Consumers,* Ames, Iowa State University, Rural Sociology Mimeo Report.–RS

GEORGE M. BEAL and others (1959a), *Agricultural Chemical Use Patterns,* Ames, Iowa State University, Rural Sociology Mimeo Report.–RS

GEORGE M. BEAL and others (1959b), *The Effectiveness of a Free Sample Coupon Promotional Technique,* Ames, Iowa State University Rural Sociology Report 6.–RS

ROBERT C. BEALER and FREDERICK C. FLIEGEL (1961), "A Meta-

Sociological Perspective for Theories of Change in Rural Sociology," paper presented at Rural Sociological Society, Ames, Iowa.–RS

JOHN C. BELCHER (1958), "Acceptance of the Salk Polio Vaccine," *Rural Sociology,* 23: 158–170.–RS

JOHN C. BELCHER and DONALD G. HAY (1959), *Use of Health Care Services and Enrollment in Voluntary Health Insurance in Hancock County, Georgia, 1956,* Athens, Georgia Agricultural Experiment Station Bulletin N.S. 72.–RS

JOHN C. BELCHER and DONALD G. HAY (1960), *Use of Health Care Services and Enrollment in Voluntary Health Insurance in Habersham County, Georgia, 1957,* Athens, Georgia Agricultural Experiment Station Bulletin N.S. 73.–RS

JAMES L. BEMILLER (1960), *Development of a Scale to Measure the Rationality Element of Farm Management Ability,* M.S. Thesis, Columbus, Ohio State University.–RS

JOSEPH BEN-DAVID (1960), "Roles and Innovations in Medicine," *American Journal of Sociology,* 65: 557–568.–MS

M. B. BENVENUTI (1958), *Farming in Cultural Change,* Ph.D. Thesis, Wageningen, Netherlands, University of Wageningen.–RS

B. BENVENUTI (1961), *Farming in Cultural Change,* Assen, Netherlands, Van Gorcum.–RS

ALVIN L. BERTRAND (1951), *Agricultural Mechanization and Social Change in Rural Louisiana,* Baton Rouge, Louisiana Agricultural Experiment Station Bulletin 458.–RS

ALVIN L. BERTRAND and others (1956), *Factors Associated with Agricultural Mechanization in the Southwest Region,* Fayetteville, Arkansas Agricultural Experiment Station Bulletin 567.–RS

BOND L. BIBLE and FRANCENA L. NOLAN (1960), *The Role of the Extension Committee Member in the County Extension Organization in Pennsylvania,* University Park, Pennsylvania Agricultural Experiment Station Bulletin 665.–RS

BOND L. BIBLE and others (1961), "Consensus on Role Definition of the County Extension Executive Committee Member," *Rural Sociology,* 26: 146–156.–RS

JOHN BLACKMORE and others (1955), *Test-Demonstration Farms and the Spread of Improved Farm Practices in Southwest Virginia,* Knoxville, Tennessee Valley Authority Report P 55-3.–RS

PETER VON BLANKENBURG (1960), *Bäuerliche Wirtschaftsfuhrug im Kraftfeld der sozialen Umwelt,* Hanover, Germany, Schaper.–RS

WESLEY BLISS (1952), "In the Wake of the Wheel: Introduction of the Wagon to the Papago Indians of Southern Arizona," in Edward H.

Spicer (ed.), *Human Problems in Technological Change*, N.Y., Russell Sage Foundation.–A

HOWARD J. BONSER (1958a), *Better Farming Practices Through Rural Community Organizations*, Knoxville, Tennessee Agricultural Experiment Station Bulletin 286.–RS

HOWARD J. BONSER (1958b), *Better Homemaking Practices Through Rural Community Organizations*, Knoxville, Tennessee Agricultural Experiment Station Bulletin 287.–RS

LALIA PHIPPS BOONE (1949), "Patterns of Innovation in the Language of the Oil Field," *American Speech*, 24: 31–37.–O

SANTI PRIYA BOSE (1961), "Characteristics of Farmers Who Adopt Agricultural Practices in Indian Villages," *Rural Sociology*, 26: 138–145.–RS

S. P. BOSE (1962), "Peasant Values and Innovation in India," *American Journal of Sociology*, 67: 552–560.–RS

FRANCIS S. BOURNE (1957), "Group Influence in Marketing and Public Relations," in Samuel P. Hayes and Rensis Likert (eds.), *Some Applications of Behavioural Research*, Paris, France, UNESCO.–O

RAYMOND V. BOWERS (1937), "The Direction of Intra-Societal Diffusion," *American Sociological Review*, 2: 826–836.–ES

RAYMOND V. BOWERS (1938), "Differential Intensity of Intra-Societal Diffusion," *American Sociological Review*, 3: 21–31.–ES One of the early empirical analyses of the spread of an innovation, amateur radios.

LOWELL BRANDNER (1960), *Evaluation for Congruence as a Factor in Accelerated Adoption of an Agricultural Innovation*, Ph.D. Thesis, Madison, University of Wisconsin.–RS

LOWELL BRANDNER and MURRAY A. STRAUS (1959), "Congruence Versus Profitability in the Diffusion of Hybrid Sorghum," *Rural Sociology*, 24: 381–383.–RS

ORVILLE BRIM (1954), "The Acceptance of New Behavior in Child-Rearing," *Human Relations*, 7: 473–492.–O

ROBERT C. BROOKS, JR. (1957), " 'Word-of-Mouth' Advertising in Selling New Products," *Journal of Marketing*, 22: 154–161.–O

RABEL J. BURDGE (1961), *Development of a Scale to Measure Leisure-Orientation*, M.S. Thesis, Columbus, Ohio State University.–RS

G. L. BURLESON (1950a), *Studying Extension Work with Farmers and Farm Homemakers in Washington Parish, Louisiana: Negro Families*, Baton Rouge, Louisiana Agricultural Extension Service Mimeo Bulletin.–RS

G. L. BURLESON (1950b), *Studying Extension Work with Farmers and Farm Homemakers in Washington Parish, Louisiana: White Fam-*

ilies, Baton Rouge, Louisiana Agriculutral Extension Service Mimeo Bulletin.–RS

TOM BURNS and G. M. STALKER (1961), *The Management of Innovation*, London, Tavistock.–I

J. B. CAIRD and H. A. MOISLEY (1961), "Leadership and Innovation in the Crofting Communities of the Outer Hebrides," *Sociological Review*, 9: 85–102.–A

HERBERT L. CAMPBELL (1959), *Factors Related to Differential Use of Information Sources*, M.S. Thesis, Ames, Iowa State University.–RS

HERBERT L. CAMPBELL (in press), *Patterns of Communication about a Farm Practice among Farmers in Iowa*, Ph.D. Thesis, Ames, Iowa State University.–RS

REX R. CAMPBELL (in press), *Attitudes and Values of Farm Operators as Related to the Adoption of Farm Practices in Two Rural Missouri Communities*, Ph.D. Thesis, Columbia, University of Missouri.–RS

REX CAMPBELL and JOHN BENNETT (1961), *Your Audience: What It's Like*, Columbia, Missouri Agricultural Experiment Station Bulletin 771.–RS

REX R. CAMPBELL and JOHN S. HOLIK (1960), "The Relationship Between Group Structure and the Perception of Community's Willingness to Change," paper presented to Rural Sociological Society, University Park, Penn.–RS

THEODORE CAPLOW (1952), "Market Attitudes: A Research Report from the Medical Field," *Harvard Business Review*, 30: 105–112.–MS

THEODORE CAPLOW and JOHN J. RAYMOND (1954), "Factors Influencing the Selection of Pharmaceutical Products," *Journal of Marketing*, 19: 18–23.–MS

C. F. CARTER and B. R. WILLIAMS (1957), *Industry and Technical Progress: Factors Governing the Speed of Application of Science*, London, Oxford University Press.–I

C. F. CARTER and B. R. WILLIAMS (1959), "The Characteristics of Technically Progressive Firms," *Journal of Industrial Economics*, 7: 87–104.–I

ALVARO CHAPARRO (1955), *Role Expectation and Adoption of New Farm Practices*, Ph.D. Thesis, University Park, Pennsylvania State University.–RS

ALVARO CHAPARRO (1956), "Soziale Aspekte des Kulturellen Wandels: Die Diffusion neuer Techniken in der Landwirtschaft," *Kölner Zeitschrift f. Soziologie und Sozialpsychologie*, 8: 567–594.–RS

S. R. CHAPDE and others (1959), "Role of Demonstration Trials on

Cultivators' Fields in the Spread of Improved Farm Practices," *Nagpur Agriculture College Magazine*, 33: 1–8.–RS

F. STUART CHAPIN (1928), *Cultural Change*, N.Y., Century.–ES The original statement of the S-shaped adopter distribution.

DENNIS CHAPMAN (1944), *Agricultural Information and the Farmer*, London, England, Social Survey Report 38.–O

LINCOLN H. CLARK (1958), *Consumer Behavior*, N.Y., Harper.–O

H. FRANKLIN CLENDENEN (1961), "Novelty Selection and Some Television Phenomena," paper presented to Northwest Anthropological Conference, Vancouver, British Columbia, Canada.–A

WALTER COCKING (1951), *The Regional Introduction of Educational Practices in Urban School Systems in the United States*, N.Y., Teachers College, Columbia University, Institute of Administrative Research Study 6.–E A nationwide study of the diffusion of education ideas.

REUBEN COHEN (1962), "A Theoretical Model for Consumer Market Prediction," *Sociological Inquiry*, 32: 43–50.–O

A. LEE COLEMAN (1946), *Some Aspects of Human Relations in Soil Conservation*, Washington, D.C. U.S.D.A., B.A.E. unpublished report.–RS

A. LEE COLEMAN (1951), "Differential Contact with Extension Work in a New York Rural Community," *Rural Sociology*, 16: 207–216.–RS

A. LEE COLEMAN and C. PAUL MARSH (1955), "Differential Communication Among Farmers in a Kentucky County," *Rural Sociology*, 20: 93–101.–RS

JAMES S. COLEMAN and HERBERT MENZEL (1955), *On the Flow of Scientific Information in the Medical Profession: A Study of the Adoption of a New Drug by the Medical Community*, N.Y., Columbia University, Bureau of Applied Social Research Mimeo Report.–MS

JAMES COLEMAN and others (1957), "The Diffusion of an Innovation," *Sociometry*, 20: 253–270.–MS

JAMES COLEMAN and others (1959), "Social Processes in Physicians' Adoption of a New Drug," *Journal of Chronic Diseases*, 9: 1–19.–MS

JAMES COLEMAN and others (in press), *Doctors and New Drugs*, N.Y., The Free Press of Glencoe.–MS

JAMES H. COPP (1956), *Personal and Social Factors Associated With the Adoption of Recommended Farm Practices Among Cattlemen*, Manhattan, Kansas Agricultural Experiment Station Technical Bulletin 83.–RS

JAMES H. COPP (1958), "Toward Generalization in Farm Practice Research," *Rural Sociology*, 23: 103–111.–RS

JAMES H. COPP and others (1958), "The Function of Information

Sources in the Farm Practice Adoption Process," *Rural Sociology*, 23: 146–157.–RS

C. MILTON COUGHENOUR (1959), *Agricultural Agencies as Information Sources for Farmers in a Kentucky County, 1950–1955*, Lexington, Kentucky Agricultural Experiment Station Progress Report 82. –RS

C. MILTON COUGHENOUR (1960a), Personal communication, Lexington, University of Kentucky.–RS

C. MILTON COUGHENOUR (1960b), "The Functioning of Farmers' Characteristics in Relation to Contact with Media and Practice Adoption," *Rural Sociology*, 25: 183–297.–RS

C. MILTON COUGHENOUR (1961), "The Practice-Use Tree and the Adoption, Drop-Out, and Non-Adoption of Recommended Farm Practices: A Progress Report," paper presented at Rural Sociological Society, Ames, Iowa.–RS

C. MILTON COUGHENOUR and N. B. PATELL (1962), *Trends in Use of Recommended Farm Practices and Farm Information Sources in 12 Kentucky Neighborhoods*, Lexington, Kentucky Agricultural Experiment Station Progress Report 111.–RS

COUNCIL ON SOCIAL WORK EDUCATION (1959), *Interprofessional Training Goals for Technical Assistance Personnel Abroad*, N.Y., Council on Social Work Education.–O

GORDON J. CUMMINGS (1950), *The Differential Adoption of Recommended Farm Practices Among Dairymen in a New York Community*, M.S. Thesis, Ithaca, N.Y., Cornell University.–RS

CLARENCE DANHOF (1949), "Observations on Entrepreneurship in Agriculture," in Harvard Research Center on Entrepreneurship History (ed.), *Change and the Entrepreneur*, Cambridge, Mass., Harvard University Press.–I

ALICE DAVIS (1940), "Technicways in American Civilization," *Social Forces*, 18: 317–330.–ES

ALVA L. DAVIS and RAUEN I. McDAVID, JR. (1949), " 'Shivaree': An Example of Cultural Diffusion," *American Speech*, 24: 249–255.–O

MORRIS DAVIS (1959), "Community Attitudes Toward Fluoridation," *Public Opinion Quarterly*, 23: 474–482.–MS

ALFRED DEAN (1958), *Some Factors Related to "Rationality" in Decision-Making Among Farm Operators*, M.A. Thesis, Chapel Hill, University of North Carolina.–RS

ALFRED DEAN and others (1958), "Some Factors Related to Rationality in Decision Making Among Farm Operators," *Rural Sociology*, 23: 121–135.–RS

LEILA CALHOUN DEASY (1956), "Socio-Economic Status and Participation in the Poliomyelitus Vaccine Trial," *American Sociological Review,* 21: 185–191.–MS

MELVIN L. DEFLEUR (1962), "Mass Communication Theory and the Study of Rumor," *Sociological Inquiry,* 32: 51–70.–O

GORDON F. DEJONG and C. MILTON COUGHENOUR (1960), "Reliability and Comparability of Two Instruments for Determining Reference Groups in Farm Practice Decisions," *Rural Sociology,* 25: 298–307.–RS

ELMER C. DENNIS (1961a), Personal communication, Doane Agricultural Service, St. Louis, Missouri.–O

ELMER C. DENNIS (1961b), *Farm Consumption and Purchase Characteristics of Petroleum Products in 1960: Attitudinal Highlights,* St. Louis, Missouri, Doane Agricultural Service.–O

PAUL J. DEUTSCHMANN (1961), "Debate Viewing, Conversation and Changes in Voting Intentions in Lansing, Michigan," East Lansing, Michigan State University, unpublished paper.–O

PAUL J. DEUTSCHMANN and WAYNE A. DANIELSON (1960), "Diffusion of Knowledge of the Major News Story," *Journalism Quarterly,* 37: 345–355.–O

PAUL J. DEUTSCHMANN and others (1961), Research Project Underway on the Diffusion and Adoption of Farm Practices in a Colombian Community, San Jose, Costa Rica, Communications Research Center.–O

ELIZABETH R. DICKINSON (1955), *A Communication Study: Characteristics of Schuyler County, New York, Farmers Using Eleven Different Media as Sources for Obtaining Information on New Farming Practices,* M.S. Thesis, Ithaca, N.Y., Cornell University.–RS

ROBERT M. DIMIT (1954), *Diffusion and Adoption of Approved Farm Practices in 11 Counties in Southwest Virginia,* Ph.D. Thesis, Ames, Iowa State University.–RS

HENRY F. DOBYNS (1951), "Blunders with *Bolsas:* A Case Study of Diffusion of Closed-Basin Agriculture," *Human Organization,* 10: 25–32.–A

STUART C. DODD (1950), "The Interactance Hypothesis: A Gravity Model Fitting Physical Masses and Human Groups," *American Sociological Review,* 15: 245–256.–O

STUART C. DODD (1953), "Testing Message Diffusion in Controlled Experiments: Charting the Distance and Time Factors in the Interactance Hypothesis," *American Sociological Review,* 18: 410–416.–O

STUART C. DODD (1955), "Diffusion Is Predictable: Testing Probability Models for Laws of Interaction," *American Sociological Review,* 10: 392–401.–O

STUART C. DODD (1958), "Formulas for Spreading Opinions," *Public Opinion Quarterly*, 22: 537–554.–O

SAMUEL A. DUM (1949), *Impact of Technological and Economic Changes on Dairy Production in Five Indiana Areas*, Ph.D. Thesis, Lafayette, Indiana, Purdue University.–O

JAMES A. DUNCAN and BURTON W. KREITLOW (1954), "Selected Cultural Characteristics and the Acceptance of Educational Programs and Practices," *Rural Sociology*, 19: 349–357.–RS

GERHARD C. EICHHOLZ (1961), *Analysis of Teacher Rejection of Audio-Visual Materials*, Ph.D. Thesis, Columbus, Ohio State University.–E

GERHARD EICHHOLZ and EVERETT M. ROGERS (in press), "Resistance to the Adoption of Audio-Visual Aids by Elementary School Teachers: Contrast and Similarities to Agricultural Innovation," in Matthew B. Miles (ed.), *The Nature of Educational Innovation*, N.Y., Columbia University Teachers College Bureau of Publications.–E

F. E. EMERY and O. A. OESER (1958), *Information, Decision and Action: A Study of the Psychological Determinants of Changes in Farming Techniques*, N.Y., Cambridge University Press. An investigation of the adoption of new farm ideas among 36 Australian farmers. –RS

JOHN L. ENOS (1958), "A Measure of the Rate of Technological Progress in the Petroleum Refining Industry," *Journal of Industrial Economy*, 6: 180–197.–I

JOHN L. ENOS (1960), "Invention and Innovation in the Petroleum Refining Industry," paper presented at the Conference on the Economic and Social Factors Determining the Rate and Direction of Inventive Activity, N.Y.–I

CHARLES JOHN ERASMUS (1952a), "Agricultural Changes in Haiti: Patterns of Resistance and Acceptance," *Human Organization*, 11: 20–26.–A

CHARLES JOHN ERASMUS (1952b), "Changing Folk Beliefs and the Relativity of Empirical Knowledge," *Southwestern Journal of Anthropology*, 8: 411–428.–A

CHARLES J. ERASMUS (1961), *Man Takes Control: Cultural Development and American Aid*, Minneapolis, University of Minnesota Press.–A

HAROLD FALLDING (1957), *Social Factors in Serrated Tussock Control: A Study of Agricultural Extension*, Sydney, Australia, University of Sydney Department of Agricultural Economics Research Bulletin 1.–RS

HAROLD FALLDING (1958), *Precept and Practice on North Coast Dairy Farms,* Sydney, Australia, University of Sydney Department of Agricultural Economics Research Bulletin 2.–RS

ORLANDO FALS BORDA (1959), *The Theory and Reality of Sociocultural Change in Colombia,* Bogotá, Colombia, Universidad Nacional de Colombia, Monografia Sociologica 2.–RS

PHILO T. FARNSWORTH (1940), *Adaptation Processes in Public School Systems as Illustrated by a Study of Five Selected Innovations in Educational Service in New York, Connecticut, and Massachusetts,* N.Y., Columbia University Teachers College Bureau of Publications.–E

ALLIE CLAY FELDER (1954), *The Acceptance of Recommended Peanut Production and Marketing Practices in Nansemond County, Virginia, Relative to Family Organization, Family Values and Related Social and Economic Status Factors,* Ph.D. Thesis, Columbus, Ohio State University.–RS

ROBERT FERBER and HUGH G. WALES (1958), *The Effectiveness of Pharmaceutical Promotion,* Urbana, University of Illinois.–O

LOYD K. FISCHER and JOHN F. TIMMONS (1959), *Progress and Problems in the Iowa Soil Conservation Districts Program,* Ames, Iowa Agricultural and Home Economics Experiment Station Research Bulletin 466.–O

GEORGE FISK (1959), "Media Influence Reconsidered," *Public Opinion Quarterly,* 23: 83–91.–O

FREDERICK C. FLIEGEL (1956), "A Multiple Correlation Analysis of Factors Associated with Adoption of Farm Practices," *Rural Sociology,* 21: 284–292.–RS

FREDERICK C. FLIEGEL (1957), "Farm Income and the Adoption of Farm Practices," *Rural Sociology,* 22: 159–162.–RS

FREDERICK C. FLIEGEL (1959), "Aspirations of Low-Income Farmers and Their Performance and Potential for Change," *Rural Sociology,* 24: 205–214.–RS

FREDERICK C. FLIEGEL (1960), "Obstacles to Change for the Low-Income Farmer," *Rural Sociology,* 25: 347–351.–RS

FREDERICK C. FLIEGEL (1961), "Traditionalism in the Farm Family and Technological Change," unpublished paper, University Park, Pennsylvania State University.–RS

FREDERICK C. FLIEGEL and JOSEPH E. KIVLIN (1961), "Farm Practice Attributes and Adoption Rates," Paper presented at the Rural Sociological Society, Ames, Iowa.–RS One of the first adequate investigations of the relationship of characteristics of innovations to their rate of adoption.

FREDERICK C. FLIEGEL and JOSEPH E. KIVLIN (1962), *Differences Among Improved Farm Practices as Related to Rate of Adoption*, University Park, Pennsylvania Agricultural Experiment Station Research Bulletin 691.–RS

WILLIAM L. FLINN (1961), *Combined Influence of Group Norms and Personal Characteristics on Innovativeness*, M.S. Thesis, Columbus, Ohio State University.–RS

ROBERT H. FOSEN (1956a), *Structural and Social Psychological Factors Affecting Differential Acceptance of Recommended Agricultural Practices: A Study in the Application of Reference Group Theory*, M.S. Thesis, Ithaca, N.Y., Cornell University.–RS

ROBERT H. FOSEN (1956b), *Social Solidarity and Differential Adoption of a Recommended Agricultural Practice*, Ph.D. Thesis, Ithaca, N.Y., Cornell University.–RS

PHILLIPS W. FOSTER (1956), *Differential Acceptance of an Extension Program as Related to Social and Economic Characteristics of a North Indian Village Population*, M.S. Thesis, Urbana, University of Illinois.–O

FOUNDATION FOR RESEARCH ON HUMAN BEHAVIOR (1956), *Group Influence in Marketing and Public Relations*, Ann Arbor, Michigan.–O

FOUNDATION FOR RESEARCH ON HUMAN BEHAVIOR (1959), *The Adoption of New Products: Process and Influence*, Ann Arbor, Michigan.–RS

LOUIS A. FOUNT and JOSEPH W. WOODLOCK (1960), "Early Prediction of Market Success for New Grocery Products," *Journal of Marketing*, 25: 31–38.–O

ROBERT FOX and others (1961), "The Introduction and Spread of Teaching Innovations to Promote Classroom Mental Health and Learning Efficiency," research project under way at University of Michigan Institute for Social Research, Ann Arbor.–E

DAVID G. FRANCIS (1960), *Communication Credibility of a Nonrecommended Innovation*, M.S. Thesis, Columbus, Ohio State University.–RS

DAVID G. FRANCIS and EVERETT M. ROGERS (1960), "Adoption of a Nonrecommended Innovation: The Grass Incubator," paper presented at the Rural Sociological Society, University Park, Penn.–RS

GEORGE GALLUP (1955), "The Absorption Rate of Ideas," *Public Opinion Quarterly*, 19: 234–242.–O

WILLIAM A. GAMSON (1961), "Public Information in a Fluoridation Referendum," *Health Education Journal*, 19: 47–54.–MS

WILLIAM A. GAMSON (1961), "The Fluoridation Dialogue: Is It an Ideological Conflict?" *Public Opinion Quarterly,* 25: 526–537.–MS

KENT GEIGER and ROBERT SOKOL (1960), "Educational Television in Boston," in Wilbur Schramm (ed.), *The Impact of Educational Television,* Urbana, University of Illinois Press.–O

C. S. GILLFILLIAN (1935), *The Sociology of Invention,* Chicago, Follett.–ES

WILLIE MAE GILLIS (1958), *The Adoption of Recommended Farm Practices in Alcorn County and Its Relationship to Other Variables,* State College, Mississippi Agricultural Experiment Station Mimeo Bulletin.–RS

MELVIN A. GLASER (1958), "A Study of the Public's Acceptance of the Salk Vaccine Programs," *American Journal of Public Health,* 48: 141–146.–MS

ROSE K. GOLDSEN and MAX RALIS (1957), *Factors Related to Acceptance of Innovations in Bang Chan, Thailand,* Ithaca, N.Y., Cornell University, Southeast Asia Program Data Paper 25.–O

BERNICE GOLDSTEIN (1959), *The Changing Protestant Ethic: Rural Patterns in Health, Work, and Leisure,* Ph.D. Thesis, Lafayette, Ind. Purdue University.–O

BERNICE GOLDSTEIN and RORERT L. EICHHORN (1961), "The Changing Protestant Ethic: Rural Patterns in Health, Work, and Leisure," *American Sociological Review,* 26: 557–565.–O

MARSHALL N. GOLDSTEIN and others (1961), *Educational Television Project: Preliminary Report Number One,* Eugene, University of Oregon Studies in Resistances to Cultural Innovations Mimeo Bulletin.–O

CARLE P. GRAFFUNDER (1961), *The Changing Role of the Agricultural Agent,* Ph.D. Thesis, East Lansing, Michigan State University.–RS

L. SAXON GRAHAM (1951), *Selection and Social Stratification,* Ph.D. Thesis, New Haven, Conn., Yale University.–O

SAXON GRAHAM (1954), "Cultural Compatibility in the Adoption of Television," *Social Forces,* 33: 166–170.–O

SAXON GRAHAM (1956), "Class and Conservatism in the Adoption of Innovations," *Human Relations,* 9: 91–100.–O

SAXON GRAHAM (1961), Personal communication, Roswell Park Memorial Institute, Buffalo, N.Y.–MS

JOSEPH H. GREENBERG (1951), "Social Variables in Acceptance or Rejection of Artificial Insemination," *American Sociological Review,* 16: 86–91.–O

Zvi Griliches (1957), "Hybrid Corn: An Exploration in the Economics of Technological Change," *Econometrica*, 25: 501–522.–O

Zvi Griliches (1958), "Research Costs and Social Returns: Hybrid Corn and Related Innovations," *Journal of Political Economy*, 5: 419–431.–O

Zvi Griliches (1960a), "Congruence Versus Profitability: A False Dichotomy," *Rural Sociology*, 25: 354–356.–O

Zvi Griliches (1960b), "Hybrid Corn and the Economics of Innovation," *Science*, 132: 275–280.–O

Zvi Griliches (1962), "Profitability versus Interaction: Another False Dichotomy," *Rural Sociology*, 27.–O

Neal C. Gross (1942), *The Diffusion of a Culture Trait in Two Iowa Townships*, M.S. Thesis, Ames, Iowa, State College.–RS

Neal Gross (1949), "The Differential Characteristics of Acceptors and Non-Acceptors of an Approved Agricultural Technological Practice," *Rural Sociology*, 14: 148–156.–RS

Neal C. Gross and Marvin J. Taves (1952), "Characteristics Associated with Acceptance of Recommended Farm Practices," *Rural Sociology*, 17: 321–328.–RS

Erna Gunther (1950), "The Westward Movement of Some Plains Traits," *American Anthropologist*, 52: 174–180.–A

Ralph Norman Haber (1961), "The Spread of an Innovation: High School Language Laboratories," unpublished paper, New Haven, Conn., Yale University.–E

Torsten Hagerstrand (1952), *The Propagation of Innovation Waves*, Lund, Sweden, Lund Studies in Geography 4.–O

Torsten Hagerstrand (1953), *Innovationsförloppet ur Korologisk Synpunkt*, Lund, Sweden, University of Lund, Department of Geography Bulletin 15.–O

Torsten Hagerstrand (1960), "On Monte Carlo-Simulation of Diffusion," unpublished paper, Lund, Sweden, University of Lund.–O

Bartlett Hague (in press), *Changing Function and Structure of Adoption of Selected Soil-Conservation and Woods Practices in Five Sample Areas*, Ph.D. Thesis, Ann Arbor, University of Michigan.–O

John Harp (1960), "A Note on Personality Variables in Diffusion Research," *Rural Sociology*, 25: 346–347.–RS

Jack S. Harris (1940), "The White Knife Shoshoni of Nevada," in Ralph Linton (ed.), *The Acculturation of Seven American Indian Tribes*, N.Y., Appleton-Century-Crofts.–A

Ruth Harris (1956), *Certain Socio-Economic Factors and Value*

Orientations as Related to the Adoption of Home Practices, M.S. Thesis, Madison, University of Wisconsin.–RS

EDWARD HASSINGER (1959), "Stages in the Adoption Process," *Rural Sociology*, 24: 52–53.–RS

A. EUGENE HAVENS (1962), *Social Psychological Factors Associated with Differential Adoption of New Technologies by Milk Producers*, Ph.D. Thesis, Columbus, Ohio State University.–RS

A. EUGENE HAVENS and EVERETT M. ROGERS (1961a), "Campaigns that Fail: Some Evidence From Past Research," paper presented at Ohio Valley Sociological Society, Cleveland, Ohio.–RS

A. EUGENE HAVENS and EVERETT M. ROGERS (1961b), "Adoption of Hybrid Corn: Profitability and the Interaction Effect," *Rural Sociology*, 26: 409–414.–RS

A. EUGENE HAVENS and EVERETT M. ROGERS (1961c), "A Theory of Adoption of Innovations," paper presented at Rural Sociological Society, Ames, Iowa.–RS

NORMAN G. HAWKINS (1959a), "Graduate Training for Health Research," paper presented at American Sociological Association, Chicago, Ill.–MS

NORMAN G. HAWKINS (1959b), "The Detailman and Preference Behavior," *Southwestern Social Science Quarterly*, 40: 213–224.–MS

FLORENCE HAWLEY (1946), "The Role of the Pueblo Social Organization in the Dissemination of Catholicism," *American Anthropologist*, 48: 407–415.–A

DONALD G. HAY and SHELDON G. LOWRY (1957), *Acceptance of Voluntary Health Insurance in Scotland Neck Community, North Carolina, 1955*, Raleigh, North Carolina Agricultural Experiment Station Progress Report, Rs–27.–RS

DONALD G. HAY and SHELDON G. LOWRY (1958), *Use of Health Care Services and Enrollment in Voluntary Health Insurance in Montgomery County, North Carolina, 1956*, Raleigh, North Carolina Agricultural Experiment Station Progress Report Rs–31.–RS

C. V. HESS and L. F. MILLER (1954), *Some Personal, Economic, and Sociological Factors Influencing Dairymen's Actions and Success*, University Park, Pennsylvania Experiment Station Bulletin 577.–O

PETER E. HILDEBRAND and EARL J. PARTENHEIMER (1958), "Socioeconomic Characteristics of Innovators," *Journal of Farm Economics*, 40: 446–449.–O

REUBEN HILL and others (1959), *The Family and Population Control: A Puerto Rican Experiment in Social Change*, Chapel Hill, University of North Carolina Press.–O

P. M. HILLEBRANDT (1958), *The Economics of the Use of Pesticides in Agriculture with Special Reference to Weedkillers on Wheat in the South Eastern Half of England,* Ph.D. Thesis, University of London.–O

DARYL J. HOBBS (1960), *Factors Related to the Use of Agricultural Chemicals on Iowa Farms,* M.S. Thesis, Ames, Iowa State University.–RS

GODFREY M. HOCHBAUM (1960), *Public Participation in Medical Screening Programs: A Socio-Psychological Study,* Washington, D.C., U.S. Public Health Service Bulletin.–MS

DONALD L. HOCHSTRASSER (1955), *The Concept of Cultural Diffusion: An Analysis Based on Contemporary Anthropological Usage,* M.A. Thesis, Lexington, University of Kentucky.–A

CHARLES R. HOFFER (1942), *Acceptance of Approved Farming Practices Among Farmers of Dutch Descent,* East Lansing, Michigan Experiment Station Special Bulletin 316.–RS

CHARLES R. HOFFER (1944), *Selected Social Factors Affecting Participation of Farmers in Agricultural Extension Work,* East Lansing, Michigan Agricultural Experiment Station Special Bulletin 331.–RS

CHARLES R. HOFFER and DALE STANGLAND (1958a), "Farmers' Attitudes and Values in Relation to Adoption of Approved Practices in Corn Growing," *Rural Sociology,* 23: 112–120.–RS

CHARLES R. HOFFER and DALE STANGLAND (1958b), *Farmers' Reactions to New Practices,* East Lansing, Michigan Agricultural Experiment Station Technical Bulletin. 264.–RS

ALLEN HOLMBERG (1960), Personal communication, Ithaca, N.Y., Cornell University.–A

DANIEL HORN and others (1959), "Cigarette Smoking Among High School Students," *American Journal of Public Health,* 49: 1497–1511. –MS

ERNA HRUSCHKA (1961), unpublished data, Stuttgart-Hohenheim, Germany, Institut für landwirtschaftliche Beratung an der Landwirtschaftlicken Hochschule.–RS

INDIAN PLANNING COMMISSION PROGRAMME EVALUATION ORGANIZATION (1958), *The Fifth Evaluation Report on Working of Community Development and N.E.S. Blocks,* Delhi, Government of India Press, P.E.O. Publication 26.–O

DON IRISH (1960), "Types and Content of Professional Oaths Used in American Medical Colleges," paper presented at the Ohio Academy of Science, Yellow Springs, Ohio.–O

KRISHMA A. JALIHAL (1960), *Some Implications of the Sociological Research on Diffusion and Adoption of Farm Practices and Their Ap-*

plication to Extension Education, M.S. Thesis, Knoxville, University of Tennessee.–RS

DONALD E. JOHNSON and ANNE W. VAN DEN BAN (1959), "The Dynamics of Farm Practice Change," paper presented to Midwest Sociological Society, Lincoln, Nebraska.–RS

DONALD E. JOHNSON and E. A. WILKENING (1961), *Five Years of Farm and Home Development in Wisconsin: A Comparison of Participating and Control Families,* Madison, Wisconsin Agricultural Experiment Station Research Bulletin 228.–RS

GWYN E. JONES (1960), *Factors Affecting the Adoption of New Farm Practices, with Particular Reference to Central Wales and the East Midlands of England,* B.Litt. Thesis, Oxford, England, Oxford University.–RS

KEMAL H. KARPAT (1960), "Social Effects of Farm Mechanization in Turkish Villages," *Social Research,* 27: 83–103.–O

ELIHU KATZ (1956), *Interpersonal Relations and Mass Communications Studies in the Flow of Influence,* Ph.D. Thesis, N.Y., Columbia University.–MS

ELIHU KATZ (1957), "The Two-Step Flow of Communication: An Up-to-Date Report on an Hypothesis," *Public Opinion Quarterly,* 21: 61–78.–MS

ELIHU KATZ (1959), "Review of *Information, Decision and Action,*" *American Journal of Sociology,* 65: 321–322.–RS

ELIHU KATZ (1960), "Communication Research and the Image of Society: Convergence of Two Traditions," *American Journal of Sociology,* 65: 435–440.–MS

ELIHU KATZ (1961), "The Social Itinerary of Technical Change: Two Studies on the Diffusion of Innovation," *Human Organization,* 20: 70–82.–MS

ELIHU KATZ (1962), "Notes on the Unit of Adoption in Diffusion Research," *Sociological Inquiry,* 32: 3–9.–O

ELIHU KATZ (in press), *The Diffusion of Innovation: An Analysis, with Case Studies,* N.Y., Wiley. An emphasis on the intellectual traditions of diffusion research.–O

ELIHU KATZ and MARTIN L. LEVIN (1959), "Traditions of Research on the Diffusion of Innovation," paper presented at the American Sociological Association, Chicago, Ill.–MS

ELIHU KATZ and HERBERT MENZEL (1954), *On the Flow of Scientific Information in the Medical Profession,* N.Y., Columbia University Bureau of Applied Social Research Mimeo Report.–MS

HAROLD F. KAUFMAN and ELLEN M. BRYANT (1958), *Characteristics*

HERBERT F. LIONBERGER (1959), "Community Prestige and the Choice of Sources of Farm Information," *Public Opinion Quarterly*, 23: 111–118.–RS

HERBERT F. LIONBERGER (1960), *Adoption of New Ideas and Practices: A Summary of the Research Dealing with the Acceptance of Technological Change in Agriculture, with Implications for Action in Facilitating Social Change*, Ames, Iowa State University Press.–RS. A summarization of rural sociological research on the diffusion of ideas completed before 1959.

HERBERT F. LIONBERGER and C. MILTON COUGHENOUR (1957), *Social Structure and Diffusion of Farm Information*, Columbia, Missouri Agricultural Experiment Research Bulletin 631.–RS

HERBERT F. LIONBERGER and EDWARD HASSINGER (1954a), "Neighborhoods as a Factor in the Diffusion of Farm Innovation in a Northeast Missouri Farming Community," *Rural Sociology*, 19: 377–384.–RS

HERBERT F. LIONBERGER and EDWARD HASSINGER (1954b), *Roads to Knowledge*, Columbia, Missouri Agricultural Experiment Station Bulletin 633.–RS

YRJO LITTUMEN (1959), "Deviance and Passivity in Radio Listener Groups," *Acta Sociologia*, 4: 17–26.–O

SHELDON G. LOWRY and DONALD G. HAY (1957), *Acceptance of Voluntary Health Insurance in Sampson County, North Carolina, 1955*, Raleigh, North Carolina Agricultural Experiment Station Progress Report Rs–28.–RS

SHELDON G. LOWRY and DONALD G. HAY (1958), *Use of Health Care Services and Enrollment in Voluntary Health Insurance in Stokes County, North Carolina, 1956*, Raleigh, North Carolina Agricultural Experiment Station Progress Report Rs-32.–RS

SHELDON LOWRY and others (1958), "Factors Associated with the Acceptance of Health Care Practices Among Rural Families," *Rural Sociology*, 23: 198–202.–RS

GEORGE J. LOVOS (1955), *A Description of Educational Practice in Metropolitan School Study Council Systems in 1954: With Special Reference to Elementary Schools*, Ed.D. Thesis, N.Y., Columbia University Teachers College.–E

N. MACCOBY and others (1959), " 'Critical Periods' in Seeking and Accepting Information," paper presented at American Psychological Association.–O

EDWIN MANSFIELD (1960), *Acceptance of Technical Change: The*

Speed of Response of Individual Firms, Pittsburgh, Carnegie Institute of Technology, Graduate School of Industrial Administration Mimeo Report.–I

EDWIN MANSFIELD (1961a), "Technical Change and the Rate of Imitation," *Econometrica*, 29: 741–766.–I

EDWIN MANSFIELD (1961b), *Innovation, Size of Firm, and Market Structure*, Pittsburgh, Carnegie Institute of Technology, Graduate School of Industrial Administration Mimeo Report.–I

C. PAUL MARSH and A. LEE COLEMAN (1954a), "Farmers' Practice-Adoption Rates in Relation to Adoption Rates of 'Leaders,'" *Rural Sociology*, 19: 180–181.–RS. A classic analysis of the effect of neighborhood norms on the innovativeness of opinion leaders.

C. PAUL MARSH and A. LEE COLEMAN (1954b), *Communication and the Adoption of Recommended Farm Practices*, Lexington, Kentucky Experiment Station Progress Report 22.–RS

C. PAUL MARSH and A. LEE COLEMAN (1954c), "The Relation of Kinship, Exchanging Work, and Visiting to the Adoption of Recommended Farm Practices," *Rural Sociology*, 19: 1–2.–RS

C. PAUL MARSH and A. LEE COLEMAN (1954d), "The Relation of Neighborhood of Residence to Adoption of Recommended Farm Practices," *Rural Sociology*, 19: 385–389.–RS

C. PAUL MARSH and A. LEE COLEMAN (1955a), "Differential Communication among Farmers in a Kentucky County," *Rural Sociology*, 20: 93–101.–RS

C. PAUL MARSH and A. LEE COLEMAN (1955b), "The Relation of Farmer Characteristics to the Adoption of Recommended Farm Practices," *Rural Sociology*, 20: 289–296.–RS

C. PAUL MARSH and A. LEE COLEMAN (1956), "Group Influences and Agricultural Innovations: Some Tentative Findings and Hypotheses," *American Journal of Sociology*, 61: 588–594.–RS

ROBERT MASON (1961), unpublished data from an investigation of the adoption of three farm ideas by about 150 farmers in one Oregon county, Corvallis, Oregon State University.–O

BERNARD MAUSNER and JUDITH MAUSNER (1955), "A Study of the Anti-Scientific Attitude," *Scientific American*, 192: 35–39.–MS

SELZ C. MAYO (1960), "An Analysis of the Organizational Role of the Teacher of Vocational Agriculture," *Rural Sociology*, 25: 334–345.–RS

THOMAS McCORKLE (1961), "Chiropractic: A Deviant Theory of Disease and Treatment in Contemporary Western Culture," *Human Organization*, 20: 20–22.–A

WALTER C. McKAIN, JR., and others (1958), *Campaigns to Increase the Milk Consumption of Older Persons*, Storrs, Conn., Storrs Agricultural Experiment Station Bulletin 344.–RS

KENNETH M. MCINTYRE (1960), "A Study to Determine Specific Sources of Resistance to the Use of Audio-Visual Materials by College and University Teachers and the Development of Procedures for Overcoming the Barriers to Optimum Use," research project under way, Chapel Hill, University of North Carolina Bureau of Audio-Visual Education.–E

DONALD R. MCNEIL (1957), *The Fight for Fluoridation*, N.Y., Oxford University Press.–MS

EDGAR C. MCVOY (1940), "Patterns of Diffusion in the United States," *American Sociological Review*, 5: 219–227.–ES

MARGARET MEAD (1955), *Cultural Patterns and Technical Change*, N.Y., New American Library.–A

HENRI MENDRAS (1956), *Attitudes des Agriculteurs du Sundgau vis-à-vis de la modernisation de l'Agriculture*, Paris, Comité d'Action pour le Progrès Economique et Social Haut Rinois.–RS

HENRI MENDRAS (1958), *Les Paysons et la Modernisation de l'Agriculture*, Paris, Centre National de la Recherche Scientifique.–RS

HERBERT MENZEL (1957), "Public and Private Conformity Under Different Conditions of Acceptance in the Group," *Journal of Abnormal and Social Psychology*, 55: 398–402.–MS

HERBERT MENZEL (1959), *Social Determinants of Physicians' Reactions to Innovations in Medical Practice*, Ph.D. Thesis, Madison, University of Wisconsin.–MS

HERBERT MENZEL (1960a), "Innovation, Integration, and Marginality: A Survey of Physicians," *American Sociological Review*, 25: 704–713.–MS

HERBERT MENZEL (1960b), Private communication, N.Y., Columbia University Bureau of Applied Social Research.–MS

HERBERT MENZEL and ELIHU KATZ (1955), "Social Relations and Innovation in the Medical Profession: The Epidemiology of a New Drug," *Public Opinion Quarterly*, 19: 337–352.–MS The first published report from the investigation of the diffusion of a new drug among doctors.

MATTHEW B. MILES (in press), *The Nature of Educational Innovation*, N.Y., Columbia University Teachers College Bureau of Publications.–E

GENEVIEVE MILLER (1957), *The Adoption of Inoculation for Smallpox in England and France*, Philadelphia, University of Pennsylvania Press.–MS

PAUL R. MORT (1946), *Principles of School Administration,* N.Y., McGraw-Hill.–E

PAUL MORT (1960), Personal communication, N.Y., Columbia University Teachers College.–E

PAUL R. MORT and FRANCIS G. CORNELL (1938), *Adaptability of Public School Systems,* N.Y., Columbia University Teachers College Bureau of Publications.–E

PAUL R. MORT and FRANCIS G. CORNELL (1941), *American Schools in Transition,* N.Y., Bureau of Publications, Teachers College, Columbia University.–E

PAUL R. MORT and TRUMAN A. PIERCE (1947), *A Time Scale for Measuring the Adapatability of School Systems,* N.Y., Columbia University Teachers College, Metropolitan School Study Council.–E

EVA MUELLER (1958), "The Desire for Innovations in Household Goods," in Lincoln H. Clark (ed.), *Consumer Behavior,* N.Y., Harper.–O

CHARLES LEE MULFORD (1959), *Relation Between Community Variables and Local Industrial Development Corporations,* M.S., Thesis, Ames, Iowa State University.–O

C. J. NAQUIN (1957), *Factors Associated with the Adoption of Selected Dairy Farming Practices, Avoyelles Parish 1956,* M.S. Thesis, Baton Rouge, Louisiana State University.–RS

NATIONAL ANALYSTS, INC. (1961), Research study under way for the U.S. Public Health Service on how communities accept fluoridation of water supplies, Philadelphia.–O

NATIONAL PROJECT IN AGRICULTURAL COMMUNICATIONS (1956), *Research and Writing on Diffusion of Farm and Home Practices,* East Lansing, Michigan State University.–RS

W. NEINHAUS (1955), *Venbreitung und Wirksamkeit von Informations und Beratungsmitteln in der westdeutschen Landwirtschaft,* Bad Godesberg, Germany, Auswerturgs und Informationdienst Bundeslandwirtschafts Ministerium Report 9.–RS

KEITH M. NICHOLS (1959), *Farming Information Sources Preferred by Iowa Farmers,* M.S. Thesis, Ames, Iowa State College.–O

N. J. NIEDERFRANK and others (1948), *The Lubbock County Study: An Evaluation of the Effectiveness of Extension Work in Lubbock County, Texas,* College Station, Texas Agricultural Extension Service Bulletin.–RS

JAMES NIELSON and R. F. BITTNER (1958), *Farm Practice Adoption in Michigan,* East Lansing, Michigan Agricultural Experiment Station Technical Bulletin 263.–O

NORTH CENTRAL RURAL SOCIOLOGY SUBCOMMITTEE FOR THE STUDY OF DIFFUSION OF FARM PRACTICES (1955), *How Farm People Accept New Ideas*, Ames, Iowa Agricultural Extension Service Special Report 15.–RS. This bulletin is probably the most-read piece of literature in the diffusion field. It is a summary of rural sociological diffusion research completed prior to 1954.

NORTH CENTRAL RURAL SOCIOLOGY SUBCOMMITTEE FOR THE STUDY OF DIFFUSION OF FARM PRACTICES (1956), *Bibliography of Research on Social Factors in the Adoption of Farm Practices*, Ames, Iowa Agricultural Extension Service Mimeo Bulletin.–RS

NORTH CENTRAL RURAL SOCIOLOGY SUBCOMMITTEE FOR THE STUDY OF DIFFUSION OF FARM PRACTICES (1959), *Bibliography of Research on Social Factors in the Adoption of Farm Practices*, Ames, Iowa Agricultural Extension Service Mimeo Bulletin.–RS

NORTH CENTRAL RURAL SOCIOLOGY SUBCOMMITTEE FOR THE STUDY OF DIFFUSION OF FARM PRACTICES (1961), *Adopters of New Farm Ideas: Characteristics and Communications Behavior*, East Lansing, Michigan Agricultural Extension Service Bulletin.–RS

IVAN NYE (1952), *The Relationship of Certain Factors to County Agent Success*, Columbia, Missouri Agricultural Experiment Station Research Bulletin 498.–RS

WILLIAM F. OGBURN (1922), *Social Change*, N.Y., Huebsch.–ES

W. F. OGBURN and COLUM S. GILFILLIAN (1933), "The Influence of Invention and Discovery," in *Recent Social Trends in the United States*, N.Y., McGraw-Hill.–ES

K. S. OLSON (1959a), *The Relation of Selected Farmers' 4-H Experience to Their Adoption of Improved Farm Practices*, Ph.D. Thesis, Madison, University of Wisconsin.–RS

K. S. OLSON (1959b), *4-H and Adoption of Improved Farm Practices*, Fargo, North Dakota Agricultural Extension Service Circular.–RS

OPINION RESEARCH CORPORATION (1959), *America's Tastemakers: A New Strategy for Predicting Change in Consumer Behavior*, Princeton, N.J.–O

MORRIS E. OPLER (1954), *Social Aspects of Technical Assistance in Operation*, Paris, UNESCO.–A

L. W. OSBORNE (1961), "County Leaflets as an Advisory Tool," *NAAS Quarterly Review*, 12: 126–132.–RS

ROSS PARISH (1954), "Innovation and Enterprise in Wheat Farming," *Review of Marketing and Agricultural Economics*, 22: 189–218.–O

ROSS PARISH (1956), "Extension Services and the Grazier on the

342   DIFFUSION OF INNOVATIONS

South-West Slope," *Review of Marketing and Agricultural Economics*, 24: 222–235.–O

BENJAMIN D. PAUL (1955), *Health, Culture and Community: Case Studies of Public Reactions to Health Programs*, N.Y., Russell Sage Foundation.–A

HAROLD A. PEDERSEN (1951), "Cultural Differences in the Acceptance of Recommended Practices," *Rural Sociology*, 16: 37–49.–RS

JAMES H. PELLEY (1948), *Invention in Education*, Ed.D. Thesis, N.Y., Columbia University Teachers College.–E

PERTTI PELTO (1960), "Innovation in an Individualistic Society," paper presented at the American Anthropological Association.–A

H. EARL PEMBERTON (1936a), "The Curve of Culture Diffusion Rate," *American Sociological Review*, 1: 547–556.–ES

H. EARL PEMBERTON (1936b), "Culture-Diffusion Gradients," *American Journal of Sociology*, 42: 226–233.–ES

H. EARL PEMBERTON (1937), "The Effect of a Social Crisis on the Curve of Diffusion," *American Sociological Review*, 2: 55–61.–ES

H. EARL PEMBERTON (1938), "Spatial Order of Cultural Diffusion," *Sociology and Social Research*, 22: 246–251.–ES

HOLLIS W. PETER and LAWRENCE E. SCHLESINGER (1959), *Using U.S. Training in the Phillipines: A Follow-Up Survey of Participants*, Washington, D.C., U.S. International Cooperation Administration Mimeo Report.–O

FRANK PETRINI (1953), *Studier av jordbrukarnas ekonomiska beteende*, Rosenbad, Sweden, Meddelanden fran jordbrukets utrednings institut Bulletin 4.–O

FRANK PETRINI (1955a), *Studier av jordbruksprodukternas utbudsforhallanden*, Rosenbad, Sweden, Meddelanden fran jordbrukets utrednings institut Bulletin 6.–O

FRANK PETRINI (1955b), *Hushallningssallskapens radgivning och upplynsning*, Rosenbad, Sweden, Meddelanden fran jordbrukets utrednings institut Bulletin 9.–O

JOHN D. PHOTIADIS (1961a), *Contacts with Agricultural Agents*, Brookings, South Dakota Agricultural Experiment Station Bulletin 493.–RS

JOHN D. PHOTIADIS (1961b), "Motivation, Contacts, and Technological Change," paper presented at Rural Sociological Society, Ames, Iowa.–RS

TRUMAN A. PIERCE (1947), *Controllable Community Characteristics Related to the Quality of Education*, N.Y., Columbia University Teachers College Bureau of Publications.–E

RONALD L. PITZER (1959), *The Influence of Social Values on the*

Acceptance of Vertical Integration by Broiler Growers, M.S. Thesis, Columbus, Ohio State University.–RS

RONALD L. PITZER and others (1959), "Values in the Adoption of Contract Farming," paper presented to the Rural Sociological Society, Ithaca, N.Y.–RS

THOMAS F. A. PLAUT (1959), "Analysis of Voting Behavior on a Fluoridation Referendum," *Public Opinion Quarterly*, 23: 213–222.–MS

LOUIS A. PLOCH (1960), *Social and Family Characteristics of Maine Contract Broiler Growers*, Orono, Maine Agricultural Experiment Station Bulletin 596.–RS

FREDERICK POLLACK (1957), *Automation: A Study of Its Economic and Social Consequences*, N.Y., Praeger.–I

ROBERT A. POLSON and AGATON P. PAL (1955), "The Influence of Isolation on the Acceptance of Technological Changes in the Dumaguete City Trade Area, Philippines," *Silliman Journal*, 2: 149–159.–RS

HILDA POTTHOFF and HANS RHEINWALD (1958), *Beratung in der Schweinmast: Untersuchungen über ein gezieltes Beratungs program*, Stuttgart-Hohenheim, Germany, Instit für landwirtschaftliche Beratung an der Landwirtschaftlicken Hochschule Bulletin 80.–RS

JACK J. PREISS (1954), *Functions of Relevant Power and Authority Groups in the Evaluation of County Agent Performance*, Ph.D. Thesis, East Lansing, Michigan State University.–RS

RAYMOND B. PRESCOTT (1922), "Law of Growth in Forecasting Demand," *Journal of American Statistical Association*, 18: 471–479.–O

CHARLES H. PROCTOR (1956), *Changing Patterns of Social Organization in a Rural Problem Area of Uruguay*, Ph.D. Thesis, East Lansing, Michigan State University.–RS

CHARLES H. PROCTOR (1960), "Did Demonstrations Alter the Diffusion of Hybrid Corn Practices in San Ramon?" unpublished paper, East Lansing, Michigan State University.–RS

JULIAN PRUNDEANU and PAUL J. ZWERMAN (1958), "An Evaluation of Some Economic Factors and Farmers' Attitudes That May Influence Acceptance of Soil Conservation Practices," *Journal of Farm Economics*, 40: 903–914.–O

B. D. PUROHIT (in press), *Human Ability, Technical Level of Production and Economic Results on Finnish Bookkeeping Farms*, Ph.D. Dissertation, Finland, University of Helsinki.–RS

SNELL W. PUTNEY and GLADYS J. PUTNEY (1961), "Prestige and Innovation in a Mexican Village," paper presented at the American Sociological Association, St. Louis, Mo.–A

CARROLL QUIGLEY (1956), "Aboriginal Fish Poisons and the Diffusion Problem," *American Anthropologist*, 58: 508–525.–A

344 DIFFUSION OF INNOVATIONS

S. A. Rahim (1961), *The Diffusion and Adoption of Agricultural Practices: A Study in a Village in East Pakistan,* Comilla, Pakistan Academy for Village Development.–RS

W. B. Rahudkar (1958), "Impact of Fertilizer Extension Programme on the Minds of the Farmers and Their Reactions to Different Extension Methods," *Indian Journal of Agronomy,* 3: 119–136.–RS

W. B. Rahudkar (1959), *Case Studies of Village Level Workers with a View to Locate the Qualities Which Make Up a Successful Extension Worker,* M.S. Thesis, Nagpur, India, Nagpur University.–RS

W. B. Rahudkar (1960), "Local Leaders and the Adoption of Farm Practices," *Nagpur Agriculture College Magazine,* 34: 1–13.–RS

W. B. Rahudkar (1961), *Testing a Culturally-Bound Model for Acceptance of Agricultural Practices,* M.A. Thesis, Manhattan, Kansas State University.–RS

Charles E. Ramsey and others (1959), "Values and the Adoption of Practices," *Rural Sociology,* 24: 35–47.–RS

Arthur Raper and Pearl Wheeler Tappan (1943), "Never Too Old to Learn New Tricks: The Canning Program in Greene County, Goergia," *Applied Anthropology,* 2: 3–11.–RS

Fritz Redlich (1953), "Ideas, Their Migration in Space and Transmittal over Time," *Kyklos,* 6: 301–322.–O

Stuart A. Rice (1928), *Quantitative Methods in Politics,* N.Y., Knopf.–ES

Everett M. Rogers (1955), Unpublished data from 148 farmers and 148 farm homemakers in one Central Iowa community.–RS

Everett M. Rogers (1957a), *A Conceptual Variable Analysis of Technological Change,* Ph.D. Thesis, Ames, Iowa State University.–RS

Everett M. Rogers (1957b), "Personality Correlates of the Adoption of Technological Practices," *Rural Sociology,* 22: 267–268.–RS

Everett M. Rogers (1957c). Unpublished data from a statewide random sample of 104 farmers and 88 farm housewives in Ohio, Columbus, Ohio State University.–RS

Everett M. Rogers (1958a), "A Conceptual Variable Analysis of Technological Change," *Rural Sociology,* 23: 136–145.–RS

Everett M. Rogers (1958b), "Categorizing the Adopters of Agricultural Practices," *Rural Sociology,* 23: 345–354.–RS. The original statement of the classification of five adopter categories.

Everett M. Rogers (1959a), "A Note on Innovators," *Journal of Farm Economics,* 41: 132–134.–RS

Everett M. Rogers (1959b), Unpublished data from a statewide random sample of 104 farmers in Ohio originally interviewed in 1957, Columbus, Ohio State University.–RS

EVERETT M. ROGERS (1961a), "The Adoption Period," *Rural Sociology*, 26: 77–82.–RS

EVERETT M. ROGERS (1961b), *Characteristics of Agricultural Innovators and Other Adopter Categories*, Wooster, Ohio Agricultural Experiment Station Research Bulletin 882.–RS

EVERETT M. ROGERS and GEORGE M. BEAL (1958a), "The Importance of Personal Influence in the Adoption of Technological Changes," *Social Forces*, 36: 329–335.–RS

EVERETT M. ROGERS and GEORGE M. BEAL (1958b), *Reference Group Influences in the Adoption of Agricultural Technology*, Ames, Iowa State College Department of Economics and Sociology Mimeo Bulletin.–RS

EVERETT M. ROGERS and GEORGE M. BEAL (1959a), "Projective Techniques: Potential Tools for Agricultural Economists?" *Journal of Farm Economics*, 41: 644–648.–RS

EVERETT M. ROGERS and GEORGE M. BEAL (1959b), "Projective Techniques and Rural Respondents," *Rural Sociology*, 24: 178–182.–RS

EVERETT M. ROGERS and RABEL J. BURDGE (1961), *Muck Vegetable Growers: Diffusion of Innovations Among Specialized Farmers*, Wooster, Ohio Agricultural Experiment Station Research Circular 94.–RS

EVERETT M. ROGERS and RABEL J. BURDGE (1962), *Community Norms, Opinion Leadership, and Innovativeness Among Truck Growers*, Wooster. Ohio Agricultural Experiment Station Research Bulletin.–RS

EVERETT M. ROGERS and HAROLD R. CAPENER (1960), *The County Extension Agent and His Constituents*, Wooster, Ohio Agricultural Experiment Station Research Bulletin 858.–RS

EVERETT M. ROGERS and A. EUGENE HAVENS (1961a), *The Impact of Demonstrations on Farmers' Attitudes Toward Fertilizer*, Wooster, Ohio Agricultural Experiment Station Research Bulletin 891.–RS

EVERETT M. ROGERS and A. EUGENE HAVENS (1961b), Unpublished paper on predicting innovativeness with data from a statewide random sample of 104 farmers, Columbus, Ohio Agricultural Experiment Station.–RS

EVERETT M. ROGERS and A. EUGENE HAVENS (1961c), *Extension Contact of Ohio Farm Housewives*, Wooster, Ohio Agricultural Experiment Station Research Bulletin 890.–RS

EVERETT M. ROGERS and A. EUGENE HAVENS (1962a), "Predicting Innovativeness," *Sociological Inquiry*, 32: 34–42.–RS

EVERETT M. ROGERS and A. EUGENE HAVENS (1962b), "Rejoinder to Griliches' Another False Dichotomy," Rural Sociology, 27.–RS

EVERETT M. ROGERS and FRANK O. LEUTHOLD (1962), *Demonstrators and the Diffusion of Fertilizer Practices,* Wooster, Ohio Agricultural Experiment Station Research Bulletin 908.–RS.

E. M. ROGERS and R. L. PITZER (1960), *The Adoption of Irrigation by Ohio Farmers,* Wooster, Ohio Agricultural Experiment Station Research Bulletin 851.–RS

EVERETT M. ROGERS and L. EDNA ROGERS (1961), "A Methodological Analysis of Adoption Scales," *Rural Sociology,* 26: 325–336.–RS.

EVERETT M. ROGERS and CONSTANTINA SAFILIOS (1960), "Communication of Agricultural Technology: How People Accept New Ideas," in Everett M. Rogers, *Social Change in Rural Society: A Textbook in Rural Sociology,* N.Y., Appleton-Century-Crofts.–RS

E. M. ROGERS and M. D. YOST (1960), *Communication Behavior of County Extension Agents,* Wooster, Ohio Experiment Station Research Bulletin 850.–RS

WAYNE C. ROHRER (1955), "On Clienteles of the Agricultural Extension Service," *Rural Sociology,* 20: 299–303.–RS

ROBERT A. ROHWER (1949), "How New Practices Spread," *Iowa Farm Science,* 4: 13–14.–RS

DONALD H. ROSS (1952), "Rate of Diffusion for Driver Education," *Safety Education,* 32: 16–32.–E

DONALD H. ROSS (1955), "Measuring Institutional Quality of School Systems," *Teachers College Record,* 57.–E

DONALD H. ROSS (1958), *Administration for Adaptability: A Source Book Drawing Together the Results of More Than 150 Individual Studies Related to the Question of Why and How Schools Improve,* N.Y., Metropolitan School Study Council.–E. The 150 studies in the education diffusion tradition at Columbia University's Teachers College are reviewed in this book, and are not listed separately in the present bibliography.

VERNON W. RUTTAN (1959), "Usher and Shumpeter on Invention, Innovation, and Technological Change," *Quarterly Journal of Economics,* 73: 596–606.–O

BRYCE RYAN (1942), *Social and Ecological Patterns in the Farm Leadership of Four Iowa Townships,* Ames, Iowa Agricultural Experiment Station Bulletin 306.–RS

BRYCE RYAN (1948), "A Study in Technological Diffusion," *Rural Sociology,* 13: 273–285.–RS

BRYCE RYAN and NEAL C. GROSS (1943), "The Diffusion of Hybrid Seed Corn in Two Iowa Communities," *Rural Sociology,* 8: 15–24.–RS. A report of the classic study of the diffusion of hybrid seed corn among 259 Iowa farmers.

BRYCE RYAN and NEAL C. GROSS (1950), *Acceptance and Diffusion of Hybrid Corn Seed in Two Iowa Communities,* Ames, Iowa Agricultural Experiment Station Research Bulletin 372.–RS

FRANK A. SANTOPOLO (1961), Personal communication, Lexington, University of Kentucky.–RS

TOM T. SASAKI (1956), "Sociocultural Problems in Introducing New Technology on a Navaho Irrigation Project," *Rural Sociology,* 21: 307–310.–A

LOIS SCANTLAND and others (1952), *A Square Look at Spokane County, Washington,* Pullman, Washington Agricultural Extension Bulletin 463.–RS

WARREN C. SCOVILLE (1951), "Minority Migrations and the Diffusion of Technology," *Journal of Economic History,* 11: 347–360.–O

WARREN C. SCOVILLE (1952), "Huguenots and the Diffusion of Technology," *Journal of Political Economy,* 15: 294–311.–O

LAURISTON SHARP (1952), "Steel Axes for Stone Age Australians," in Edward H. Spicer (ed.), *Human Problems in Technological Change,* N.Y., Russell Sage Foundation.–A

DAVID SHEPPARD (1960a), *A Survey Among Grassland Farmers,* London, Central Office of Information Social Survey 274.–RS

DAVID SHEPPARD (1960b), "Neighbourhood Norms and the Adoption of Farm Practices," *Rural Sociology,* 25: 356–358.–RS

DAVID SHEPPARD (1961), "Farmers' Reasons for Not Adopting Controversial Techniques in Grassland Farming," *Journal of the British Grassland Society,* 16: 6–13.–RS

DAVID SHEPPARD (in press), "The Importance of 'Other Farmers,' " *Sociologia Ruralis.*–RS

MAURICE L. SILL (1957), *Personal, Situational, and Communicational Factors Associated with the Farm Practice Adoption Process,* Ph.D. Thesis, University Park, Pennsylvania State University.–RS

DAVID L. SILLS and RAFAEL E. GILL (1959), "Young Adults' Use of the Salk Vaccine," *Social Problems,* 6: 248–253.–MS

LESLIE J. SILVERMAN and WILFRID C. BAILEY (1961), *Trends in the Adoption of Recommended Farm Practices,* State College, Mississippi Agricultural Experiment Station Bulletin 617.–RS

SIMULMATICS CORPORATION (1961a), "Simulation of the Adoption or Rejection of Flouridation by U.S. Communities," Research project under way for the U.S. Public Health Service, Washington, D.C.–O

SIMULMATICS CORPORATION (1961b), "Simulation of Communication Processes in the U.S. Farm Population," research proposal to the U.S. Department of Agriculture, Washington, D.C.–O

LEONARD M. SIZER and WARD F. PORTER (1960), *The Relation of*

Knowledge to Adoption of Recommended Practices, Morgantown, West Virginia Agricultural Experiment Station Bulletin 446.–RS

WALTER L. SLOCUM and others (1958), *Extension Contacts, Selected Characteristics, Practices, and Attitudes of Washington Farm Families,* Pullman, Washington Agricultural Experiment Station Bulletin 584.–RS

ROBERT SOKOL (1959), "The Television Behavior and Attitudes of Influentials," paper presented at American Sociological Association, Chicago.–RS

LAUREN SOTH (1952), *How Farm People Learn New Methods,* Washington, D.C., National Planning Association Pamphlet 79.–RS

IRVING A. SPAULDING (1955), *Farm Operator Time-Space Orientations and the Adoption of Recommended Farming Practices,* Kingston, Rhode Island Agricultural Experiment Station Bulletin 330.–RS

IRVING A. SPAULDING (1960), *Motivation for Communication Behavior,* Kingston, Rhode Island Agricultural Experiment Station Bulletin 354.–RS

GEORGE ELWOOD SPENCER (1958), *Value-Orientations and the Adoption of Farm Practices,* Ph.D. Thesis, Ithaca, N.Y., Cornell University. –RS

GEORGE M. STABLER (1958), *Bejucal: Social Values and Changes in Agricultural Practices in a Cuban Rurban Community,* Ph.D. Thesis, East Lansing, Michigan State University.–RS

BERNARD J. STERN (1927), *Social Factors in Medical Progress,* N.Y., Columbia University Press.–MS

BERNARD J. STERN (1937), "Resistances to the Adoption of Technological Innovations," in Natural Resources Committee, *Technological Trends and National Policy,* Washington, D.C., Government Printing Office.–MS

JOHN T. STONE (1952), *How County Agricultural Agents Teach,* East Lansing, Michigan Agricultural Extension Service Mimeo Bulletin.–O

W. PAUL STRASSMAN (1959), *Risk and Technological Innovation: American Manufacturing Methods During the Nineteenth Century,* Ithaca, N.Y., Cornell University Press.–I

MURRAY A. STRAUS (1953), "Cultural Factors in the Functioning of Agricultural Extension in Ceylon," *Rural Sociology,* 18: 249–256.–RS

MURRAY A. STRAUS (1960a), "Family Role Differentiation and Technological Change in Farming," *Rural Sociology,* 25: 219–228.–RS

MURRAY A. STRAUS (1960b), "Analytical Model of the Components of a Social System Necessary for Understanding the Process of Technological Change," unpublished paper, Ithaca, Cornell University.–RS

MURRAY A. STRAUS and ALLEN J. ESTEP (1959), *Education for*

Technological Change Among Wisconsin Farmers, Madison, Wisconsin Agricultural Experiment Station Technical Bulletin 214.–RS

SUBCOMMITTEE ON THE DIFFUSION AND ADOPTION OF FARM PRACTICES, Rural Sociological Society (1952), *Sociological Research on the Diffusion and Adoption of New Farm Practices,* Lexington, Kentucky, Agricultural Experiment Station Mimeo Bulletin RS–2.–RS

ALISTAIR SUTHERLAND (1959), "The Diffusion of an Innovation in Cotton Spinning," *Journal of Industrial Economics,* 7: 118–135.–I

WAYNE SUTTLES (1951), "The Early Diffusion of the Potato Among the Coast Salish," *Southwestern Journal of Anthropolgy,* 7: 272–288.–A

W. D. TOUSSAINT and P. S. STONE (1960), "Evaluating a Farm Machine Prior to Its Introduction," *Journal of Farm Economics,* 42: 241–251.–O

CARLOS F. TUCKER (1961), *Prediction of Rate of Adoption from Characteristics of Farm Innovations,* M.S. Thesis, Columbus, Ohio State University.–RS

W. J. VAN DE VEN (1957), *Problemen rond de verbreiding van de kunstmatige inseminatie,* M.S. Thesis, Wageningen, Netherlands, University of Wageningen.–RS

A. W. VAN DEN BAN (1953), "Wie worden door de landbouwvoorlichtingsdienst bereikt?" (Who Are Influenced by the Agricultural Extension Service?), *Landbouwkundig Tijdschrift,* 65: 317–327.–RS.

A. W. VAN DEN BAN (1956), *Enkele kenmerken en eigenschappen van de vooruitstrevende boeren,* Wageningen, Netherlands, University of Wageningen Department of Rural Sociology Bulletin 5.–RS

A. W. VAN DEN BAN (1957a), *Boer en Landbouwonderwijs: De Landbouwkundige Ontwikkeling van de Nederlandse Boeren (Vocational Training in Agriculture of the Dutch Farmers),* Wageningen, Netherlands, University of Wageningen Department of Rural Sociology Bulletin 6.–RS

A. W. VAN DEN BAN (1957b), "Some Characteristics of Progressive Farmers in the Netherlands," *Rural Sociology,* 22: 205–212.–RS

A. W. VAN DEN BAN (1958), *Regionale Verschillen in de Toepassing van Enkele Landbouwmethoden (Regional Differences in the Adoption of Some Farm Practices),* Wageningen, Netherlands, University of Wageningen Department of Rural Sociology Bulletin 9.–RS

A. W. VAN DEN BAN (1960a) "Aufgaben und Ziele der Agrarsoziologie in den Niederlanden," *Fachgebiet,* 16: 1–8.–RS

A. W. VAN DEN BAN (1960b), "Locality Group Differences in the Adoption of New Farm Practices," *Rural Sociology,* 25: 308–320.–RS

A. W. VAN DEN BAN (1961a), "Research in the Field of Advisory Work," *Netherlands Journal of Agricutural Science,* 9: 122–133.–RS

A. W. VAN DEN BAN (1961b), Personal communication, Wageningen, Netherlands, University of Wageningen.–RS

A. W. VAN DEN BAN (in press), *Boer en landvoorlichting: De communicatie over nieuwe landouwmethoden,* Assen, Netherlands, Van Gorkum.–RS. An analysis of the adoption of farm ideas in three Netherlands communities with different norms on innovativeness.

FRED VOGET (1948), "Individual Motivation in the Diffusion of the Wind River Shoshone Sundance to the Crow," *American Anthropologist,* 50: 634–646.–A

FRED VOGET (1950), "A Shoshone Innovator," *American Anthropologist,* 52: 53–63.–A

ODELL L. WALKER and others (1960), *Application of Game Theory Models to Decisions on Farm Practices and Resource Use,* Ames, Iowa Agricultural Experiment Station Research Bulletin 488.–O

CHESTER R. WASSON (1960), "What Is 'New' about a New Product?" *Journal of Marketing,* 25: 52–56.–O

GEORGE H. F. WELIKALA (1959), *An Analysis of the Adoption of Some Agricultural, Medical, Public Health and Cooperative Practices in Six Selected Villages of Ceylon,* M.A. Thesis, East Lansing, Michigan State University.–RS

EDWARD WELLIN (1955), "Water Boiling in a Peruvian Town," in Benjamin D. Paul (ed.), *Health, Culture and Community,* N.Y., Russell Sage Foundation.–A

WILLIAM H. WHYTE, JR. (1954), "The Web of Word of Mouth," *Fortune,* 50: 140–143, 204–212.–O

A. J. WICHERS (1956), *De beoefening van de bloemisterij en groententeelt te Beesd (Management of Floriculture and Vegetable Growing at Beesd),* Wageningen, Netherlands, University of Wageningen Department of Rural Sociology Bulletin 5.–RS

A. J. WICHERS (1958), *De Evaluatie van een Voorlichtingscampagne in de Betuwe (The Evaluation of an Extension Campaign),* Wageningen, Netherlands, University of Wageningen Department of Rural Sociology Bulletin 11.–RS

EUGENE A. WILKENING (1949), *The Acceptance of Certain Agricultural Programs and Practices in a Piedmont Community of North Carolina,* Ph.D. Thesis, University of Chicago.–RS

EUGENE A. WILKENING (1950a), "Sources of Information for Improved Farm Practices," *Rural Sociology,* 15: 19–30.–RS

EUGENE A. WILKENING (1950b), "A Sociopsychological Approach to the Study of the Acceptance of Innovations in Farming," *Rural Sociology*, 15: 352–364.–RS

EUGENE A. WILKENING (1951), "Social Isolation and Response of Farmers to Agricultural Programs," *American Sociological Review*, 16: 836–837.–RS

EUGENE A. WILKENING (1952a), *Acceptance of Improved Farm Practices*, Raleigh, North Carolina Agricultural Experiment Station Technical Bulletin 98.–RS. One of the best early statistical analyses of the adoption of farm ideas.

EUGENE A. WILKENING (1952b), "Informal Leaders and Innovators in Farm Practices," *Rural Sociology*, 17: 272–275.–RS

EUGENE A. WILKENING (1953), *Adoption of Improved Farm Practices as Related to Family Factors*, Madison, Wisconsin Experiment Station Research Bulletin 183.–RS. Analyzes the role of the family in farmers' adoption decisions.

EUGENE A. WILKENING (1954a), "Techniques of Assessing Farm Family Values," *Rural Sociology*, 19: 39–49.–RS

EUGENE A. WILKENING (1954b), "Change in Farm Technology as Related to Familism, Family Decision Making, and Family Integration," *American Sociological Review*, 19: 29–37.–RS

EUGENE A. WILKENING (1956), "Roles of Communicating Agents in Technological Change in Agriculture," *Social Forces*, 34: 361–367.–RS

EUGENE A. WILKENING (1957), *The County Extension Agent in Wisconsin*, Madison, Wisconsin Experiment Station Research Bulletin 203.–RS

EUGENE A. WILKENING (1958a), "An Introductory Note on the Social Aspects of Practice Adoption," *Rural Sociology*, 23: 97–102.–RS

EUGENE A. WILKENING (1958b), "Consensus in Role Definition of County Extension Agents Between the Agents and Local Sponsoring Committee Members," *Rural Sociology*, 23: 184–197.–RS

EUGENE A. WILKENING (1958c), "Joint Decision-Making in Farm Families as a Function of Status and Role," *American Sociological Review*, 23: 187–192.–RS

EUGENE A. WILKENING (1958d), "Communication and Technological Change in Rural Society," in Alvin L. Bertrand (ed.), *Rural Sociology: An Analysis of Contemporary Rural Life*, N.Y., McGraw-Hill.–RS

EUGENE A. WILKENING (1958e), "Process of Acceptance of Technological Innovations," in Alvin L. Bertrand (ed.), *Rural Sociology: An Analysis of Contemporary Rural Life*, N.Y., McGraw-Hill.–RS

E. A. WILKENING and DONALD JOHNSON (1958), "A Case Study in Decision-Making among a Farm Owner Sample in Wisconsin," paper presented at the Rural Sociological Society, Pullman, Washington.–RS

E. A. WILKENING and DONALD JOHNSON (1961), *Goals in Farm Decision-Making as Related to Practice Adoption*, Madison, Wisconsin Agricultural Experiment Station Research Bulletin 225.–RS

EUGENE A. WILKENING and FRANK A. SANTOPOLO (1952), *The Diffusion of Improved Farm Practices from Unit Test-Demonstration Farms in the Tennessee Valley Counties of North Carolina*, Raleigh, North Carolina Agricultural Experiment Station Mimeo Bulletin.–RS

E. A. WILKENING and others (1960), "Use and Role of Information Sources among Dairy Farmers of Northern Victoria," paper presented at the Rural Sociological Society, University Park, Penn.–RS

EUGENE A. WILKENING and others (1962), "Communication and Acceptance of Recommended Farm Practices among Dairy Farmers of Northern Victoria," *Rural Sociology*, 27: 116–197.–RS

M. M. WILLEY and S. A. RICE (1933), *Communication Agencies and Social Life*, N.Y., McGraw-Hill.–ES

D. B. WILLIAMS (1958), "Facts, Fancies and Fallacies, for Unscientific Scientists," *Journal of the Australian Institute of Agricultural Science*, 24: 124–131.–RS

M. C. WILSON (1927), *Influence of Bulletins, News Stories, and Circular Letters upon Farm Practice Adoption with Particular Reference to Methods of Bulletin Distribution*, Washington, D.C., U.S.D.A. Extension Circular 57.–RS

M. C. WILSON (1928), *Distribution of Bulletins and Their Use by Farmers*, Washington, D.C., U.S.D.A. Extension Circular 78.–RS

M. C. WILSON and GLADYS GALLUP (1955), *Extension Teaching Methods and Other Factors That Influence Adoption of Agricultural and Home Economics Practices*, Washington, D.C., U.S.D.A. Federal Extension Service Circular 495.–RS

CHARLES WINICK (1961), "The Diffusion of an Innovation Among Physicians in a Large City," *Sociometry*, 24: 384–396.–MS

SANFORD WINSTON (1933), *Culture and Human Behavior*, N.Y., Ronald Press.–A

CLARK WISSLER (1923), *Man and Culture*, N.Y., Crowell.–A

E. R. WOLF (1955), "Types of Latin American Peasantry," *American Anthropologist*, 57: 452–471.–A

CONSTANTINE A. YERACARIS (1961), "Social Factors Associated with the Acceptance of Medical Innovations," paper presented at the American Sociological Association, St. Louis, Mo.–MS

RUTH YOUNG (1959a), "Observations on Adoption Studies Reported in June, 1958, Issue," *Rural Sociology*, 24: 272–274.–RS

JAMES N. YOUNG (1959b), *The Influence of Neighborhood Norms on the Diffusion of Recommended Farm Practices*, Ph.D. thesis, Lexington, University of Kentucky.–RS

JAMES N. YOUNG and A. LEE COLEMAN (1959), "Neighborhood Norms and the Adoption of Farm Practices," *Rural Sociology*, 24: 372–380.–RS

JAMES N. YOUNG and C. PAUL MARSH (1956), *The Adoption of Recommended Farm Practices and Sources of Farmer Information*, Lexington, Kentucky Agricultural Experiment Station Progress Report 40.–RS

WIQAR H. ZAIDI (1961), *Adoption of Improved Methods of Paddy Cultivation in Comilla Development Area II*, Comilla, Pakistan Academy for Village Development Technical Publication 6.–RS

PAUL J. ZWERMAN and JULIAN PRUNDEANU (1956), "Obstacles to Soil Conservation," *Journal of Soil and Water Conservation*, 11: 127, 129, 1956.–O

GENERAL REFERENCES CITED

HERBERT I. ABELSON and W. DONALD RUGG (1958), "Self-Designated Influentiality and Activity," *Public Opinion Quarterly*, 22: 556–567.

R. L. ANDERSON and T. A. BANCROFT (1952), *Statistical Theory in Research*, N.Y., McGraw-Hill.

SOLOMON E. ASCH (1952), "Affects of Group Pressure upon the Modification and Distortion of Judgments," in Guy E. Swanson and others (eds.), *Readings in Social Psychology*, N.Y., Holt, Rinehart & Winston.

NORMAN T. J. BAILEY (1957), *The Mathematical Theory of Epidemics*, N.Y., Hafner.

HOWARD C. BECKER (1940), "Constructive Typology in the Social Sciences," in Harry Elmer Barnes and Howard C. Becker, *Contemporary Sociological Theory*, N.Y., Appleton-Century-Crofts.

RUTH BENEDICT (1934), "Anthropology and the Abnormal," *Journal of Genetical Psychology*, 10: 55–60.

B. R. BERELSON and others (1954), *Voting*, Chicago, University of Chicago Press.

JEAN BODDEWYN (1961), "Galbraith's Wicked Wants," *Journal of Marketing*, 25: 14–18.

ALVIN BOSKOFF (1957), "Social Change," in Howard Becker and Alvin Boskoff (eds.), *Modern Sociological Theory in Continuity and Change*, N.Y., Holt, Rinehart & Winston.

WALTER B. CANNON (1945), *The Way of an Investigator*, N.Y., Norton.

ALBERT K. COHEN (1959), "The Study of Social Disorganization and Deviant Behavior," in Robert K. Merton and others (eds.), *Sociology Today*, N.Y., Basic Books.

LEONARD S. COTTRELL, JR., (1942), "Analysis of Situational Fields in Social Psychology," *American Sociological Review*, 7: 370–382.

PHILLIP CUTRIGHT and PETER H. ROSSI (1958), "Grass Roots Politicians and the Vote," *American Sociological Review*, 23: 171–179.

KINGSLEY DAVIS (1940), "The Sociology of Parent-Youth Conflict," *American Sociological Review*, 5: 523–535.

JOHN L. DILLON and EARL O. HEADY (1961), "Free Competition, Uncertainty and Farmer Decisions," *Journal of Farm Economics*, 43: 643–651.

ROBERT DUBIN (1959), "Deviant Behavior and Social Structure," *American Sociological Review*, 24: 147–163.

HORACE B. ENGLISH and AVA CHAMPNEY ENGLISH (1958), *A Comprehensive Dictionary of Psychological and Psychoanalytical Terms*, N.Y., Longmans, Green.

LEON FESTINGER and others (1950), *Social Pressures in Informal Groups*, N.Y., Harper.

THOMAS FORD (1960), "Status, Residence, and Fundamentalist Religious Beliefs in the Southern Appalachians," *Social Forces*, 39: 41–49.

ROBERT W. GILLESPIE (1961), *Simulation of Economic Growth with Alternative Balance of Payments Policies*, Ph.D. Thesis, Cambridge, Massachusetts Institute of Technology.

JOHN L. GILLIN and JOHN P. GILLIN (1945), *An Introduction to Sociology*, N.Y., Macmillan.

WALTER GOLDSCHMIDT (1952), "The Interrelations Between Cultural Factors and the Acquisition of New Technical Skills," in Bert F. Hoselitz (ed.), *The Progress of Underdeveloped Areas*, Chicago, University of Chicago Press.

R. L. GREEN and N. L. LeRAY (1960), "Development and Application," in USDA (ed.), *The Yearbook of Agriculture, 1960,* Washington, D.C., Government Printing Office.

ERNEST R. HILGARD (1956), *Theories of Learning,* N.Y., Appleton-Century-Crofts.

GEORGE C. HOMANS (1950), *The Human Group,* N.Y., Harcourt, Brace & World.

GEORGE C. HOMANS (1961), *Social Behavior: Its Elementary Forms,* N.Y., Harcourt, Brace & World.

BERT F. HOSELITZ (1961), "Tradition and Economic Growth," in Ralph Braibanti and Joseph J. Spengler (eds.), *Tradition, Values, and Socio-Economic Development,* Durham, N.C., Duke University Press.

CARL I. HOVLAND (1953), "Social Communication," in Bernard Berelson and Morris Janowitz (eds.), *Reader in Public Opinion and Communication,* N.Y., The Free Press of Glencoe.

MARIE JAHODA and others (1951), *Research Methods in Social Relations,* N.Y., Holt, Rinehart & Winston.

GLENN L. JOHNSON and CECIL B. HAVER (1953), *Decision-Making Principles in Farm Management,* Lexington, Kentucky Agricultural Experiment Station Bulletin 593.

JOSEPH A. KAHL (1957), *The American Class Structure,* N.Y., Holt, Rinehart & Winston.

GEORG KARLSSON (1958), *Social Mechanisms: Studies in Sociological Theory,* N.Y., The Free Press of Glencoe.

ELIHU KATZ and PAUL F. LAZARSFELD (1955), *Personal Influence,* N.Y., The Free Press of Glencoe.

HAROLD H. KELLEY and EDMUND H. VOLKHART (1952), "The Resistance to Change of Group-Anchored Attitudes," *American Sociological Review,* 17: 453–465.

JOSEPH T. KLAPPER (1960), *The Effects of Mass Communication,* N.Y., The Free Press of Glencoe.

CLYDE KLUCKHOHN (1951), "Values and Value-Orientations in the Theory of Action," in Talcott Parsons and E. A. Shils (eds.), *Toward a General Theory of Action,* Cambridge, Harvard University Press.

RICHARD T. LAPIERE (1954), *A Theory of Social Control,* N.Y., McGraw-Hill.

PAUL F. LAZARSFELD and others (1944), *The People's Choice,* N.Y., Duell, Sloan, & Pearce.

PAUL F. LAZARSFELD and MORRIS ROSENBERG (1955), *The Language of Social Research,* N.Y., The Free Press of Glencoe.

EDWIN M. LEMERT (1951), *Social Pathology,* N.Y., McGraw-Hill.

KURT LEWIN (1936), *Principles of Topological Psychology,* N.Y., McGraw-Hill.

KURT LEWIN (1952), "Group Decision and Social Change," in Guy E. Swanson and others (eds.), *Reading in Social Psychology,* N.Y., Holt, Rinehart & Winston.

ALFRED LINDESMITH and ANSELM STRAUSS (1956), *Social Psychology,* N.Y., Holt, Rinehart & Winston.

RONALD LIPPITT and others (1958), *The Dynamics of Planned Change,* N.Y., Harcourt, Brace & World.

CHARLES P. LOOMIS and J. ALLAN BEEGLE (1957), *Rural Sociology: The Strategy of Change,* Englewood Cliffs, N.J., Prentice-Hall.

JAMES G. MARCH and HERBERT A. SIMON (1958), *Organizations,* N.Y., Wiley.

DON MARTINDALE (1959), "Sociological Theory and the Ideal Type," in Llewellyn Gross (ed.), *Symposium on Sociological Theory,* Evanston, Ill., Row, Peterson.

GEORGE HERBERT MEAD (1956), "Stages in the Act: Preliminary Statement," in Anselm Straus (ed.), *The Social Psychology of George Herbert Mead,* Chicago, Phoenix Books.

ROBERT K. MERTON (1957), *Social Theory and Social Structure,* N.Y., The Free Press of Glencoe.

ROBERT K. MERTON (1959), "Social Conformity, Deviation, and Opportunity Structures: A Comment on the Contributions of Dubin and Cloward," *American Sociological Review,* 24: 177–189.

GUY H. ORCUTT and others (1961), *Microanalysis of Socioeconomic Systems: A Simulation Study,* N.Y., Harper.

TALCOTT PARSONS (1951), *The Social System,* N.Y., The Free Press of Glencoe.

TALCOTT PARSONS and E. A. SHILS (1952), *Toward a General Theory of Action,* Cambridge, Massachusetts, Harvard University Press.

ITHIEL DE SOLA POOL and ROBERT ABELSON (1961), "The Simulmatics Project," *Public Opinion Quarterly,* 25: 167–183.

ANATOL RAPOPORT (1956), "The Diffusion Problem in Mass Behavior," in Ludwig von Bertalanffy and Anatol Rapoport (eds.), *General Systems,* Ann Arbor, Mich., Braun-Brumfield.

WALTER C. RECKLESS and others (1956), "Self Concept as an Insulator Against Delinquency," *American Sociological Review,* 21: 744–746.

ROBERT REDFIELD (1930), *Tepoztlan, A Mexican Village: A Study of Folk Life,* Chicago, University of Chicago Press.

ROBERT REDFIELD (1956), *Peasant Society and Culture,* Chicago, University of Chicago Press.

CRAIG A. REED (1961), *The Impact of Mass Society on Rural Communities,* M.S. Thesis, Columbus, Ohio State University.

ALBERT J. REISS, JR., and ALBERT LEWIS RHODES (1961), "The Distribution of Juvenile Delinquency in the Social Structure," *American Sociological Review*, 26: 720–732.

EVERETT M. ROGERS (1960), *Social Change in Rural Society*, N.Y., Appleton-Century-Crofts.

A. ROMEIN (1937), "De dialectiek van de voormitgang" (The Dialectics of Development), in *Het onvoltooid verleden, Kultuur-historische Studien*, Amsterdam, Netherlands.

FRANK R. SCARPITTI and others (1960), "The 'Good' Boy in a High Delinquency Area: Four Years Later," *American Sociological Review*, 25: 555–558.

BURT SCHORR (1961), "The Mistakes: Many New Products Fail Despite Careful Planning, Publicity," *Wall Street Journal*, April 5, pp. 1, 22.

GEORGE SIMPSON (1959), *Sociologist Abroad*, The Hague, Netherlands, Martinus Nijhoff.

BRUCE L. SMITH and others (1946), *Propaganda, Communication and Public Opinion*, Princeton, N.J., Princeton University Press.

PITIRIM A. SOROKIN (1959), *Social and Cultural Mobility*, N.Y., The Freee Press of Glencoe.

FRANK A. STEWART (1947), "A Sociometric Study of Influence in Southtown," *Sociometry*, 10: 11–31.

ROBERT P. STUCKERT (1958), "A Configurational Approach to Prediction," *Sociometry*, 21: 225–237.

HARRY STACK SULLIVAN (1953), *The Interpersonal Theory of Psychiatry*, N.Y., Norton.

GABRIEL TARDE (1903), *The Laws of Imitation* (trans. Elsie Clews Parsons), N.Y., Holt, Rinehart & Winston.

WILSON L. TAYLOR (1956), "Recent Developments in the Use of 'Cloze Procedure,'" *Journalism Quarterly*, 33: 42–48.

HENRY DAVID THOREAU (1906), *The Writings of Henry David Thoreau*, Boston, Houghton Mifflin.

JOHN VON NEUMANN and OSKAR MORGANSTERN (1953), *Theory of Games and Economic Behavior*, Princeton, N.J., Princeton University Press, 1953.

MAX WEBER (1947), *The Theory of Social and Economic Organization*, (trans. A. M. Henderson and Talcott Parsons). N.Y., The Free Press of Glencoe.

MAX WEBER (1958), *From Max Weber: Essays in Sociology*, (trans. Hans Gerth and C. Wright Mills), N.Y., Oxford University Press.

JAMES E. WERT and others (1954), *Statistical Methods in Educational and Psychological Research*, N.Y., Appleton-Century-Crofts.

DELOS D. WICKENS and DONALD R. MEYER (1955), *Psychology*, N.Y., Holt, Rinehart & Winston.

JOHN T. ZADROZMY (1959), *Dictionary of Social Science*, Washington, D.C., Public Affairs Press.

Abell, Helen C., 37
Abelson, Herbert I., 229, 232
Abelson, Robert, 298
Accessibility, personal information sources, 100
Ackerman, Joseph, 4
Active adopters, 210
Active rejectors, 210
Adams, Richard N., 193, 194, 200
Adaptability, 39
Adler, David, 41, 53, 89, 91, 125, 134
Adopter categories, 19, 35, 43, 148–192
  age, 172–174
  awareness-to-trial period, 113–118
  changes over time, 189
  characteristics of, 171–186
  closer contact, 181
  composite portrait, 185–186
  cosmopolite information sources, 179–181
  cosmopoliteness, 182–184
  definition, 19, 148
  deliberation, 304
  dominant values, 304
  financial position, 175–176
  impersonal information sources, 179
  incomplete adoption, 165
  length of adoption period by, 111
  mental ability, 177–178
  more information sources, 181–182
  need for standardization, 149
  nonsymmetry, 164
  opinion leadership, 184
  perception of divisibility, 131–132
  respect, 304
  self-images, 188–189
  situational fields, 303–305
  skepticism, 305
  social relationships, 182–186
  social status, 174
  specialization, 177
  titles for, 150–151

tradition, 305
trial-to-adoption period, 112–118
venturesomeness, 304
Adopter categories as ideal types, 168–171
Adopter categorization, 159
Adopter distribution, deviation from normality, 164
  normal, 41, 152–159
  S-shaped, 37, 54, 55, 152
  testing for normality, 158
Adoption, 307
  of change agents, 261
  consequences of, 96
  definition, 17
  on the installment plan, 116
  unit of, 124
Adoption dates, recall accuracy, 116, 160–161
Adoption leaders, 209
Adoption of innovations theory, 305–307
Adoption period, 2, 18, 34, 41, 105–120, 261
  definition, 18, 105
  of innovators, 111
  in the diffusion process, 118–119
  length of, 108, 111
Adoption process, 76–120
  definition, 17
  stages in, 34, 80, 81–86
Adoption rate, 56, 69, 73, 108, 134–142, 296
  characteristics and, 134–142
  definition, 134
  measures of, 134
  prediction of, 122
Adoption stage, 86
  example of, 86–88
  existence of, 95–98
Age, time of adoption, 173
  time of interview, 173
Agriculture crazes, 143

Allen, Harley Earl, 41, 89
Anderson, R. L., 161
Antecedents, 305
Anthropology, 23, 24–28, 55, 272
Apodaca, Anacleto, 58
Armstrong, Joseph B., 73, 258, 288, 289
Asch, Solomon E., 203
Awareness, rate of, 108
Awareness stage, 81
Awareness-to-trial period, 112–118

Bailey, Norman T. J., 90, 91, 129, 130, 217, 298
Bancroft, T. A., 161
Barnabas, A. P., 37, 184, 243
Barnett, Homer G., 27, 53, 121, 130, 194, 255
Barriers to the flow of ideas, 247–250
Barrington, Thomas M., 41
Barton, Allan, 42, 43
Beal, George M., 5, 80, 83, 84, 95, 96, 97, 98, 99, 100, 101, 102, 105, 106, 108, 110, 112, 151, 156, 172, 177, 179, 181, 201, 218, 219, 220, 221, 224, 263
Bealer, Robert C., 78
Becker, Howard C., 60, 168
Beegle, J. Allan, 255
Belcher, John C., 37, 52, 174
Bemiller, James L., 64, 178
Ben-David, Joseph, 205
Benedict, Ruth, 196
Bennett, John W., 193
Benvenuti, M. B., 63, 64, 150, 182
Berelson, B. R., 238, 241
Bertrand, Alvin L., 125, 275
Bible, Bond L., 256
Blackmore, John, 176
Bliss, Wesley, 28, 273
Boddewyn, Jean, 100
Bonser, Howard J., 37
Bose, Santi Priya, 37, 63, 64, 269
Boskoff, Alvin, 133
Bowers, Raymond V., 5, 29, 30, 53, 179, 222
Brandner, Lowell, 136, 137, 144, 184, 243
Brim, Orville, 5, 81

Burdge, Rabel J., 64, 68, 69, 70, 71, 74, 148, 172, 174, 176, 177, 178, 181, 183, 184, 187, 200, 201, 227, 229, 232, 233, 235, 238, 239, 242, 243, 244. 246, 251, 270
Burns, Tom, 80
Business Week, 285

Campaigns, 281
Campbell, Herbert L., 102, 181
Campbell, Rex R., 68, 69
Canning campaign, 86
Cannon, Walter B., 76
Capener, Harold R., 238, 270
Caplow, Theodore, 45, 49, 53, 150, 151
Carter, C. F., 2, 44, 53, 150, 151, 181, 183, 289
Change agent, commercial, 261–267
  definition, 17, 254
  factors in the success of, 256–257, 268
  promotion efforts by, 257–260
  rate of adoption related to, 257–260
  role of, 254–284
  social consequences, 271–278
  strategy, 278–282
Chaparro, Alvaro, 148, 150, 151, 160, 174, 184, 227, 229, 242, 243, 248, 269
Chapin, F. Stuart, 29, 53, 54, 89, 152, 153
Clendenen, H. Franklin, 42
Cocking, Walter, 39, 41, 42, 53, 150, 183
Cohen, Albert K., 196, 203
Cohen, Reuben, 150, 289
Coleman, A. Lee, 36, 60, 68, 106, 108, 174, 176, 182, 184, 186, 209, 229, 233, 235, 243, 244, 246, 247, 270, 286
Coleman, James S., 5, 46, 47, 48, 49, 50, 51, 53, 82, 140, 150, 172, 176, 181, 187, 209, 211, 215, 218, 223, 229
Communicability, 132–133
Communication
  behavior, 178–182, 291
  impersonal, 99
  personal, 98
Community norms, measurement of, 235

Compatibility, 127–130, 136
  definition, 127
  versus profitability, 136–142
Complexity, 130–131
Computer simulation, 297–299
Concept
  definition, 308
  development of, 79–81
Conceptual variable analysis, 308–316
Configurational approach to prediction, 292–295
Conformity, 197
Consequences
  of adoption, 298
  direct or manifest, 274–276
  indirect or latent, 274–276
  unexpected, of the canning campaign, 88
Copp, James H., 63, 80, 84, 95, 98, 99, 101, 174, 176, 178, 182, 186, 187, 222, 263, 288
Cornell, Francis G., 22, 35, 39, 40, 41, 53, 150, 151
Cosmopolite, 42, 44, 51, 228
Cosmopoliteness, 51, 310
  definition, 17, 102
Cottrell, Leonard S., Jr., 302, 303
Coughenour, C. Milton, 74, 89, 93, 99, 104, 172, 174, 175, 176, 178, 182, 186, 242, 296
Council on Social Work Education, 255, 272
Credibility, 145, 265–267
  personal information sources, 100
Crisis, 125
Cross-cultural diffusion, 267–271
Cultural values, 278–279
Culture, 57
Cutright, Phillip, 258

Danhof, Clarence, 43, 44, 53, 148, 150, 151
Danielson, Wayne A., 99
Davis, Alice, 29, 153
Davis, Kingsley, 174
Davis, Morris, 15, 52
Dean, Alfred, 64, 178
Deasy, Leila Calhoun, 52
Decay function, 155
Decision-making, 77-78
Dennis, Elmer C., 150–151

Dependent variable, 287
Detail men, 47
Deutschmann, Paul J., 99, 225
Deviancy from norms, 235
Deviation, 196–198
Diffusion, 57
  definition, 13
  elements of, 12–20
  of an innovation, 303–305
  period, 118
  process, 13, 18
Diffusionists, 25
Dillon, John L., 298
Dimit, Robert M., 106, 112, 113, 156
Discontinuances, 88–91, 307
  later adopters, 91
Divisibility, 131–132
Dobyns, Henry F., 28, 280
Dodd, Stuart C., 140, 154
Drug study, 46–51
Dubin, Robert, 197
Duncan, James A., 37, 174, 176

Early adopters, 19
  values, 169
Early majority, 19
  values, 170
Early sociologists, 152
Early sociology, 23, 28–31, 55
Ecology of diffusion, 29
Economic advantage, 59
Education, 23, 39–43, 56
Eichholz, Gerhard, 42, 90
Eichhorn, Robert L., 144, 178
Emery, F. E., 64, 80, 81, 104, 178, 182, 183, 186, 209, 227, 236, 238, 242, 256, 270, 293, 296, 305
Empathy, 61
Empirical hypothesis, 309
English, Ava Champney, 77
English, Horace B., 77
Enos, John L., 44, 53, 150, 151, 175, 196, 205
Epistemic relationship, 309
Erasmus, Charles J., 28, 132, 271
Estep, Allen J., 281
Evaluation stage, 83

Farnsworth, Philo T., 41, 53
Ferber, Robert, 266

Festinger, Leon, 203
Fliegel, Frederick C., 78, 174, 176, 182, 186, 187, 242, 288
Fluoridation, 15
Followers, 232, 248, 250
Ford, Thomas, 63
Foster, Phillips N., 183, 269, 270
Fount, Louis A., 122
Fox, Robert, 42, 296, 305
Francis, David G., 145, 206, 255

Gallup, Gladys, 32
Game theories, 297–299
  Monte Carlo, 298
Gammanyn, 47–51
Gamson, William A., 15, 52
Geiger, Kent, 127
Generalizations, 7, 308
  complete listing of, 311–315
Gill, Rafael E., 52
Gillespie, Robert W., 298
Gilfillian, C. S., 153, 274
Gini ratio, 227
Glaser, Melvin A., 52
Goldschmidt, Walter, 278
Goldsen, Rose K., 5, 183, 269
Goldstein, Bernice, 144, 178
Goldstein, Marshall N., 42
Graham, L. Saxon, 92, 127, 131, 174
Grass incubators, 145, 206, 255
Green, R. L., 2
Griliches, Zvi, 134, 136, 137, 139, 140, 158
Gross, Neal C., 2, 4, 5, 32, 33, 34, 35, 38, 46, 50, 53, 79, 80, 85, 102, 106, 108, 112, 113, 117, 131, 138, 139, 149, 150, 151, 153, 157, 158, 172, 173, 174, 179, 183, 186, 215, 263, 277, 286, 309, 310
Group adoption decision, 14

Haber, Ralph N., 42, 107, 111, 116
Hagen, Everett E., 194
Hagerstrand, Torsten, 154, 298
Hamlin, Robert, L., 308
Harp, John, 178
Harris, Jack S., 59
Harris, Ruth, 37, 64
Hassinger, Edward, 82, 110

Havens, A. Eugene, 37, 49, 134, 136, 140, 161, 187, 193, 217, 224, 232, 270, 281, 285, 289, 300
Haver, Cecil B., 78
Hawkins, Norman G., 49, 53, 266
Hawley, Florence, 60, 128
Hay, Donald G., 37, 52
Heady, Earl O., 298
Hess, C. V., 278
Hildebrand, Peter E., 105, 189, 278
Hilgard, Ernest R., 77, 153
Hill, Reuben, 5, 64
Hobbs, Daryl J., 63, 175, 176, 288, 296, 305
Hochbaum, Godfrey M., 52
Hochstrasser, Donald L., 22
Hoffer, Charles R., 32, 35, 53, 64, 104, 172, 175, 176, 258
Holik, John S., 68, 69
Holmberg, Allen, 81
Homans, George C., 143, 197, 233
"Hot" and "cold" food complex, 9
Hovland, Carl I., 99
Hruschka, Erna, 132, 182, 243, 251, 282
Hybrid seed corn, 33–35

Ideal types, 60
Ideas
  characteristics of, 56
  complexity of new, 129–130
Independent variable, 287
Indian Planning Commission Programme Evaluation Organization, 89–90
Industrial tradition of diffusion research, 23, 43–45, 56
Industrial engineers, 272
Infectious disease, 217
Inflection, point of, 161
Influence
  distribution of, 226
  sociometric, 227
Information sources, 35, 44, 307
  cautions about, 104–105
  cosmopoliteness of, 102–104
  impersonal, at awareness stage, 99
  institutionalized, 99
  noninstitutionalized, 99
  personal, at evaluation stage, 99
  sequence of, 101–102

Innovation, 13
  characteristics of, 73, 121–147
  nonrecommended, 3, 205
  theory of the adoption and diffusion of, 300–316
  two-step flow of, 211–214
Innovation-use tree, 93
Innovativeness, 40, 44, 51, 55, 67, 73, 159, 287, 310
  average, 68
  consistency of, 186
  definition, 19
  predicting, 285–299
Innovativeness scale, 41, 166
  internal consistency, 167
  reliability, 167
  undimensionality, 167
  validity, 166
Innovators, 19, 43, 111, 193–194, 276–278
  attitude toward, 68
  cosmopoliteness of, 203–205
  deviancy of, 194
  nonagricultural, 205
  reference groups, 203
  research inadequacies on, 195
  self-images, 201
  values, 169
Interaction effect, 138–142, 154–155, 215–217
  definition, 138
Interest stage, 82
Inventors, 195–196
Irrational overadopters, 142
Irrational underadopters, 142

Jahoda, Marie, 161
Johnson, Donald E., 90, 91, 125, 137
Johnson, Glenn L., 78
Jones, Gwyn E., 71, 150, 151, 165, 172, 174, 176, 177, 183

Kahl, Joseph A., 168
Kardiner, Abraham, 275
Karlsson, George, 217
Karpat, Kemal H., 275
Katz, Elihu, 12, 14, 16, 21, 22, 23, 24, 30, 31, 35, 36, 38, 46, 47, 48, 50, 52, 53, 54, 64, 99, 102, 116, 117, 118, 131, 150, 151, 183, 184, 209,

214, 218, 222, 227, 229, 231, 232, 236, 238, 239, 241, 242, 243, 244, 251, 263, 266
Kelley, Harold H., 203
Key informants, 229
Kivlin, Joseph E., 124, 130, 131, 134, 135, 287, 296
Klapper, Joseph T., 210, 218, 224
Klietsch, Ronald, 64, 66, 298
Klonglan, Gerald, 113
Kollmorgen, Walter M., 32
Koontz, Donald H., 107
Kreitlow, Burton W., 37, 174, 176
Kroeber, A. L., 25, 31, 53
Krug, Larry L., 136

Lackey, Alvin S., 104, 189, 191, 286
Laggards, 19, 276
  deviants, 197
  values, 171
LaPiere, Richard T., 197
Larson, Olaf F., 104, 286
Larson, Otto N., 150
Late majority, 19
  values, 170
Lavidge, Robert J., 81, 83, 84, 86
Lazarsfeld, Paul F., 95, 111, 209, 211, 218, 224, 227, 230, 231, 232, 236, 238, 239, 241, 243
Learning, 76–77
Learning curves, 153
LeRay, N. L., 2
Lerner, Daniel, 60, 63, 66
Lemert, Edwin M., 196
Leuthold, Frank O., 102, 181, 239, 244, 265
Levin, Martin L., 14, 23, 24, 30, 35, 47, 50, 52
Lewin, Kurt, 209, 300
Lindesmith, Alfred, 303
Lindstrom, David E., 37, 176
Linkage, 268–269, 279
Linton, Ralph, 25, 39, 53, 57, 133, 194, 275
Lionberger, Herbert F., 5, 6, 36, 38, 53, 99, 100, 129, 150, 151, 172, 174, 176, 183, 184, 209, 227, 228, 235, 238, 239, 240, 242, 243, 244, 246, 249
Lippitt, Ronald, 255
Littumen, Yrjo, 200
Localite, 228

Loomis, Charles P., 60, 255
Lovos, George, 41
Lowie, Robert, 31
Lowry, Sheldon G., 37, 52, 172, 174

Maccoby, N., 5
McCorkle, Thomas, 128
McIntyre, Kenneth, 42
McKain, Walter C., Jr., 100
McNeil, Donald R., 15, 52
McVoy, Edgar C., 29, 53
Mansfield, Edwin, 44, 45, 53, 134, 135, 150, 151, 158, 175, 187
March, James G., 77, 83, 84
Marsh, C. Paul, 60, 68, 174, 176, 182, 184, 186, 209, 229, 233, 235, 243, 244, 246, 247, 286
Martindale, Don, 60
Mason, Robert, 98
Mass society, 211
Mead, Margaret, 28, 278, 280
Mediascope, 208
Medical sociology, 23, 45–55, 56
Mendras, Henri, 64, 270
Menzel, Herbert, 46, 47, 48, 49, 53, 121, 133, 150, 151, 160, 197, 200, 205, 222, 229, 238, 244, 251, 266
Merton, Robert K., 60, 196, 197, 209, 218, 228, 229, 236, 241, 285, 308
Meyer, Donald R., 77
Miller, Genevieve, 5, 45, 205
Miller, L. F., 278
Modern norms, 59–75
Morganstern, Oskar, 62, 298
Mort, Paul R., 22, 35, 39, 40, 41, 53, 150, 151, 163
Mueller, Eva, 150
Mulford, Charles Lee, 125, 175
Multiple correlation, 251, 287–292
   criteria for selecting variables, 290

National Analysts, Inc., 15, 297
Neinhaus, W., 270
Niederfrank, N. J., 270
Nolan, Francena L., 256
Nonfollowers, 250
Nonrecommended innovations, 3, 206
Normality, 29
Norms, 15, 57, 290, 292
   definition, 16, 57, 196

measuring, 67–70
on innovativeness, 246
traditional and modern, 59–75
North Central Rural Sociology Subcommittee (NCRS), 38, 53, 80, 83, 84, 149, 150, 151
Nye, Ivan, 237

Oeser, O. A., 64, 81, 104, 178, 182, 183, 186, 209, 227, 236, 238, 242, 256, 270, 293, 296, 305
Ogburn, William F., 39, 53, 133, 274
Olson, K. S., 150, 151, 281
Opinion leaders, 72 208–212, 281–282
   active roles, 209
   consensually validate, 304
   definition, 16, 208
   passive roles, 209
Opinion leadership, 35, 50, 56, 169, 218, 291
   conformity to norms, 233
   cosmopoliteness, 239
   example among physicians, 211
   information sources, 238
   innovativeness, 242
   lack of overlap, 236
   measurement of, 228–232
   needed research on, 250
   social participation, 240
   social status, 241
Opinion Research Corporation, 5, 187, 209
Opler, Morris E., 272
Orcutt, Guy H., 298
Osborne, L. W., 270
Overadoption, 142–145

Pal, Agaton P., 37, 269
Parameters, 161
Parish, Ross, 129, 187, 270
Parsons, Talcott, 197, 301
Partenheimer, Earl J., 105, 189, 278
Passive adopters, 210, 215
Passive rejectors, 210
Paul, Benjamin D., 269
Pedersen, Harold A., 58, 80, 166
Pelley, James H., 41
Pelto, Pertti, 194, 200
Pemberton, H. Earl, 29, 53, 126, 153
Perception, 140–142, 303

Personal influence, 217–223
    as a process, 218
    at evaluation stage, 219
    definition, 217–218
    from peers, 219
    functions of, 223
    later adopters, 220
    uncertain situations, 222
Peter, Hollis W., 267
Petrini, Frank, 111
Pfizer, Charles, and Company, 46, 47
Photiadis, John D., 174, 178, 186
Pierce, Truman A., 41, 53, 150, 151, 163, 289
Pitzer, Ronald L., 84, 99, 106, 116, 175, 176, 204
Plaut, Thomas F. A., 15
Pollack, Frederick, 275
Polson, Robert A., 37, 269
Pool, Ithiel de Sola, 298
Porter, Ward F., 174, 176, 177, 186, 288
Prediction, 285–299
    and theory, 296
    future approaches, 295–299
    usefulness, 299
Preiss, Jack J., 256
Profitability
    definition, 136
    measure of, 138–139
    versus compatibility, 136–142
Prundeanu, Julian, 129
Public health, 7, 11, 23, 37
Putney, Gladys J., 194, 200
Putney, Snell W., 194, 200

Rahim, S. A., 83, 99, 107, 158, 175, 176, 179, 184, 220, 221, 229, 237, 238, 241, 242, 243, 269
Rahudkar, W. B., 37, 60, 68, 104, 172, 184, 218, 235, 237, 240, 243, 246, 268, 269, 296, 305
Ralis, Max, 5, 183, 269
Ramsey, Charles E., 64
Raper, Arthur, 86
Rapoport, Anatol, 118, 217
Rate of adoption, 56, 69, 73, 108, 134–142, 296
Rate of awareness, 108
Ratings, judges', 68
Rational adopters, 142

Rational rejectors, 142, 207
Rationality, 61, 91
Raymond, John J., 45, 49
Reckless, Walter C., 71
Redfield, Robert, 60
Reed, Craig A., 1
Reference groups, 302
Reiss, Albert J., Jr., 71
Rejection, 19, 88, 307
Relative advantage, 124–126, 258
    definition, 124
Research expenditures, 2
Rhodes, Albert Lewis, 71
Rice, Stuart A., 29, 53
Rogers, Everett M., 4, 5, 37, 41, 53, 68, 69, 70, 71, 74, 84, 96, 97, 98, 99, 100, 101, 102, 105, 106, 108, 110, 111, 112, 116, 134, 136, 140, 148, 150, 151, 156, 157, 158, 166, 167, 172, 174, 175, 176, 177, 178, 179, 181, 183, 184, 186, 187, 188, 189, 191, 195, 198, 200, 201, 202, 204, 209, 217, 218, 219, 220, 221, 224, 226, 227, 229, 230, 232, 233, 235, 239, 240, 242, 243, 244, 246, 251, 255, 261, 263, 265, 270, 278, 281, 288, 289, 308
Rogers, L. Edna, 166, 167, 187
Rohrer, Wayne C., 279
Rohwer, Robert A., 34
Romein, A., 74
Rosenberg, Morris, 95
Ross, Donald H., 2, 5, 6, 23, 39, 40, 126, 148, 150, 151, 175, 183, 186, 209, 258
Rossi, Peter H., 258
Rugg, W. Donald, 229, 232
Rural sociology, 23, 31–38, 56, 272, 287
Ruttan, Vernon W., 13, 196
Ryan, Bryce, 2, 4, 5, 32, 33, 34, 35, 37, 46, 50, 53, 79, 80, 85, 107, 108, 111, 115, 117, 131, 150, 151, 153, 156, 157, 158, 179, 183, 215, 236, 263, 309, 310

S-shaped curve, 37, 152, 261
Safilios, Constantina, 209
Santopolo, Frank A., 89, 106, 108, 111, 126
Scantland, Lois, 270

Scarpitti, Frank R., 71
Schlesinger, Lawrence E., 267
Schorr, Burt, 122
Selective exposure, 109, 225
Selective perception, 225
Selective retention, 225
Selectivity, 224–226
Self-designating opinion leadership scale, 229
Self-identity, 302
Sharp, Lauriston, 25, 26, 27
Sheppard, David, 89, 155, 172, 174, 175, 176, 187, 188, 209, 220, 229, 246, 247, 250
Shils, E. A., 301
Sill, Maurice L., 79, 101
Sills, David L., 52
Silverman, Leslie J., 90, 91, 129, 130
Simon, Herbert A., 77, 83, 84
Simpson, George, 285
Simulmatics Corporation, 15, 297, 299
Situational field, 302
Sizer, Leonard M., 174, 176, 177, 186, 288
Slocum, Walter L., 270
Smirnov test, 158
Smith, Bruce L., 12
Snowball effect, 215
Social consequences, 25, 271–278, 282
    of the wheel among the Papago, 273–276
    windfall profits, 276–278
Social status, 290
Social system, 61–62, 303
    definition, 14
    dropping out of the, 191
    measuring norms of, 67–70
    norms, 73, 170
Sociometric influence, 227
Sociometric techniques, 228
Sokol, Robert, 127, 229
Sorokin, Pitirim, 60, 158, 159
Sources of information, by adoption stages, 98–105
Spicer, Edward H., 25
Stabler, George M., 255
Stalker, G. M., 80
Standard deviation, 161, 235
Standard scores, 163–164
Stangland, Dale, 64, 172, 175, 176
Steel axe, 25–28
Steiner, Gary, 81, 83, 84, 86

Stern, Bernard J., 45
Stewart, Frank, A., 209, 229, 232, 239, 241
Stone, John T., 259, 260
Stone, P. S., 144, 278
Strassman, W. Paul, 44, 53, 85, 196
Strategy of change, 278–282
Straus, Murray A., 136, 144, 150, 151, 175, 176, 269, 281, 289, 292, 296, 305
Strauss, Anselm, 303
Stuckert, Robert P., 292
Sullivan, Harry Stack, 301
Survey experiments, 315
Sutherland, Alistair, 5, 44, 125, 151, 175, 178
Suttles, Wayne, 27

Tappan, Pearl Wheeler, 86
Tarde, Gabriel, 1, 28, 29, 42, 53, 54, 184, 241
Taves, Marvin J., 34, 183, 186, 286
Taylor, Wilson L., 177
Technical assistance, 23, 28, 267–269
Theory of the middle range, 315
Thomas, W. I., 230
Thoreau, Henry David, 193
Time lag, 40
Toennies, Ferdinand, 60
Toussaint, W. D., 144, 278
Traditional-modern dimension
    at individual level, 62–67
    in social systems, 67–70
    measurement of, 62–70
Traditional neighborhoods, 233
Traditional norms, 59–75
Traditions, lack of diffusion between, 54
Traditions of diffusion research, 21–56, 317–353
    definition, 22
    interrelations among, 53
Trial-to-adoption period, 49, 112–118
Trial stage, 84–85, 263–267
Tucker, Carlos F., 124, 134, 135
Two-step flow of communication, 211–214

Unit of adoption, 124
Useem, John, 193

Value homophily, 243
Van de Ven, W. J., 64, 67
Van den Ban, A. W., 37, 60, 63, 64, 68, 69, 71, 72, 74, 90, 91, 99, 101, 160, 165, 174, 176, 177, 179, 184, 186, 200, 223, 224, 227, 229, 235, 237, 238, 239, 240, 241, 242, 243, 244, 246, 248, 249, 250, 266, 270, 279
Voget, Fred, 15
Volkhart, Edmund H., 203
vom Blankenburg, Peter, 270
vom Neumann, John, 62, 298

Wales, Hugh G., 266
Walker, Odell L., 298
Wall Street Journal, 122
Wassen, Chester R., 123
Water-boiling. 7–12
Weber, Max, 60, 62
Welikala, George H. F., 269, 270, 282
Wellin, Edward, 7
Wert, James E., 164
Wichers, A. J., 64, 72, 270
Wickens, Delos D., 77

Wilkening, Eugene A., 36, 37, 53, 80, 81, 89, 99, 100, 102, 105, 106, 108, 111, 125, 126, 135, 137, 142, 179, 184, 186, 187, 199, 200, 209, 223, 227, 229, 237, 243, 244, 256
Williams, B. R., 2, 44, 53, 148, 150, 151, 181, 183, 289
Williams, D. B., 148
Wilson, M. C., 31, 32, 53
Windfall profits, 276–278
Winston, Sanford, 255
Wissler, Clark, 25, 31, 39, 53
Wolf, E. R., 60
Woodlock, Joseph W., 122

Yeracaris, Constantine A., 52, 127, 174
Yir Yoront, 26–27
Yost, M. D., 84, 106, 111, 261
Young, James N., 184, 243, 246
Young, Ruth, 280, 281

Zadrozmy, John T., 196
Zwerman, Paul J., 129